THE DARK FANTASTIC

THE DARK FANTASTIC

*Race and the Imagination
from Harry Potter to
the Hunger Games*

EBONY ELIZABETH THOMAS

NEW YORK UNIVERSITY PRESS
NEW YORK

NEW YORK UNIVERSITY PRESS
New York
www.nyupress.org

References to Internet websites (URLs) were accurate at the time of writing. Neither the author nor New York University Press is responsible for URLs that may have expired or changed since the manuscript was prepared.

Library of Congress Cataloging-in-Publication Data
Names: Thomas, Ebony Elizabeth, 1977– author.
Title: The dark fantastic : race and the imagination from Harry Potter to the hunger games / Ebony Elizabeth Thomas.
Description: New York : New York University Press, [2019] | Series: Postmillennial pop | Includes bibliographical references and index.
Identifiers: LCCN 2018042917 | ISBN 9781479800650 (cl : alk. paper)
Subjects: LCSH: Fantasy fiction, American—History and criticism—Theory, etc. | Fantasy fiction, English—History and criticism—Theory, etc. | African Americans— Intellectual life. | Literature and race. | Storytelling in mass media.
Classification: LCC PS374.F27 T475 2019 | DDC 813/.8766093552—dc23
LC record available at https://lccn.loc.gov/2018042917

Manufactured in the United States of America

Also available as an ebook

Dedicated to
Jalen, Daija, Alexzis, Kellen, Danielle, Jr., and Dylon
And all the children of tomorrow
who deserve fantastic worlds
endarkened and whole.

CONTENTS

INTRODUCTION

The Dark Fantastic: Race and the Imagination Gap

"There is no magic."

This statement, perhaps most famously attributed to Harry Potter's uncle Vernon Dursley, is also something that my mother has said to me since I was a child. Magic has long been under siege in my culture, social class, and hometown. The eldest daughter of an African American, working-class, Detroit family, I was born in the late 1970s just as the fires of the Civil Rights era were smoldering to ashes.[1] My mother was doing me a favor by letting me know that magic was inaccessible to *me*. The real world held trouble enough for young Black girls, so there was no need for me to go off on a quest to seek it.[2] I was warned against walking through metaphoric looking glasses, trained to be suspicious of magic rings, and assured that no gallant princes were *ever* coming to my rescue. The existential concerns of our family, neighbors, and city left little room for Neverlands, Middle-Earths, or Fantasias. In order to survive, I had to face reality.

My life has been intentionally constructed to prove my mother's words wrong. Among my earliest memories are snapshots taken from behind the spectacles of my younger self, seeking desperately for any traces of magic in the real world, even when magic did not seem to search for—or take much notice of—me. Secret passageways remained closed off to me, but I continued to dream. Books were my ticket to the realm of the imagination; reading, a welcomed escape. Although I grew up in urban America during the height of the crack epidemic of the 1980s and 1990s, my heart, mind, and soul were almost always somewhere else. In the realm of the fantastic, I found meaning, safety, catharsis—and hope. Though it eluded me, I *needed* magic.

My emerging critical consciousness as a reader, creative writer, and fangirl were soon on a collision course with my experiences as a teacher, scholar, and critic. The promise from Disney's classic *Cinderella* film, "In dreams you will lose your heartache . . . whatever you wish for, you keep," was obscured by the real conditions of my existence as a young Black woman in early twenty-first century America. It was also obscured in the lives of my family and friends, and in the lives of many children and adults whom I knew. Perhaps this is why some of my students, family members, and friends have been especially ambivalent about speculative fiction. They prefer to read and view stories that are, in their words, "true to life" or "keeping it real." Although there are many exceptions to this conventional wisdom about Black readers' and viewers' genre preferences—the recent *Black Panther* phenomenon for one—I have been told throughout my lifetime that stories like the ones I preferred were "for White people."

When people of color seek passageways into the fantastic, we have often discovered that the doors are barred. Even the very act of dreaming of worlds-that-never-were can be challenging when the known world does not provide many liberating spaces. A poignant example comes from Marlon Riggs's Emmy-award winning 1986 documentary about racial representation in media, *Ethnic Notions*.[3] Toward the end of the film, there is a haunting sequence in which Dr. Martin Luther King's "I Have a Dream" speech is interposed over Ethel Waters's ethereal performance of "Darkies Never Dream" in the 1943 movie *Cabin in the Sky*. While others have read her performance through the lens of minstrelsy, for me, it was almost as if Ethel's haunting melody was audaciously pointing to the possibility of the endarkened future of King's March on Washington, and beyond it to our time—a time when all people would ostensibly have access to the pleasures of dreaming.

But are the cartographies of dreams truly universal? When we dream inside the storied worlds of printed and digital books, fanfiction, fanart, fan videos, television shows, movies, comics, graphic novels, online fandom communities, and fan "cons," do those worlds offer all kinds of people escape from the world as we know it? Could they offer catharsis for some of our most pressing human problems? Might they help us collectively imagine our world anew?

This conversation is even more critical in today's social media environment, described by media theorist Henry Jenkins as *convergence culture*, in which traditional and new media forms thrive together. Since today's young people are as likely to be engaged in virtual social worlds as they are in face-to-face communication, the ways that stories are told and retold in convergence culture are more significant than ever for shaping the collective consciousness. As Jenkins notes:

> Transmedia storytelling is the art of world making. To fully experience any fictional world, consumers must assume the role of hunters and gath-erers, chasing down bits of the story across media channels, comparing notes with each other via online discussion groups, and collaborating to ensure that everyone who invests time and effort will come away with a richer entertainment experience.[4]

Today's teens and young adults are increasingly using new forms of com-munication to read and tell stories. They engage in textual and visual production that is collaborative, shared in what has been characterized as environments of *digital intimacy*.[5] Digitally intimate virtual communi-ties have their own ever-evolving rules, norms, and assumptions about meaning-making processes, authorship, and composing. As people par-ticipate with one another across these affinity spaces and networked publics,[6] they engage in participatory cultures in which "everyday citizens have an expanded capacity to communicate and circulate their ideas . . . [and] networked communities can shape our collective agendas."[7] This participatory turn has made it possible for more people to produce indi-vidual and collaborative content as part of their everyday lives, using a wide variety of multimodal tools to make meanings that are increasingly decentralized, crowdsourced, and situated in a multiplicity of contexts. A wide variety of communicative channels, modalities, and meanings helps to expand the stories that get told, circulated, and remixed, thereby challenging single stories about individuals and groups, and opening up interpretive space for multiple possible meanings.[8]

While digitally networked culture affords more scope for the imag-inations of young people, this is not universally the case. Although a sense of the infinite possibilities inherent in fantasy, science fiction, comics, and other imaginative genres draws children, teens, and adults from all backgrounds to speculative fiction, not all people are equally represented in these genres. This problem of representation has created

discord in the collective imagination. As I describe later in this introduction, the dark fantastic is my attempt to understand that discord as
it plays out in stories for young adults and in audience interactions with
those stories. But before journeying into the dark, I first want to call attention to one of the most pressing problems in all genres of young adult
literature, media, and culture—a long-entrenched lack of diversity—and
its implications for young people who aren't mirrored in those texts.

The Imagination Gap in Youth Literature, Media, and Culture

Conversations about the lack of diversity in children's stories are not new.
New York Times op-eds written by notable Black children's author Walter
Dean Myers and his son, Christopher Myers, in the spring of 2014 were
among the latest developments in decades-long struggles over disparities
in children's publishing and media. Walter Dean Myers's and Christopher
Myers's powerful essays, "Where Are the People of Color in Children's
Books?" and "The Apartheid of Children's Literature," referenced their
work with children as well as their lifelong commitments as writers to
represent diverse kids' lives.[9] Both authors cited statistics collected by the
University of Wisconsin's Cooperative Children's Book Center, which has
analyzed trends in children's publishing on an annual basis for more than
two decades. The center has found that every year, over 85 percent of all
books published for children and young adults feature White characters—a statistic that has barely moved since the 1960s.[10]

After the Myers father-and-son editorials appeared, a number of the
largest publishers remained silent. In May 2014, a bold new hashtag
began circulating on social media websites—#WeNeedDiverseBooks,
launched by authors Ellen Oh, Malinda Lo, Aisha Saeed, and others in
response to BookCon's choice to feature only White male authors on
their children's literature panel.[11] Other prominent voices within the
children's publishing industry rose to the forefront of social media conversations around diversity in media.[12] These more recent efforts are
connected to a protest tradition launched decades ago by leaders in the
multicultural children's literature movement such as Augusta Baker,
Pura Belpré, Nancy Larrick, Jella Lepman, Charlemae Hill Rollins, and
Rudine Sims Bishop, as well as many other authors, librarians, educa-

tors, and community activists who work with some of our world's most vulnerable young people.

The problem of the diversity gap extends far beyond the mere lack of representation of characters of color in children's publishing and media. Many diverse characters that actually *do* show up on the page, on a tablet, on a television or movie screen, or on the computer are often problematic, as recurring controversies about picture books featuring smiling slaves demonstrate.[13] Stereotyping, caricature, and marginalization of people of color, poor and working-class children and families, gender and sexual minorities, immigrants, and other minoritized groups have been persistent problems in children's literature.[14] Additionally, the Cooperative Children's Book Center's annual reports show a troubling trend of books that feature diverse characters not being written by authors from that background, leading to questions about who has the right to tell diverse stories.[15] Even within the sparse numbers of diverse texts that make it into print every year, disparities remain.

As author, creative writing professor, and activist Daniel José Older has pointed out during heated discussions since the Myers editorials, calling for diversity is not enough:

> The question industry professionals need to ask themselves is: "How can I use my position to help create a literary world that is diverse, equitable, and doesn't just represent the same segment of society it always has since its inception? What concrete actions can I take to make actual change and move beyond the tired conversation we've been having for decades?"[16]

As one of those industry professionals—a professor responsible for designing, teaching, and evaluating courses on children's and young adult literature and comics in education, and a former reviewer for *Kirkus Reviews*' children's section—I hope to use this book as an occasion to take up Older's call. Inspired by a 2010 *Horn Book* article by children's and young adult author Zetta Elliott, I have described the diversity crisis in children's and young adult media as an *imagination gap*.[17] Over the past decade, much has been made of the persistence of racial and ethnic achievement gaps in literacy and educational attainment. These conversations have extended from classrooms and communities to the White House, prompting inquiry about other gaps, such as in empathy, opportunities, resources, and technology.[18] Building on these efforts, I have begun to theorize a corresponding imagination gap in literature and media for young people.[19] This imagination gap is caused in part by the lack of diversity in childhood and teen life depicted in books, television, and films. When youth grow up without seeing diverse images in the mirrors, windows, and doors of children's and young adult literature, they are confined to single stories about the world around them and, ultimately, the development of their imaginations is affected. [20]

I have long suspected, and I am assuredly not alone, that racialized disparities in literacy attainment among kids and teens may be ultimately rooted in a massive failure of the collective imagination.

I wish to be perfectly clear here. I am not referring to any failure in the imaginations of young people. From the time I began teaching in Detroit in the late 1990s to my work with students in Philadelphia today, I have rarely encountered a young person without the capacity to imagine and dream even in the direst of life circumstances. Among children and young adults, storytelling and play are humming right along as always, as kids and teens all over the world are now using new media to inscribe themselves into existence (more on that later). Our young people have certainly not failed.

I am referring to the failures of adults:

- There is an imagination gap when nine out of every ten books published in the juvenile market feature the same kinds of characters that have been spotlighted since the inception of children's publishing in the United States.[21]
- There is an imagination gap when we cannot fathom that a young Black girl could be the symbolic mockingjay who inspires a revolution in one of today's most popular young adult adapted megaseries, *The Hunger Games*.[22]
- There is an imagination gap when one of the most visible Black female characters on teen television is stripped of agency, marginalized within the larger story, and becomes a caricature of her literary counterpart, as in *The Vampire Diaries*.[23]
- There is an imagination gap when a Korean Canadian woman's slam poetry critique of a popular character from an iconic fantasy series was seen by many fans as more of an issue than the author's troubling handling of one of her few characters of color in *Harry Potter*.[24]

- There is an imagination gap when children's and young adult literature critics' and sensitivity readers' perspectives on fantasy novels misrepresenting Native and First Nations people are seen as more problematic than the world-building itself (as in *Thirteenth Child*, *The Continent*).[25]

These are but a few of the many imagination gaps that I have seen as a teacher, fangirl, creative writer, scholar, critic, and researcher. The problem extends far beyond the mere lack of representation of characters of color in children's publishing and media. Often, the characters of color who *do* appear on the page or screen are stereotypes or caricatures. Marginalization has been a persistent problem in literature for children and adolescents throughout history. Therefore, even within the sparse numbers of diverse texts that make it into print every year, disparities remain.

Is it any wonder that some kids and teens of color don't like to read much?

Here is a radical, potentially dangerous thought: Maybe it's not that kids and teens of color and other marginalized and minoritized young people don't like to read. Maybe the real issue is that many adults haven't thought very much about the racialized mirrors, windows, and doors that are in the books we offer them to read, in the television and movies we invite them to view, and in the fan communities we entice them to play in. There has not been much sustained scholarly conversation about how kids and teens of color are affected by their representation in books, movies, comics, and online. Nor have previous studies of popular culture critically considered how those story representations shape not only the lives of young people today but whether they will want to pick up the next book, or the other media associated with it, tomorrow. One way we can begin this important conversation is by exploring the dark fantastic.

Critical Race Counterstorytelling for a Digital Age

The dark fantastic is my term for the role that racial difference plays in our fantastically storied imaginations. The fantastic—and here, I have been influenced by fantasy writers from J. R. R. Tolkien to J. K. Rowling and Philip Pullman, fantasy theorists from Tzvetan Todorov to Brian Attebery and Farah Mendlesohn, and author-critics from Toni Morrison to Ursula K. LeGuin and Kevin Young—includes fantasy fiction but goes beyond it to include all stories-about-worlds-that-never-were, whether they are marketed, shelved, or classified as fairy tales, horror, superhero comics, "soft" science fiction, alternate histories, or otherwise. I prefer *the fantastic* as a concept and a term to the more common designation of "speculative fiction." Words matter, and the fantastic has multiple resonant connotations. The fantastic captures the wonder of stepping into a world-that-never-was, and immersing yourself in it in a way that speculative fiction does not.

Other scholars, artists, and activists have focused on multicultural fantasy, the postcolonial fantastic, and the Black fantastic.[26] Prior to 2014, much of the important work on this topic was more taxonomic and descriptive than theoretical and conceptual, and was designed to raise awareness of the work of creators of color from Afrofuturist multimedia storytellers to Black comics artists and writers.[27] While some of the literature that I touch upon in *The Dark Fantastic* has been categorized by literary theorists as multicultural fantasy, Afrofuturism, or the Black fantastic, I distinguish the dark fantastic from these constructs.

The Black fantastic has historically been liberating, activist artistic production in the face of erasure and marginalization. Originators of the Black fantastic tradition in North America include W. E. B. Du Bois, Amiri Baraka, Octavia Butler, Samuel R. Delany, Virginia Hamilton, Tananarive Due, Tina McElroy Ansa, Nisi Shawl, Sheree Renee Thomas, and Nalo Hopkinson. Newer authors include noted Hugo Award winners N. K. Jemisin and Nnedi Okorafor, as well as emerging stellar talent for young adult readers, such as Zetta Elliott, Tomi Adeyemi, Dhonielle Clayton, Alaya Dawn Johnson, Tracey Baptiste, Sherri L. Smith, Justina Ireland, and L. L. McKinney. To characterize how these authors, as well as Black speculative transmedia stories such as *Black Panther*, *Luke Cage*, and *Black Lightning*, are transforming the literary and popular culture landscape is beyond the scope of this project. While the aforementioned stories are still being told and transmediated, the texts that I focus on in this book have run their course and are considered to be "closed canons" in online fandom. The narratives of *The Hunger Games*, the BBC's version of *Merlin*, *The Vampire Diaries*, and *Harry Potter* are complete as of early 2018. All of these stories were featured on screens large and small—and in the case of the first three, on the page—during the first two decades of the 2000s, long before the Afrofuturistic renaissance of the late 2010s.

Afrofuturism is both an aesthetic and an activist movement in the arts. While the term first appeared in Mark Dery's 1993 cyberculture essay "Black to the Future," Alondra Nelson was among those who initiated conversations about the intersections between speculative fiction, futurism, and African Diaspora culture. I view the Black fantastic as part of the larger Afrofuturist project, which responds to and transcends what I describe in this book as "the dark fantastic cycle" in the Western imagination. Recent key critical works on Black American and African Diaspora speculative fiction include Ytasha L. Womack's *Afrofuturism: The World of Black Sci-Fi and Fantasy Culture* (2013) and Andre L. Carrington's *Speculative Blackness: The Future of Race in Science Fiction* (2016), among others.[28] Taken together, these and other critical works, such as Helen Young's *Race in Popular Fantasy Literature: Habits of Whiteness* (2015), form an important new canon for the study of race in contemporary science fiction, fantasy, and horror.[29]

The Dark Fantastic, while informed by these and other projects and taking heart in the rise of Afrofuturism, is a different project altogether. *The Dark Fantastic* is not about the Black fantastic or Afrofuturism. Both are burgeoning and important genres that I value, and my own emerging creative work is in conversation with these and other traditions. But the fact remains that the vast majority of speculative narratives read and viewed in the United States are still written by White authors and screenwriters and consumed by mass audiences. Most youth digital media culture surrounding these works is centered in fandoms like those I explore in this book. Thus *The Dark Fantastic* considers the work of mainstream authors, television writers, and other storytelling creatives through the networked communities—such as fandoms—where such work is discussed, and the attendant implications for the larger culture.

As a literacy scholar working in the tradition of reader response theorists such as Louise Rosenblatt and Lawrence R. Sipe, I study transactions between readers, writers, and texts using qualitative research methods such as ethnography, autoethnography, and discourse analysis. While authorial intention is important, my role as a professor in a school of education, where I am preparing teachers for the classroom, means that I must take the experiences of readers into account. Therefore, in the tradition of memoirs by readers of color, such as Karla Holloway's *BookMarks* and Richard Rodriguez's *Hunger of Memory*, my theorization of the con-

struct of the dark fantastic is autoethnographic as well as phenomeno-
logical, grounded in my experiences as a child and adult participant in
communities of the fantastic (both as a reader transacting with authors
and as a writer of original fiction and fanwork) and in the virtual social
communities of the digital world. A generation of scholarship in critical
race theory and qualitative research informs my analytic approach in *The
Dark Fantastic*: critical counterstorytelling for a digital age.

In order to bring critical race theory into conversations about young
adult literature, media, fandom, and popular culture, counterstories, or
alternative narratives, must be foregrounded.[30] First theorized by legal
scholars Derrick Bell, Kimberlé Crenshaw, Mari Matsuda, Richard Del-
gado, and others in the 1980s, critical race theory emerged from the need
to explain the persistence of racial discrimination and social suffering in
the United States long after the classical Civil Rights movement ended.
Critical race theory uses storytelling and personal narrative as method,
following a long intellectual tradition in African American letters beginning with the slave narratives. Critical race counterstorytelling, according to Daniella Cook and Adrienne Dixson, provides the following
affordances for the contemporary study of race in texts, schools, and
society. It

1. provides psychic preservation by not silencing the experiences of
   the oppressed and thus exposing neglected evidence;
2. challenges normative reality through an exchange that overcomes
   ethnocentrism and the dysconscious conviction of viewing the
   world one way;
3. privileges the voices of people of color as the basis for understanding how race and racism function; and
4. purposefully attempts to disrupt liberal ideology.[31]

In *The Dark Fantastic*, I bring this rich restorying tradition to bear in
my analysis of the fantastic as both genre and social construct, narrating my experiences as a Black woman interlocutor before moving to the
interplay among the voices of texts, critics, and researchers, and finishing
with the voices of the characters of color themselves. In order to theorize
the role of race in the collective literary imagination, I privilege the fictional, imagined "Africanist Others" Toni Morrison describes in *Playing*

in the Dark in each of the texts and genres I examine. This choice is intentional: shifting focus away from White heroic protagonists and illuminating the imaginary stories of people of color at the margins can reveal much, especially for today's youth. Thus, in my chapter on *The Vampire Diaries* television show, I am more interested in the way that Bonnie Bennett is constructed in and by the text than the positioning of protagonist Elena Gilbert. And as I analyze racial innocence in *The Hunger Games*, it is Katniss's friend Rue, not Katniss herself, whose positionality I seek to privilege. The marginalization of these dark fictional girls within these multimedia texts is analogous to the marginalization of people of color in schooling and society. I examine how race and the imagination bend such texts at the seams, contorting both space and time.[32]

Tracing the dark fantastic cycle for this book required not only critical race counterstorytelling and case study as method, but also an intimate familiarity with highly popular texts consumed by youth and young adults, as well as the contested digital contexts of fandom communities and social media. As Karen Hellekson and Kristina Busse note about autoethnographic work produced by fans who are also scholars:

> We hope to shift the concerns from a dichotomy of academic and fannish identity to subject positions that are multiple and permit us to treat the academic and fannish parts as equally important. Our identities are neither separate nor separable. We rarely speak as fan or scholar; we rarely differentiate between an academic and fannish audience, except perhaps in formality of tone. . . . The act of performing fandom parallels the act of performing academia. Both rely on dialogue, community, and intertextuality. . . . We contend that our self-definition as participants and observers does not hinder us from seeing but rather helps us to see a more comprehensive picture of fandom.[33]

Analysis of race in speculative fiction should include counterstories that narrate stories from the perspectives of readers, writers, fans, and audiences who are racialized. It is my hope that this counterstorying approach—moving from an autoethnography of reading and participation toward critical and empirical perspectives in the field, and then concluding with an exploration of the stories being told about race and difference through the vantage point of the Dark Other—might serve as a launching point for further empirical work in reading and literacy education, as well as illuminate the participatory experiences of people of color as they interact with media of all kinds and engage in the myriad social communities of the digital age.

Tour of *The Dark Fantastic*

In chapter 1, "Toward a Theory of the Dark Fantastic," I begin by defining and describing the construct of the dark fantastic. A dark fantastic reading reveals an eerie cycle that moves inevitably from spectacle to hesitation, from violence to haunting, and can only be subverted through emancipation. Grounding the project in my lived experiences as an insider/outsider of the genre, I use Morrison's *Playing in the Dark*, as well as other key texts across disciplines, as a guide for framing the dark fantastic as I have encountered it in operation across texts, authors and creators, genres and modes, and affinity groups.

Thus, chapter 2, "Lamentations of a Mockingjay: *The Hunger Games'* Rue and Racial Innocence in the Dark Fantastic," is my critical examination of race in terms of digital age reader/viewer response and associated fan cultures through the lens of Robin Bernstein's concept of *racial innocence*. I theorize that racial innocence is one of the reasons why it has been difficult to racially integrate the fantastic.

After examining how the dark fantastic is refracted because of the necessity of innocence in fantastic narratives, chapter 3, "A Queen out of Place: Dark Fantastic Dreaming and the Spacetime Politics of Gwen in BBC's *Merlin*," moves to the issue of *location*. Although some fantasy authors and screenwriters have begun to look beyond an exclusively European past to dream and imagine, Angel Coulby being cast as Gwen, the servant girl who would grow up to become Queen Guinevere on *Merlin*, led to consternation on the part of some viewers. I look at fan and viewer reactions to Gwen as a princess out of place, eliciting questions about accuracy and authenticity, and raise questions about the challenges of location for an emancipatory Black fantastic. I conclude by making the case for why Gwen matters in our considerations of the role that race plays in fairy tales, given the enduring presence of fairy stories in the culture and how they ultimately shape the popular imagination.

Chapter 4, "The Curious Case of Bonnie Bennett: *The Vampire Diaries* and the Monstrous Contradiction of the Dark Fantastic," considers how the intersections among race, gender, and desire are commodified within the auspices of the fantastic, thereby illustrating how Black girl characters are uniquely subjected to *violence* even in a horror narrative. Theories of race in horror from Kinitra Brooks and others are essential for understanding what happens as Irish American Bonnie McCullough in the book series is transformed into African American Bonnie Bennett on the television screen. Bonnie's curious case is framed by conversations that I had with my niece about race, fangirling, and the dark fantastic worlds that we choose for ourselves.

Chapter 5, "Hermione Is Black: A Postscript to Harry Potter and the Crisis of Infinite Dark Fantastic Worlds," moves from ideological concepts to concrete action by showcasing the ways that audiences respond to textual erasure and misrepresentation by using social media to create new worlds—and how creatives are in turn starting to think about the implications of race and difference in participatory culture. After reflecting on my own experiences as a prominent participant in Harry Potter fandom in the early 2000s and my subsequent ostracism from the community, I speculate on the implications of expanding canons and characters in science fiction, fantasy, horror, comics, and graphica across media forms, and point toward a new way that today's young people and new authors are ensuring that we have *all* kinds of characters in *all* kinds of stories.

The Dark Fantastic is intended to be the opening of a conversation, not the culmination of it. It is my hope that this book helps people across fields consider how to address the diversity crisis in young adult literature, media, and fan cultures much more critically by thinking through some of the reasons why, until recently, the fantastic has not been a site of liberation and transcendence for many people.

Examining examples of today's dark fantastic may help us understand how profound our societal crisis of imagination has become. Theorizing the dark fantastic may provide some answers for why magical stories seem to be written for some people and not for others. Working toward a fantastic that is restorative, transformative, and emancipatory has the power to remake our world.

TOWARD A THEORY OF THE DARK FANTASTIC

"I nearly reached the point of believing": that is the formula which sums up the spirit of the fantastic. Either total faith or total incredulity would lead us beyond the fantastic: it is *hesitation* which sustains its life.

—Tzvetan Todorov, *The Fantastic: A Structural Approach to a Literary Genre*, 1973

If the *spectacle* of the lynched Black body haunts the modern age, then the slow disintegration of Black bodies and souls in jail, urban ghettos, and beleaguered schools haunts our postmodern times.

—Hazel Carby, *Race Men*, 1998

In Him was life, and that life was the light of all mankind. The light shines in the darkness, and the darkness has not overcome it.

—John 1:4–5

The Dangers of Myth-Making: Why We Need to Examine the Dark Fantastic

In her landmark essay, *Playing in the Dark: Whiteness and the Literary Imagination*, Toni Morrison explained that she could understand and theorize Whiteness in American literature only when she "stopped reading as a reader and began to read as a writer."[1] It was only when I began to read fantasy and fairy tales as an aspiring author that I began to understand the function of darkness in the fantastic. My first fanfiction was sparked by the Ron/Hermione versus Harry/Hermione shipping wars in the Harry Potter fan communities of the early 2000s (discussed in chapter 5).[2] It was a crowdsourced story, with beta readers from England to Brazil, and fandom personalities showing up as characters—and lampooned caricatures—in every chapter. Although I conceded that Rowling would likely put Ron and Hermione together in the end, I shipped Harry and Hermione together for reasons that I wanted to show in my take on things. As a fan of color, I was also curious about what the wizarding world might be like outside England. Without colonialism or slavery, how on earth did Black children end up at Hogwarts with English names? Adoption? Immigration? Or had witches and wizards of color been somehow subjugated—was their magic less powerful? As a young writer, I audaciously dreamed about someday creating and publishing my own fantasy stories that weren't based primarily on European folklore or myth.

Wanting to know more about the possibilities of characters that had been focalized only through Harry's point of view in the book series, I set my second fanfiction in the most magical place I could think of at the time—Brazil. Of course, I had never actually *visited* Brazil. As I was growing up, my parents had neither the money nor the desire to travel abroad. After college and graduate school, there were student loans and the financial realities of striking out on my own. Yet like many other African Americans, I was enthralled with the prospect of making my pilgrimage to Brazil—Salvador, Bahia, to be exact. It was thought that in Salvador the cultural loss and trauma of slavery had been far less severe than it had been in the United States, and that Brazilians of African descent had retained more of their memories from our Motherland. Just as my Irish American friends made pilgrimages to Dublin, and my Italian American friends regularly visited their relatives in Sicily, I hoped to someday travel to Brazil and then West Africa to reclaim a part of my heritage, perhaps experiencing a bit of what I believed was authentic magic along the way.[3]

While browsing the Brazzil.net forum in the early 2000s, I read a heated exchange between two participants. One was a Brazilian man, an anthropologist living in Rio de Janeiro and using the alias of Macunaima. The other was a Black American woman who shared the same vision of Bahia as a racism-free Afrotopia that I had internalized. The more this woman posted her fantasies about visiting Brazil, the more offended Macunaima seemed to become. Finally, he wrote something on that thread that affected me so profoundly that I saved it to mull over:

> Myth-making is not a good cure for amnesia. In fact, given your original statement as to "stagnant" African culture, it seems that your amnesia has resulted in your unconscious incorporation of some incredibly racist opinions and beliefs. *This is why myth-making is dangerous for subordinate peoples: your imagination is more controlled by the dominant social formation than you're probably willing to admit.* Only by deep and wide engagement with history can we begin to reconstruct a reasonable notion as to what has happened and why.[4]

The idea that my imagination had been controlled in any way floored me. As a child and teen, I had been an omnivorous reader, seeking my own bliss without much concern about the politics of my reading. The cartography of my imagination had been inscribed by Tove Jansson's *Moominland Midwinter* as much as it had been by Julius Lester's *To Be a Slave*. I greatly enjoyed reading Virginia Hamilton's lyrical retellings of traditional Black American folktales but counted Lucy Maud Montgomery's idealized Edwardian-era Prince Edward Island story girls as my favorite characters of all. I dutifully read Mildred Taylor's *Roll of Thunder, Hear My Cry* series in order to learn about my ancestors' plight, but when it was time for imaginative escape, I turned to Michael Ende's *Neverending Story*. When it came to works that made the leap from page to screen, I watched the film adaptation of William Howard Armstrong's *Sounder* once while in school, but I have watched *The Princess Bride* and *Labyrinth* so many times that I have both movies memorized. Although I grew up in the first generation after the classical phase of the Civil Rights movement, my literate imagination was quite segregated. Books and movies about children and teens who looked like me were read and viewed out of duty, in order to learn something about the past.[5] Books and movies that showcased the pleasures of dreaming, imagination, and escape were stories about people who did not look like me.

And yet I was most drawn to those magical stories, for I longed to dream.

Macunaima's online post was the first moment I began thinking deeply about the myth-making that all human beings engage in to make sense of an oft-nonsensical world. This myth-making process—which fantasist Brian Attebery described as creating "stories *about* stories"—forms metanarratives that shape society, culture, and ultimately, the imagination. For, as Attebery notes, "Fantasy is an arena—I believe the primary arena—in which competing claims about myth can be contested and different relationships with myth tried out."[6] Literary historian Farah Mendlesohn further theorizes the relationships between the reader and the fantastic metanarrative as rhetorical.[7] A reader or viewer of the fantastic can enter a portal and go on a quest. He or she can be immediately immersed within the fantasy world from the first page, the first scene, or the first swell of the movie score. The fantastic can intrude upon the world the reader knows, or the reader can choose to remain in the liminal space between the real and the unreal.

What unites all of these paths into the fantastic is *belief*: one must *believe* the world that one is entering. This common thread, found in scholarship by Attebery and Mendlesohn, has its genesis in Todorov: "'I nearly reached the point of believing': that is the formula which sums up the spirit of the fantastic. Either total faith or total incredulity would lead us beyond the fantastic: it is *hesitation* which sustains its life."[8] This point of hesitation—whether it is the first flutter of a dragon's wing, blood dripping from a fang, the shimmer of fairy dust, or an otherworldly glow in a character's eyes—is very familiar to readers, viewers, and fans of fantasy, fairy tales, and other imaginative works. From our earliest years, we are inclined toward finding that point of hesitation that signals the fantastic.

But not everyone is positioned the same way *in* or *by* the fantastic. As Nigerian author Chimamanda Ngozi Adichie so aptly noted in her popular TED Talk about the dangers of a single story:

> I wrote exactly the kinds of stories I had been reading. All my characters were White and blue-eyed. They played in the snow. They ate apples and they talked a lot about the weather: how lovely it was that the sun had come out! Now, this despite the fact that I had never left Nigeria. . . . We didn't have snow, we ate mangoes, and we never talked about the weather because there was no need to. . . . What this demonstrates, I think, is how impressionable and vulnerable we are in the face of a story, particularly as children.[9]

The positioning of readers, viewers, and fans within the "stories about stories" of the fantastic is vital. While there has been some critical attention to the ways that women are positioned within fantasy, Adichie points to another problem: What happens when neither characters nor narrators in the fantastic seem to imagine *you* as a possible interlocutor?

Although it is generally assumed that audiences are positioned to identify with the heroes and heroines in "stories about stories," I began to wonder how the fantastic shapes the collective consciousness toward perceptions of difference. When might young readers experience moments of dissonance? Specifically, when might young readers of color realize that *the characters I am rooting for are not positioned like me in the real world, and the characters that are positioned like me are not the team to root for*? How do these readers respond to this absence? Do they assume an assimilationist stance? *People are people—I can relate to any character.* Do they assume a stance of resistance? *This story contains no one like me—therefore, it is not for me.* More research is needed on what happens when children and teens of color read texts where either they are not represented, or their representation is problematic.[10]

Recent conversations about diversity in publishing and the media advocate for greater inclusion of people of color within stories, especially stories written for young people. But the challenge of getting readers to voluntarily *choose* to identify with the Dark Other is a perennial one. For those of us who are always already positioned as monsters, even current theories of the monstrous fall short. To demonstrate their limits, I provide the following counterstory from the monster's perspective.

Through a Looking Glass, Darkly: Theorizing Fantasy from the Monster's Point of View

The traditional purpose of darkness in the fantastic is to disturb, to unsettle, to cause unrest. This primal fear of darkness and Dark Others is so deeply rooted in Western myth that it is nearly impossible to find its origin. Some scholars have traced the fear of darkness to ancient Greece and the classical tradition,[11] while others locate a corresponding valuation of Whiteness and lighter skinned peoples in the Christianization of the late Roman Empire and Dark Ages Europe, and in the emergence of the Islamic world.[12] No matter what the reasons were for the way our culture came to view all things dark in the past, the consequences have been a nameless and lingering fear of dark people in the present.[13]

In the West, the mysterious unknowability of darkness in nature was extended to a corresponding fear of unknown and unknowable dark things, including imaginary monsters beyond the boundaries of the known world during medieval times and, in the modern period, conquered and enslaved people from its margins. "Darky," a colloquial term for people of African descent during the late eighteenth century, signals that in modern English, darkness has never been just a metaphor. Darkness is personified, embodied, and most assuredly racialized.

My quest for the origins of fantastic darkness within history, culture, and society is part of a long intellectual tradition. Jeffrey Jerome Cohen's *Monster Theory* is but one of many influential texts that posits fantastic beasts, witches, zombies, vampires, dragons, manticores, shades, and the rest of a monstrous menagerie as analogous to those who are positioned as different in the real world. Cohen's seven theses of monster culture echo some of the observations that I began making as I read text after text. If monsters and people of color inhabit the same place in our stories, what would it be like to read monster theory from the monster's perspective? Thus, I offer the following call and response to Cohen's seven theses of monster culture:

1. *The monster's body is a cultural body.* Cohen notes that "the monster's body quite literally incorporates fear, desire, anxiety, and fantasy . . . giving them life and an uncanny independence. The monstrous body is pure culture. A construct and a projection, the monster exists only to be read."[14] From my experiences with the fantastic, this echoes my suspicion that the Dark Other is constructed through text primarily as a spectacle. The Dark Other occupies the same space in reality that the monster occupies in fantasy. Hazel Carby's observation that the Black body is the spectacle of the modern age and Toni Morrison's illustration of the Africanist Other as always already imagined by the dreamer seem to warrant this countertheorization.

2. *The monster always escapes.* "The monster's body is both corporeal and incorporeal; its threat is its propensity to shift."[15] From Henry

Louis Gates's groundbreaking critical text *The Signifying Monkey*, I knew that the role of the Dark Other in the West has been that of the Trickster—African American language, rhetoric, and culture has had this shapeshifting quality since its inception.[16] While this escapist tendency may be frustrating from the point of view of the heroic protagonist, from the point of view of the monster, it is an essential strategy for self-preservation.

3. *The monster is the harbinger of category crisis.* The monster's "refusal to participate in the classificatory 'order of things' is true of monsters generally: they are disturbing hybrids whose externally incoherent bodies resist attempts to include them in any systematic structuration. And so the monster is dangerous, a form suspended between forms that threaten to smash distinctions."[17] From the monster's point of view, the language of this thesis is slanted toward the perspective of the gallant hero and the fair maiden, *not* the monster. The monster is said to refuse ordered participation, but the monster has already been excluded from the Great Chain of Being. The embodied hybridity that is positioned as disturbingly incoherent has been laminated into construction of the Other as monstrous.

4. *The monster dwells at the gates of difference.* "The monster is difference made flesh, come to dwell among us. In its function as dialectal Other . . . the monster is an incorporation of the Outside, the Beyond—of all those loci that are rhetorically placed as distant and distinct but originate Within."[18] Although this thesis provides insight into the construction of the monster through identity difference, again, the monster is only different from the perspective of those who have labeled the monster as monstrous. Even as Cohen walks us through the construction of racial Otherness in the Western imagination, I find myself wondering how these monstrous Dark Others might have viewed the *Westerners*. (After all, in our world, it is not those positioned as monstrous in the fantastic who engaged in modern-era conquest or colonization.)

5. *The monster polices the borders of the possible.* "The monster prevents mobility (intellectual, geographic, or sexual), delimiting the social spaces through which private bodies may move. To step outside this official geography is to risk attack by some monstrous

border patrol or (worse) to become monstrous oneself."[19] The monster is policed whenever it leaves terra incognita—the liminal spaces monsters are allowed to inhabit. It is deemed unreasonable for the monster to defend her home, unseemly for her to travel outside her delimitations, or unthinkable for her to enjoy her own monstrous culture. From the hero's point of view, this policing makes sense. From the perspective of the monster, it is nonsense.

6. *Fear of the monster is really a kind of desire.* "The monster is con-tinually linked to forbidden practices . . . the monster also attracts. The same creatures who terrify and interdict can evoke potent escapist fantasies; the linking of monstrosity with the forbidden makes the monster all the more appealing as a temporary egress from constraint."[20] From the heroic perspective, the monster provides an enticement, a poisonous lure that *makes* her deserving of destruction. But does the monster feel the same lure toward the hero? What the hero reads as simultaneous seduction and threat may not be what the monster is really communicating. Because we rarely receive the monster's point of view in fantastic narratives, the motives of the monstrous are a mystery.

7. *The monster stands at the threshold . . . of becoming.* "Monsters are our children. They can be pushed to the farthest margins of geog-raphy and discourse, hidden away at the edges of the world and in the forbidden recesses of our mind, but they always return."[21] This makes sense to the hero, center of the universe in his or her own mind, but just before this, the question, "Do monsters really exist? Surely they must, for if they did not, how could we?" raises a subsequent, unanswered question: Is the monster *truly* parent, child, neither, or both? For if the monster is a figment of the hero's imagination, then the imagination of the monster is truly unex-plored terrain.[22]

I have found much value in considering monster theory, color the-ory, and the history of racial analogies in speculative fiction. However, when we read literary and cultural texts from the perspective of the monster, *not* the protagonist, we find ourselves in a completely different ballgame.[23] This is why taking a supposedly "neutral" or "objective" ap-proach to theorizing the dark fantastic is problematic; the default position is to allow those who are used to seeing themselves as heroic and desired the power and privilege of naming, defining, and delimiting the entire world and everything that is in it. We never notice that monsters, fantastic beasts, and various Dark Others are silenced because we have never been taught the language that they speak. Critical race counterstorytelling provides both translation and amplification for these subsumed narratives.

From this perspective, the central claim that I am making about the dark fantastic is this: in the Anglo-American fantastic tradition, the Dark Other is the spectacle, the monstrous Thing that is the root cause of *hesitation, ambivalence,* and the *uncanny*. The Dark Other is the present-absence that lingers at the edges of every fairy tale. She stalks the shadows of the futurist visions of science fiction, lurks along the margins of the imagined magical pasts of high fantasy, and renders the uchronia of alternate history into a nonsensical cipher. What is most chilling is that *even when those who are endarkened and Othered dream in the fantastic, the Dark Other is* still *the obstacle to be overcome*. And most chilling of all, even in stories where all of the characters are "White and blue-eyed" (recalling Adichie's influential talk), *the Dark Other is always already there*.

When readers who are White, middle class, cisgender, heterosexual, and able-bodied enter the fantastic dream, they are empowered and afforded a sense of transcendence that can be elusive within the real world. If this is the case, then readers and hearers of fantastic tales who have been endarkened and Othered by the dominant culture can never be plausible conquering heroes nor prizes to be won in the fantastic. Unless the tale is meant to be comedic, tongue-in-cheek, a wink and a nod that breaks the fourth wall and assures audiences that this is a parody of the fantastic, not the *real* story . . .

. . . the implicit message that readers, hearers, and viewers of color receive as they read these texts is that *we are the villains. We are the horde. We are the enemies.*

We are the monsters.

For many readers, viewers, and fans of color, I suspect that, at the level of consciousness, to participate in the fantastic is to watch *yourself* be slain—and justifiably so, as the story recounts. After all, in fairy tales, it was *you* who terrorized the hapless villagers, who kidnapped the fair princess, who dared wage war against the dashing hero. You are the jealous darker sister who wishes to steal the fair maiden's pedestal for yourself. If you are present in the story at all, you are relegated to the margins; rarely is the narrative focalized through your eyes, and you are rendered abject. To watch a science fiction film is to learn that you have no future—there are only two or three people of color on most spaceships. Very often, when you appear on the page or on the screen, you are a slave, a servant, or a prostitute—your body is not your own. If you have words, your speech serves only to support the narrative, never to subvert it.

You are the alien Other. You are the Orc. You are the fell beast.

The very presence of the Dark Other in a text of speculative fiction, across genre and mode, creates a profound ontological dilemma. This dilemma is inescapable, for readers and for writers, and must be reconciled. It is most often resolved by enacting symbolic and/or actual violence against the Dark Other. This is what readers and hearers of the fantastic expect, for it mirrors the spectacle of violence against the endarkened and the Othered in our own world. It is a familiar template, an archetype that comforts, especially when the position of the Other in the real world is uncertain.

When one is positioned as the Dark Other by the dominant culture, the fantastic presents a cipher, a puzzle that must be solved. Some people of color resolve this tension by rejecting the fantastic for the desert of the Real (to borrow a term from *The Matrix* trilogy). For many, a viable fantastic may be the dream of a world where they are not judged by the color of their skin, the language of their parents, the God they pray to (or not), or whom they choose to love, but rather by the kind of persons they are, or are becoming, or wish to be someday. For many, the long struggle for liberation in the world that we know is epic enough without imagining a completely different world, with different rules and different outcomes. However, it is because the fantastic is often positioned as universal in our culture that its deconstruction and transformation are essential.

The fantastic has need of darkness, for these innocent "stories about stories" require both heroes *and* villains, fair princesses *and* evil crones, valiant steeds *and* nightmarish beasts. The fantastic requires Medusas *and* Grendels, chimaeras *and* manticores, cunning tricksters *and* cowardly fools. It needs the Dark Other as its source of hesitation, the very spectacle that causes the heart to skip in fear. It desires the Dark Other's violent end in a form of ritual sacrifice, purging the very source of the darkness and righting the wrongs of the world before returning to haunt the happy ending.

This haunting means that people of color are not incidental to the fantastic. Without Dark Others—either embodied or as shades—fairy tales, science fiction, high fantasy, superhero comics, and graphic novels as we know them simply would not exist. Any impetus toward whitewashing the imagination, memory, dreams, and magic is futile, for any work of the fantastic that is all White signals (if not *screams*) that darkness lingers just beyond the turn of a page, the flicker of a frame, or the click of a thumb.

To understand the work that the fantastic does in our world, the position of the Dark Other—and of the shadows cast by the presence of imagined darkness—must be centered. Reading fantastic narratives from a critical race counterstorytelling perspective, the Dark Other becomes the Dark One, the subject, the focalizer, and the narrator of the *shadow book* that poet Kevin Young imagines as "a book that we don't have, but know of, a book that may haunt the very book we have in our hands."[24] The tales told by darkness, by the shadows, by the Dark Ones are never completely erased or removed, but are simply "hidden in plain sight." For it is not only history that has been irrevocably inscribed by its victors, but also memory and imagination itself.

Once upon a time, I believed that people of color were incidental to the English language fantasy tradition. I believed that for the most part, the speculative genres did not deal directly with race, which was why I liked them. In digital fandom, I could shed my skin and just *be*. But when you begin to read the fantastic as a writer and a critic, you begin to notice the presence of dark shadows *everywhere*. Therefore, in contrast to readings of young adult literature, media, and culture that position human and nonhuman characters of color as marginal, I wish to position all endarkened characters and characterizations as central to both the fantastic and the construction of imagined Whiteness. The Dark Other is the engine that drives the fantastic.

Sympathy for the Monster:
How the Dark Fantastic Cycle Works

Observing the role of Dark Others in the fantastic, I have noticed a pattern—a cycle of the dark fantastic—in text after text. The cycle, which I revisit in subsequent chapters of this book, is as follows: (1) spectacle, (2) hesitation, (3) violence, (4) haunting, and (5) emancipation.

The first step of the dark fantastic cycle, *spectacle*, extends beyond the marble halls of the fantastic into the real world.[25] As Daphne Brooks and Qiana Whitted observe, audiences in the West have long marveled at the presence of the Dark Other in genres ranging from theater to comics.[26] Visual difference has fueled the Western fantastic imagination since medieval times, creating what Stuart Hall terms the "spectacle of the Other."[27] Hall argues, "What is visually produced, by the practices of representation, is only half the story. The other half—the deeper meaning—lies in *what is not being said, but is being fantasized, what is implied but cannot be shown.*"[28] Even if we cannot *see* this awesome persona of the Dark Other, there is one certainty: she is dark.

In the second step, *hesitation*, the presence of the Dark Other interrupts the waking dream of the fantastic. Philosopher Paul Ricoeur posits that imagination alters our memories, because imagination is directed toward the fantastic, the fictional, the unreal, the possible, and the utopian.[29] Ricoeur further notes that imagination has to be uncoupled from memory, and I believe this uncoupling is the source of hesitation—there is no way of imagining our way out of the trauma and suffering of our fraught collective history. This creates a profound dilemma for writers and readers. Although the Dark Other is necessary for the fantastic, her presence is unsettling. She is not supposed to be there (although she *must* be), wreaking havoc on the order, harmony, and happiness of all that is right and light (and White). She must be contained, subjugated, and ultimately destroyed.

This leads to the third phase of the cycle: the dilemma created by the presence of the Dark Other must be resolved with *violence*. Postcolonial theorists from Robert J. C. Young to Anne McClintock might say that this violence occurs because we cannot deal with the strong fear, desire, and longing that the Dark Other elicits.[30] Whether driven by desire, fear, longing, or another impulse, darkness must be destroyed, or there *is* no story. Black feminist scholars from Hazel Carby to Michelle Alexander and Dorothy Roberts have noted the ways that the containment and destruction of Black bodies works in the real world.[31] The fantastic is driven by similar imperatives at the symbolic level. Thus, the Dark Other is subject to textual violence, which often results in character death.

Yet this death is not permanent. When the Dark Other is defeated and catharsis is reached, their present-absence nonetheless haunts the story, which represents the fourth step in the cycle of the dark fantastic. Toni Morrison referred to this haunting as "Romancing the Shadow" in *Playing in the Dark*:

> These speculations have led me to wonder whether the major and championed characteristics of our national literature—individualism, masculinity, social engagement versus historical isolation; acute and ambiguous moral problematics; the thematics of innocence coupled with an obsession with figurations of death and hell—are not in fact responses to a dark, abiding, signing Africanist presence.[32]

This haunting presents another dilemma for the fantastic, which remains ambivalent toward the presence of darkness in the narrative. The Dark Other *must* die, but she *cannot* die. The Dark One haunts the text because she cannot escape. She is fettered to the story; without her, there is neither conflict nor climax, neither rising action nor resolution. The Dark Other gives the story its excitement, its promise, its very meaning. Morrison once again provides insight into this pernicious fettering, which leads to the nonexistent existence of racialized characters:

> The ways in which artists—and the society that bred them—transferred internal conflicts to a "blank darkness" consisting of conveniently bound and violently silenced black bodies is a major theme in American literature. . . . Black slavery enriched the country's creative possibilities. For in that construction of Blackness and enslavement could be found not only the not-free, but also with the dramatic polarity created by skin color, the projected of the not-me. The result was a playground for the imagination.[33]

Although the Dark Other elicits both fear and desire, her continuing presence is necessary for creating and sustaining these "playgrounds for the imagination." It is this dilemma that ultimately repositions the Dark Other as the spectacle that creates hesitation and elicits violence anew. Hence, the first four phases of this cycle repeat, spawning sequels, spinoffs, and authorial success.

The final step of the dark fantastic cycle is *emancipation*. It is reached only when the Dark Other is liberated from spectacle, embodied hesitation, violence, and haunting. Narratives with liberated Dark Others are rare, and are rarely as popular as those that feature trapped dark subjectivities. This is because subverting the traditional positioning of the Dark Other in the fantastic requires radical rethinking of everything that we know. It is why, I suspect, when characters of color appear in atypical roles, they are often challenged, disliked, and rejected. The principles of the dark fantastic are so ingrained in our collective consciousness that when the expected pattern is subverted, most audiences cannot suspend disbelief. Readers and viewers complain that dark heroic protagonists are not *likable*. Critics observe that the characters, settings, circumstances, and resolutions are *unbelievable*. Agents regret that they *just cannot connect* with the characters. Television and movie studios, as well as publishing houses, tell writers that their stories are not *marketable*. Thus, whether the story in question is a novel, a television show, or a graphic novel, the Dark Other remains caged.

Everything in our culture, as well as in modern history and contemporary life of the West, demands the positioning of the Dark Other as an antagonist. As Edward Said observed, "Without empire . . . there is no European novel as we know it."[34] Within American literature, Morrison contends, "there is no romance (and no Gothic) free of what Herman Melville called 'the power of blackness.'"[35] Connecting Morrison's observations to Maria Nikolajeva's claims that fantasy's origins can be located in Romanticism, I believe there can be no fantastic without the Dark Other. The Dark Other is the counterbalance, the counterweight that makes the entire enterprise of the fantastic work. Even when the Dark Other is not present, her present-absence nonetheless haunts the story. This goes beyond a mere cursory consideration of the lack of Black characters, characters of color, or characters who are different in the story. Even if darkness and light—or Black and White—seem to have exchanged places in the narrative, *the Dark Other is always already there. Darkness is the source that powers the fantastic.*

And so it is that any artist or writer who wishes to write an emancipatory fantastic faces an uphill journey if seeking mainstream readership and viewership. The template of the fantastic is our imperfect, messy, postmodern, and postcolonial world. The charge of the fantastic is to bedazzle the landscapes of childhood. But, as postcolonial theorist Shaobo Xie observes, "If this is the truth of the postmodern moment, then children are perhaps the most victimized and most urgently need to be postcolonized . . . because they are most violently subjected to colonialist ideas of racial-ethnic Otherness at the most formative years of their [lives]."[36] These colonialist ideas are inscribed in the generic conventions of the fantastic. Therefore, would-be storytellers must somehow liberate the Dark Other from her imprisonment and impending doom, not only in the text itself, but also in the imaginations of his or her readers.

In contemporary culture, the project of emancipating the dark fantastic may be even more challenging than the myth-making project J. R. R. Tolkien assigned for himself. Liberating the fantastic from its fear and loathing of darkness and Dark Others not only requires new narratives for the sake of endarkened readers. It requires emancipating the imagination itself.

The Shadow with a Thousand Faces: Locating the Dark Other in the Fantastic

How can one find the Dark Other in the fantastic, especially when many traditional fantasy novels, fairy tales, comics, and fantastic television shows and movies seem not to have any discernible characters of color? Again, Toni Morrison's *Playing in the Dark* provides a good starting point:

> The situation is aggravated by the tremor that breaks into discourse on race. It is further complicated by the fact that the habit of ignoring race is understood to be a graceful, even generous liberal gesture. To notice is to recognize an already discredited difference. To enforce its invisibility through silence is to allow the black body a shadowless participation in the dominant cultural body. According to this logic, every well-bred instinct argues *against noticing* and forecloses adult discourse.[37]

In other words, the reason our culture does not often notice the ways that race, difference, and darkness are hailed in the fantastic is because we have been carefully taught not to notice it. The supposedly raceless terrain of the fantastic thus becomes a means of escape from our raced, embodied existences, even for White readers and viewers. However, enforced invisibility through colormuteness in the fantastic does *not* render Black bodies shadowless.[38] Quite the contrary. The shadow cast becomes darker and more ominous still for its very unspeakability.

Beyond the magical landscapes of fantasy, stories set in the future and on alien worlds seem to uncannily imagine alien Others subjugating the West in the same way that Europe did to the "rest."[39] John Rieder observes in *Colonialism and the Emergence of Science Fiction* that "scholars largely (though not universally) agree that the period of the most fervid imperialist expansion in the late nineteenth century is also the most crucial period for the emergence of [science fiction]."[40] From H. G. Wells's radio play *The War of the Worlds* to the cinematic blockbuster *Star Trek* Kelvinverse movies, themes of invasion, conquest, and colonization are the bread and butter of science fiction. Fantasy and fairy tales are not exempt. Mark Bould and Sherryl Vint, drawing on José Monleón, find that fantasy emerges from dialectics of reason and unreason that arose with modernity, dividing the world into "us" and "them."[41]

In the fantastic, vampires and werewolves, witches and wizards, and seers and shifters often function as recognizable stand-ins for majorities and minorities and the inevitable conflicts that emerge between identity groups. Bould and Vint also suggest that Mendlesohn's organization of the fantastic into four broad rhetorical types—portal-quest, intrusion, immersion, and liminal—may be useful for thinking about what kind of political work might be done in each.[42] Yet the Dark Other crosses all of these boundaries—generic, categorical, and rhetorical —with both thrill and threat, and can be found in some of the most popular books, television shows, and movies:

- In *Once Upon a Time*, an ABC postmodern fairy tale drama popular with teens and young adults, folkloric figure Rumpelstiltskin becomes the Dark One, entwined in a relationship with the lovely Belle from *Beauty and the Beast*.

- The main antagonists of vampires in the *Twilight* movie series as well as the CW television shows *The Vampire Diaries* and *The Originals* are were-wolves. In all of these mythologies, werewolves are directly connected to Native Americans and/or First Nations people.
- In the first few seasons of *The Vampire Diaries* television show, the majority of witches and warlocks had visible African ancestry. This was revised only with the introduction of *The Originals* characters, storylines, and spinoff series. (As I show in chapter 4, this is a departure from the books, where witch sidekick Bonnie McCullough is of Irish Celtic—and likely Druidic—heritage).

These are but a few of the locations of the Dark Other in the early twenty-first-century mainstream fantastic. In these examples, I focus on visual narratives (television shows and movies) because it seems that when the fantastic is transmediated from page to screen, conventions become that much more amplified, especially in the post–*Harry Potter* age. It is one thing to *read* and *imagine* a character who is the site of difference; it is quite another to *see* that character on the small or large screen. Participatory culture also plays a role in this: when Morrison asked rhetorically about what happens as we imagine "an Africanist Other," she might not have foreseen that twenty years later, not only would fans run to social media to share their reactions after finishing a narrative but they would also use social media to discuss books and shows *during* readings and viewings. Thus, reader, viewer, and fan responses are being shaped much more collectively than at any time in the recent past. While there are some affordances to this crowdsourcing of imagination, there may also be a greater tendency to affirm what is traditional. As media scholar Henry Jenkins said in an interview marking the twentieth anniversary of his landmark publication *Textual Poachers*, "Fandom is an imagined community, but if so, it is a community that is constructed through *the collective imagination*. Its utopian imagination often fuels fandom's resistances to corporate efforts to commodify its cultural productions and exchanges. If we downplay the utopian aspects of fandom, we may also lose some of its critical edge."[43]

Those who respond to the fantastic may be collectively shaping imagination and resisting the commodification of stories from a commitment to utopia. However, the pervasive belief that fandoms for the imaginative genres represent postracial utopias also suppresses efforts to decolonize and emancipate the imagination. This presents a real challenge. Children's and young adult literature, particularly fairy tales, myths, and folklore, are powerful agents of social reproduction in our culture. I passionately believe that examining the dark fantastic through critical scholarship of books, films, magazines, websites, comics, and graphic novels intended for children and young adults is indeed one of the most effective postcolonial and critical projects in the long run, for as Xie reminds us, "The world ultimately belongs to children."[44]

Songs of Endarkened Girlhoods:
Rue, Gwen, Bonnie, Hermione—and Beyond

I did not set out to focus on the intersectional roles of gender and race in the dark fantastic. However, as I surveyed speculative texts outside of comics, I quickly found that the vast majority of the Black protagonists I encountered were girls and women—#BlackGirlMagic.[45] In comics, perhaps the most famous Black character of the past quarter century is mutant heroine Ororo Munroe, best known as Storm from Marvel Comics' lucrative *X-Men* series. Clearly, there is something about endarkened girlhood and womanhood that especially anchors the fantastic, from H. Rider Haggard's colonialist boys' adventure novel *She* to the growing number of Black female protagonists in today's science fiction and horror television shows. Black Girls' Literacies Collective co-founder Yolanda Sealey-Ruiz writes:

The brutality against Black girls has a long and deep history in the United States. Dating back centuries to the sanctioned system of slavery that began in 1619, acts of violence against Black female bodies, including death at the hands of slave traders, were a common occurrence. The historical research of [Daima] Berry, [Deborah] Gray White, and [Saidiya] Hartman, among others, details the brutality Black girls and women experienced under the system of chattel slavery. Varying degrees of inhumane treatment experienced by Black girls have continued throughout history; however, in recent times, there has been a heightened attack on them, particularly in schools.[46]

Given this recent history in the era of #BlackLivesMatter, #SayHerName, and other permutations of activism targeted toward the intersections of race and gender, inspired by the foundational research of scholars from Kimberlé Crenshaw and Patricia Hill Collins to Kyra Gaunt and Venus Evans-Winters, *The Dark Fantastic* takes up calls by the Black Girls' Literacies Collective in my field to "center Black girls in literacy research by speaking to the invisibility of girls in schools, classrooms, and research literature, the ways in which they are misrepresented and dehumanized in the public media. . . . Researchers have pointed to the intricacies of Black girlhood and how their literacies are deeply complex and the need to center their ways of knowing and being in the world."[47] While most research in this area rightly focuses on the experiences, needs, and outcomes of living Black girls, past and present, in this project, I have focused my critical lenses on the story-lives of Black girl characters. As a literacy scholar, I concur with the Black Girls' Literacies Collective, and contend that how Black girls show up on the page and on the screen matters for the ways that Black girls are treated in the world.

My choice *not* to focus on Black male characters, Black nonbinary characters, and Black trans characters in this project was solely due to their limited number in popular speculative transmedia during the period of research and writing (2013–2017). Until recently, the presence of Black male protagonists in the fantastic beyond the ubiquitous and safe Will Smith seemed too fearsome even for our storied nightmares. Audience reactions to Finn in the final *Star Wars* trilogy are worth tracking by researchers and critics, as are Black male protagonists emerging from the expanded Marvel cinematic universe, including T'Challa, King of Wakanda in *Black Panther*, his antagonist, fan favorite Erik "Killmonger" Stevens, and Luke Cage. Further criticism and research is warranted, especially given the phenomenal, record-breaking success of *Black Panther*. Similarly, I anticipate an explosion of critical work on non-Black and/or Indigenous characters, as well as queer characters of color in fantastic narratives for youth and young adults in the near future.

The balance of *The Dark Fantastic* explores the fantastic from the perspectives of four stories, four fantastic worlds, and four protagonists. I begin with the heartbreaking racial innocence of young tribute Rue from Suzanne Collins's *The Hunger Games*, whose very existence was an affront to audiences when she emerged from the page to appear as dark skinned on the big screen. Moving from contemporary young adult literature rendered on screens large and small, I turn to Gwen in the BBC's *Merlin* to highlight some of the challenges inherent in locating an emancipatory dark fantastic in both time and space. Transmediation also reveals the plight of Bonnie Bennett, the heroine of Alloy, Inc.'s and the CW's *The Vampire Diaries*, whose incredible transformation from page to screen points to the trouble with heterosexual beauty and desirability politics in a late-capitalist, televised dark fantastic.

I conclude by revisiting my time in Harry Potter fandom when I chose as my avatar one of the most famous Black girls in a mainstream fantasy narrative, Angelina Johnson from J. K. Rowling's *Harry Potter* series—incidentally, the first-viewpoint narrator whose perspective I tried to capture in my ill-fated fanfiction from long ago.

Angelina joins Gwen, Rue, and Bonnie in an exclusive club of dark girls in the shadows of our contemporary billion-dollar fantastic, sacrificing life, limb, and love for protagonists fair, fueling the lucrative franchises from which they hail. Yet they are also the harbingers of a new generation of Black girl protagonists who are emerging from the imaginations of writers from all over the world to become the center of their own stories, as diverse audiences immersed in today's participatory cultures begin to demand more from education, entertainment, and society.

Myth-making may be dangerous indeed for those of us who play in the dark.

But let's play anyway.

2

LAMENTATIONS OF A MOCKINGJAY

The Hunger Games' *Rue and Racial Innocence in the Dark Fantastic*

Are you, are you,
Coming to the tree,
Where I told you to run
So we'd both be free.
Strange things have happened here
No stranger would it be
If we met at midnight in the hanging tree.
—Suzanne Collins, *Mockingjay* (2010)

What is a Black child? In the United States, conservatives simultaneously call for an end to abortion and extol the imagined virtues of it. . . . This is an execrable arithmetic, a violent accounting. Another indication that the meaning of *child*, as it abuts blackness, falls . . . apart.
—Christina Sharpe, *In the Wake: On Blackness and Being* (2016)

While they were eating, Jesus took bread, and when he had given thanks, he broke it and gave it to his disciples, saying, "Take and eat; this is my body." Then he took a cup, and when he had given thanks, he gave it to them, saying, "Drink from it, all of you. This is my blood of the covenant, which is poured out for many for the forgiveness of sins. I tell you, I will not drink from this fruit of the vine from now on until that day when I drink it new with you in my Father's kingdom."
—Matthew 26:26–29a

During the first decade of the twenty-first century, three transmedia franchises for young audiences were colloquially known as the Big Three—*Harry Potter*, *Twilight*, and *The Hunger Games*. Among the Big Three, the world of Suzanne Collins's *Hunger Games* trilogy (*The Hunger Games*, *Catching Fire*, and *Mockingjay*) is perhaps the most eerily close to our own. Unlike Gene Roddenberry's optimistic futuristic vision in *Star Trek*, *The Hunger Games* presents worst-case scenario answers for the most pressing questions of our day.[1] Set in the fictional dystopia of Panem (a thinly veiled take on a postnuclear United States), the eponymous first book recounts Katniss Everdeen's participation in the annual Hunger Games, a televised gladiatorial fight to the death. After a failed rebellion that took place nearly a century earlier (aptly known as the Dark Days), each of Panem's twelve districts is forced to send two of its children to the Capitol to participate as tributes in the games. At the annual Reaping, when tributes are chosen, or Reaped, by lottery, Katniss volunteers in place of her younger sister, Prim. The second book, *Catching Fire*, details Katniss's participation in an all-star version of the games known as the "Quarter Quell," while the final book, *Mockingjay*, traces Katniss's rise as the revolutionary leader who takes down the oppressive Capitol.

Although I was not completely satisfied with the conclusion of the series, the dystopian setting was appealing and familiar. Katniss hails from District 12, the poorest of Panem's regions, distant from the Capitol culturally and politically. I grew up in one of the District 12s of the United States—Detroit, Michigan. Much like Katniss, I came of age in the aftermath of a rebellion that occurred long before my earliest memories but that nonetheless shaped my childhood.[2] The 12th Street Rebellion of July 1967, also known as the "Detroit race riots," happened ten years before I was born, and its afterlife structured every element of our lives. As in Panem's outlying districts, there was the unspoken sense in 1980s Detroit that we were being collectively punished for past actions that had begun to fade into mythic significance. Everything that we lacked, from chain stores to safe streets and neighborhoods, was colloquially said to be the result of "the riots." White suburbanites and the media blamed Black criminality. In public, Black Detroiters blamed White flight. But when we conversed in our homes and neighborhoods, many of us in Black Detroit blamed ourselves. Although I have since learned more about the conditions that led to the social unrest and the role that internalized racism and anti-Blackness plays in self and community perception, when I was younger, I sincerely believed that Detroit's troubles were our fault. More than half a century has passed in real time, but in the collective imagination of Detroiters, 1967 was only yesterday. Even today, discourse about Detroit is laden with blame and shame about an event that occurred when my *mother* was only fifteen years old.

Despite these similarities, the Detroit of my childhood wasn't exactly like District 12. There wasn't *technically* an electrified fence around my neighborhood—although 8 Mile Road formed a barrier so formidable that the rapper Eminem made it the title of his biographical movie, and the affluent suburb of Grosse Pointe actually *did* build a wall between it and the city of Detroit. There was no *real* danger of being Reaped, but there was a legitimate risk of getting caught in the crossfire of drug-related violence. Yet while the world of my childhood differed from Katniss's in the details, it was similarly positioned as dystopian by the structures of power: politicians, the media, the educational establishment, and the criminal justice system. After all, Detroit, the 1980s Murder Capital of the United States, famously gave the nation the spectacle of an annual arson-fest popularly known as "Devil's Night." Violence reported on a daily basis by our all-too-diligent local media Othered us from Reagan's "Morning in America." As much of the rest of the United States basked in post-malaise prosperity, Detroiters suffered the consequences of being on the wrong side of the Reagan revolution.

By the time the cyberpunk film *RoboCop* portrayed Detroit as the quintessential near-future American nightmare in 1987, the line between fictional dystopia and reality was blurred. Within the United States of the late twentieth century, the discursive positioning of Detroit was similar to the Capitol's positioning of the fictional District 12 in *The Hunger Games* books. Many cities in the United States had suffered from disinvestment after World War II, but not all cities suffered in the same way. The variety of urban decline that we experienced in the Rust Belt was particularly acute. In Detroit, the metropolis that was known as the "Arsenal of Democracy" during the Second World War unraveled into what seemed like post-apocalyptic chaos during the final quarter of the twentieth century. By the early 2000s, it was among the cities discussed as evidence that the world had moved past the American century.[3] Thus, my interpellation of the dystopian Panem as a fictionalized version of my hometown is deeply rooted in my childhood experiences of attempting to make sense of a city that appeared to defy American notions of progress. Beyond any personal identification with the fictional setting of *The Hunger Games*, part of the novel's appeal to a mass audience is that it asks those immersed in the narrative to sympathize with a heroine who takes matters into her own hands. Through Katniss Everdeen, a people who are viewed as abject by totalitarian power liberate themselves through protest and eventually a second revolution, as detailed in the final two books of the trilogy, *Catching Fire* and *Mockingjay*. The liberation of Panem mirrors many of our own unfulfilled dreams of equity and justice. As Black feminist writer Roxane Gay observes, *The Hunger Games* "offers the kind of tempered hope everyone who survives something unendurable hungers for."[4]

Having equated conditions of District 12 with the struggles of postmodern Black Detroit, I was in for a surprise when I watched the first movie in *The Hunger Games* series: the vast majority of District 12 residents would very likely be classified as White in the contemporary United States. Seeing the Reaping rendered on the big screen created quite a bit of dissonance for me as a viewer: the film tacitly requires its audience to imagine that White people in this dystopian future not–United States were being subjected to a kind of social death analogous to that experienced mainly by contemporary people of color, especially those of us who are dark skinned.[5] Although the vast popularity of the movie franchise shows that most readers accepted this swap without question, for me, it was quite a stretch. After all, most media fail to show impoverished White people.[6] In my viewing experiences, Whiteness had typically been equated with middle-class norms, wealth, privilege, beauty, and desirability. In fact, I had so deeply projected the racial politics of the contemporary United States onto Collins's fictional setting as I read, that I experienced this viewing dissonance *twice*—the first time when I saw virtually no people of color at the famous Reaping where Katniss volunteers in the stead of her sister, Prim, and the second time when I was pleasantly surprised by the casting of mixed-race actor Lenny Kravitz as Cinna, a character whom I had somehow imagined during multiple readings of the series as pale skinned and red haired![7]

Given my difficulty imagining the residents of District 12 and the Capitol as White before seeing the movie version of *The Hunger Games*,

I should have been unsurprised that other readers had difficulty reading race, ethnicity, and other visible markers of difference as Collins had imagined them. What left me most surprised and dismayed was the negative online reaction of some viewers to the casting of Amandla Stenberg—a young mixed-race actress—as Rue, a young girl befriended by Katniss at a critical moment of the games.[8] Moreover, I was bewildered that many readers and fans of *The Hunger Games* didn't realize that Rue would probably be considered (and treated as) Black if she lived in the contemporary United States.[9] Perhaps that is because I am so used to searching for the faintest traces of myself in stories (including reading White characters described as "dark" as being dark skinned when I was a child).[10] I have long been clued in to science fiction and fantasy writers' myriad ways of signaling non-White characters, many of them problematic and stereotypical.[11] There can be a fine line between subversion and creating what has been theorized as a "magical Negro character,"[12] but I felt that Collins walked it better than some when it came to Rue.

In the balance of this chapter, I first look at the way that race and ethnicity are constructed in *The Hunger Games* and consider some of the literature on Collins's project to highlight the intersections between televised state violence and the neoliberal imperative of using visual technologies to market the body (in this case, through becoming a contestant on reality TV). Next, I show how the novel's moral center of gravity is transferred from Rue to Katniss, as the benefits of Rue's sacrifice provide not only the impetus for Katniss's revolution but also directly enable it. Moving from the page to the screen, I then note how some readers responded to Rue in the book and in the movie using social media. I conclude by showing how the problem of racial innocence in our culture leads to such reader responses, and ultimately traps Rue and other characters like her in the dark fantastic cycle.

Dark Days, Dark People:
How Race and Class Are Constructed in *The Hunger Games*

Because the fantastic reflects the concerns of our own world, it is not surprising that racial and ethnic difference is signaled in ways that are eerily familiar. Early in the first novel, the reader learns that class differences in District 12 are marked by physical appearance. Katniss is described as having "straight black hair, olive skin . . . gray eyes. . . . Most of the families who work the mines resemble one another the same way."[13] In our world, many people with White, Asian, Middle Eastern, and/or African ancestry could be described using the same terms. Thus, as represented in the text, the District 12 "look" is racially ambiguous. In the movie version of *The Hunger Games*, Jennifer Lawrence, a blue-eyed blonde actress, was cast as Katniss, and her hair was dyed brunette for the role. Media scholars Sarah Projansky and Kent A. Ono characterize this phenomenon as *strategic whiteness*. It involves re-centering White people within our popular media without explicitly calling attention to that fact.[14] In a narrative of a dystopian future that is purportedly post-racial, the racial hierarchies of our own world are reinscribed.

In the novels, Katniss's physical appearance, which is typical for District 12 residents, is specifically contrasted with her mother's and sister's looks: "That's why my mother and Prim, with their light hair and blue eyes, always look out of place. They are. My mother's parents were part of the small merchant class that caters to officials, Peacekeepers, and the occasional Seam customer."[15] Katniss resembled her late father, a miner who married above his social class. After the marriage, Katniss's mother was relegated to a life of poverty among the mining families of the Seam. Akin to Katniss and her father in appearance is her best friend and hunting companion, Gale, who is also from a mining family in the district. Other than Katniss's mother and Prim, no poor characters are described as blonde or blue eyed. Due to the casting choices for the film trilogy—and despite the fact that Lawrence's hair was dyed brunette for the role—much of the visual contrast between Katniss and the rest of her family that is evident in the novels gets lost on the screen.

Other District 12 residents from the merchant and managerial classes are described as having features resembling Katniss's mother and sister, including Katniss's male counterpart in the games and eventual love interest, fellow District 12 tribute Peeta Mellark. The mayor of District 12 has a daughter, Madge, who is blonde: "Today her drab school outfit has been replaced by an expensive white dress, and her blonde hair is done up with a pink ribbon. Reaping clothes."[16] This description of Madge emphasizes her pale appearance, signaling innocence and purity. Madge has adorned her "Reaping clothes" with a pin in the shape of a mockingjay—the bird that will become so central to the *Hunger Games* narrative.

After her initial shock at Prim's name being called during the Reaping, Katniss volunteers to serve as her district's female tribute in her younger sister's place. Here, it is significant that Prim's fair hair signals the Everdeen girls' merchant-class heritage.[17] Many merchants favor Prim, including District 12's baker, who promises Katniss, "I'll keep an eye on the little girl. Make sure she's eating."[18] Even as Katniss relaxes because of the baker's assurances to take care of her family, she reflects upon the difference between the ways people see her and the ways they see Prim: "People deal with me, but they are genuinely fond of Prim. Maybe there will be enough fondness to keep her alive."[19] Katniss explicitly connects Prim's ability to elicit sympathy to her ability to survive after Katniss leaves for the games. While Katniss must become the heroine of the games in order for her people to embrace her, Prim's natural qualities lead people to love her. The meaning is clear: the darker sister must earn our sympathy, while the fair one deserves it simply because she *is* fair. This is one way that, in the words of performance scholar Robin Bernstein, "whiteness . . . derives power from its status as an unmarked category."[20] Although Katniss and Prim are both of the same race, the opposition between dark girls and lighter ones is set up early in the reader's imagination, before other tributes who are racialized differently are introduced. Because these associations mirror the way that our own world is stratified, most casual readers would be unlikely to notice them.

Katniss is but one of the twenty-four tributes whose sacrifice will quench the Capitol's thirst for televised state violence. Within Panem's totalitarian state, the games serve both as retribution for the districts' failed revolution several generations before and as a shared sacrifice to bind civilization together. Some districts are more favored in the games than others. While the neo-Spartan Districts 1 and 2 supply the Capitol with "Peacekeeper" soldiers and the games with professional youth killers known as "Career Tributes," District 12 provides the fuel to power the Capitol's advanced technology. As Katniss observes: "In school, they tell us the Capitol was built in a place once called the Rockies. District 12 was in a region known as Appalachia. Even hundreds of years ago, they mined coal here. Which is why our miners have to dig so deep."[21] Just as Appalachia (like Detroit) is considered an abject place within our own United States, associated with those who labor with their hands,

District 12 is also denigrated. This disparaging attitude is made explicit by the effervescent Effie Trinket, a Capitol native and the moderator of each district's Reaping. As she says to Katniss and Peeta: "I've done my best with what I had to work with. How Katniss sacrificed herself for her sister. How you've both successfully struggled to overcome the barbarism of your district."[22] The contrast between the glitter of the Capitol and the grit of District 12 serves as an illuminating backdrop for Katniss's transformation from the authentically appealing girl who hunts and trades to feed her family into the sensational "girl on fire" for the games. Dubrofsky and Ryalls note that "altered bodies—bodies marked as surgically transformed or adorned with makeup and clothing—are constructed as deviant, in opposition to Katniss' unaltered White femininity, dangerously entrenching notions of naturalized embodied feminine Whiteness."[23] The narrative does not reveal how the other female tributes respond to their makeovers, but Katniss's resistance endears her to the reader in ways that are not accessible to characters of color.

One notable feature of the construction of Whiteness in Panem is the contrast between the honorable poverty of District 12 and the ill-gotten wealth of the Capitol. Appalachian Whiteness is not often positioned as desirable within metadiscourses of American Whiteness, but as Dubrofsky and Ryalls note, "The wealth, excess, and privilege of the people in the Capitol and the richer districts make them hyper-visible, marked by an undesirable and inauthentic White racial identity."[24] Furthermore, this wealth, excess, and privilege are positioned as deviant and nonnormative. It acts as a foil for the natural, *authentic* Whiteness embodied by Katniss in the books and amplified when the narrative is transmediated from page to screen. This positioning inverts the hierarchies of class often found in youth literature—privilege is seen as undesirable for this heroine because of the inauthenticity of the ruling class. This obscuring of White privilege serves to authenticate Katniss's Whiteness by its very omission.[25] Therefore, Katniss and District 12, with whom the reader is supposed to identify, have been positioned as more authentic than the oppressive multiracial, multiethnic Capitol.

If Whiteness has been equated with authenticity, what are the racial politics of *The Hunger Games*? In the books, it is significant that the first time we see Rue through Katniss's eyes is the televised account of her Reaping from the neighboring district:

And most *hauntingly*, a twelve-year-old girl from District 11. She has dark brown skin and eyes, but other than that, she's very like Prim in size and demeanor. Only when she mounts the stage and they ask for volunteers, all you can hear is the wind whistling through the decrepit buildings around her. There's no one willing to take her place.[26]

Katniss is haunted by Rue at first sight. Yet Rue is no ghost or monster. She is the most vulnerable character in the first book, the youngest of the twenty-four tributes. Her vulnerability reminds Katniss of the innocence of her own sister, Prim. The fact that Katniss is able to see Rue's innocence contributes to her heroism, as I illustrate in the next section. But no one is willing to sacrifice themselves on Rue's behalf as Katniss has done for Prim. Therefore, from her first appearance, the doom of Rue, the darkest girl in the story, is foreshadowed. Without Rue's presence, however, Katniss's heroism in the games, and her later revolution, would have been impossible. For it's not only the girls' friendship that inspires Katniss to action, but also the practical skills and strategic information she learns from the little girl from District 11.

Readers are positioned by stories to identify with protagonists like Katniss. Like many protagonists in young adult literature, Katniss is presented as defiant, courageous, self-sacrificing, and refreshingly authentic[27]—all qualities that most readers admire and wish to see in themselves. But the tantalizing glimpses of secondary characters don't just provide insight into the fictional world of Panem. They also offer a glimpse into the way that race, class, and freedom are perceived in society. Among a wide array of secondary characters, Rue is the story girl who haunts the narrative the most. As much as Katniss's story is a critique of the inauthenticity of the Capitol and its exploitation of its districts, Rue's story, if counterstoried through a critical race lens, is a critique of Katniss's heroism. For in a very real sense, Rue was, and is, the first mockingjay of *The Hunger Games*.

In the next section, I trace Rue's evolution from uncannily innocent little dark girl, likened to a flower and a bird, to the dark sacrifice that haunts the narrative. In doing so, I once again invoke Toni Morrison's assertion that our literature has been written in response to "a dark, abiding, signing Africanist presence."[28] As I will do in each subsequent chapter, I turn the spotlight from the White female protagonist to the dark girl in the shadows, in the expectation that if we behold her presence and hear her speak, we will be able to understand more about how race shapes the imagination.

The Mockingbird Becomes the Mockingjay: Rue as Dark Sacrifice on the Page and the Big Screen

Spectacle

As with other transmedia intended for young adult audiences, *The Hunger Games* is not often noted for its literary quality. This is most unfortunate, for I can't help but hear echoes of Harper Lee's quintessential novel *To Kill a Mockingbird* in the name Collins created for her fictional avian symbol.[29] Birds in religion, myth, and folklore have varied symbolic meanings: the soul, paradise, metamorphosis or transformation, beauty, vulnerability, dreams and the afterlife, omens, flight, or escape—just to list a few. Some birds are considered noble and majestic (the eagle), while others are silly or absurd (usually the flightless ones, like the extinct dodo). Still others symbolize peace (doves), humility (sparrows), predation (hawks), fear (ravens and owls), or opportunism (vultures).[30] It is interesting, then, that it is the cunning blue jay with which Atticus Finch contrasts the mockingbird:

> Atticus said to Jem one day, "I'd rather you shot at tin cans in the backyard, but I know you'll go after birds. Shoot all the blue jays you want, if you can hit 'em, but remember it's a sin to kill a mockingbird." That was the only time I ever heard Atticus say it was a sin to do something, and I asked Miss Maudie about it. "Your father's right," she said. "Mockingbirds don't do one thing except make music for us to enjoy. They don't eat up people's gardens, don't nest in corn cribs, they don't do one thing but sing their hearts out for us. That's why it's a sin to kill a mockingbird."[31]

The mockingbird is a symbol of innocence for all the reasons that Miss Maudie famously stated. Notice that the mockingbirds, who sing sweetly, are contrasted with blue jays, whose calls are more jarring. Just as the doomed mockingbird, Tom Robinson, is the central symbol of Harper

Lee's classic, little Rue from District 11 is the first doomed mockingjay of the games. Tracing the development of the mockingjay as symbol of revolutionary self-sacrifice throughout Collins's books illustrates this clearly.

The genesis of the mockingjay itself is imbued with symbolic resistance. Katniss reflects on the evolution of the mockingjay within Panem's culture soon after the Reaping:

> During the rebellion, the Capitol bred a series of genetically altered animals as weapons. . . . One was a special bird called a jabberjay that had the ability to memorize and repeat whole human conversations. They were homing birds, exclusively male, that were released into regions where the Capitol's enemies were known to be hiding. After the birds gathered words, they'd fly back to centers to be recorded. . . . The [male] jabberjays mated with female mockingbirds, creating a whole new species that could replicate both bird whistles and human melodies. They had lost the ability to enunciate words but could still mimic a range of human vocal sounds, from a child's high-pitched warble to a man's deep tones.[32]

Difference is encoded in the mockingjay's very DNA. In addition to its association with the mockingbird, already powerfully associated with the African American struggle in the United States thanks to Harper Lee, the mockingjay also recalls the blue jay, whose patterns of migration elude even skilled ornithologists.[33] Albeit bred from tools of their subjugation, the mockingjay is beloved among the people in the districts.

It is also significant that the very first appearance of the mockingjay in *The Hunger Games* is as the golden pin worn by the mayor's daughter, Madge. In the previous section, I recounted the ways that Prim is positioned as the ultimate symbol of purity within the narrative, her physical features signaling her membership in District 12's merchant class. Madge is described as having similar features. After Katniss volunteers as tribute on her sister's behalf, Madge gifts her with the golden pin:

> "They let you wear one thing from your district in the arena. Will you wear this?"
>
> She holds out the circular gold pin that was on her dress earlier. I hadn't paid much attention to it before, but now I see it's a small bird in flight.[34]

Madge pins the golden mockingjay on Katniss's dress and then gives her a kiss. With this gift, the mayor's daughter confers not only some of her own purity and innocence upon Katniss but also her privilege. Katniss repeatedly forgets the presence of the pin, only to remember it at key moments in the story. The first such time is on the train to the Capitol. After ruminating upon the class differences within both Panem and District 12, Katniss notices the pin she has been wearing since she left her family behind: "For the first time, I get a good look at it. It's as if someone fashioned a small golden bird and then attached a ring around it. The bird is connected to the ring only by its wing tips. I suddenly recognize it. A mockingjay."[35] Now that it is in Katniss's possession, the mockingjay pin is associated not only with innocence but also with memory and history. It reminds Katniss of her father, who was noted for his singing voice and his displeasure with the Capitol:

> My father was particularly fond of mockingjays. When we went hunting, he would whistle or sing complicated songs to them and, after a polite pause, they'd always sing back. . . . Whenever my father sang, all the birds in the area would fall silent and listen. . . . There's something comforting about the little bird.[36]

Katniss's father's angelic singing voice will become significant later in the narrative. In her memories the mockingjay and her father seem to engage in call and response—a pattern that will be repeated in Katniss's story but that will be modeled first in Rue's.[37]

A cursory reading may lead to the conclusion that Katniss has, in a sense, "become" the mockingjay right after being pinned by Madge. But Katniss becomes so emotional as she says good-bye to District 12 that she has forgotten about the pin until she has been on the train to the Capitol for some time. After reflecting on the mockingjay's significance to the districts and her father, and having dinner on the train, Katniss watches the other districts' tributes being Reaped—selected for the games. Her attention is immediately drawn to Rue.[38]

From her first introduction, Rue is tied to Katniss's innocent sister Prim, and by narrative proximity, to the defiant, sweet-singing mockingjay. In order to emphasize these associations, and *not* the fact that Rue is Katniss's competition in the games, there is no mention of Rue during the opening ceremonies, beyond an indirect one: "The tributes from District 11 are just rolling out when Cinna appears with a lighted torch."[39] Although Rue is not mentioned by name, the first appearance of the flames that will become associated with Katniss, the "girl on fire," is actually *in the same sentence* as Rue's entrance into the ceremonies. This foreshadowing is quite clever. While there is oddly no mention of whether Cinna's torch is real, the flames that will engulf Katniss and Peeta moments later are artificial. Thus, when Effie Trinket opines about doing her best with Katniss because she "sacrificed herself for her sister" and "successfully struggled to overcome the barbarism of [her] district," the reader is led to think of Katniss as the symbolic sacrifice for the sake of Prim and District 12.[40] The very point of a sacrifice is that the *sacrifice is supposed to die*. But from her very first scene in the forest with Gale, Katniss is positioned as a hunter, not the hunted. Distancing ourselves from her viewpoint narration reveals that Katniss is no one's prey; she is a predator. Her hunting skills allow her to survive the game but, unless mitigated, make her a less than plausible sacrifice.

If Katniss is not by nature a sacrificial victim, then who might be? It is significant that Rue begins to watch Katniss and Peeta during training, and that she does this without being seen at first. Much like a bird that is subject to apex predators and human hunters, Rue observes those who might be a threat to her. When Peeta first notices Rue, he tells Katniss: "I think we have a shadow."[41] Shadows are associated with all the aspects of the dark fantastic, including haunting.

As soon as Peeta points Rue out, Katniss's attention is drawn to her. Once again, Katniss describes Rue in terms that the reader has previously seen Katniss associate with Prim:

> The little girl from District 11 [was] standing back a bit, watching us. She's the twelve-year-old, the one who reminded me so of Prim in stature. Up close she looks about ten. She has bright, dark eyes and satiny brown skin and stands tilted up on her toes with her arms slightly extended to her sides, as if ready to take wing at the slightest sound. It's impossible not to think of a bird.[42]

Rue's slight stature and body movements remind Katniss of a bird, creature of her beloved woods, while her very name brings up memories of home: "I bite my lip. Rue is a small yellow flower that grows in the Meadow. Rue. Primrose. Neither of them could tip the scale at seventy pounds soaking wet."[43] The connection to Katniss's little sister could not be more specific. Both Katniss and Rue have the names of flower that exist in the real world. While Katniss is the colloquial name for *Saggitaria*, a genus of water plant native to the Americas, Rue's floral name also has deep resonance. *Rue graveolens* has been associated with healing and sacrifice since the beginning of recorded human history.[44] Rue, also known as "herb-of-grace," is a yellow flower. One of the most famous songs of the early Republic, the "Yellow Rose of Texas," was written in honor of a multiracial woman of African heritage, Emily D. West, and the "yellow" color explicitly refers to her skin.[45] By conjuring up the fair Primrose Everdeen in close proximity to this newest flower of a girl, Collins evokes the most famous Yellow Rose of all—a girl of color.

Rue soon joins Katniss and Peeta in their training. Much like Katniss, Rue is "clever with plants, climbs swiftly, and has good aim."[46] Rue's weapon of choice is the slingshot, famously used by a young David in his fight against the gargantuan Goliath in the biblical narrative. Katniss's assessment of Rue's abilities seems to specifically recall the encounter between child and giant: "She can hit the target every time with a slingshot. But what is a slingshot against a 220-pound male with a sword?"[47] Katniss's observations make clear that Rue's success against the giants in the Hunger Games arena depends upon divine providence. Fortunately, Rue is quite talented, earning an impressive seven of a possible ten points during the showcase for the judges.[48] Much as a hunter may wonder how the quarry manages to elude its fate, Katniss wonders what the little girl could have done to impress the judges. Rue provides one possible answer after she "flutters" over to the host of the games, Caesar Flickerman, in her evocative winged costume:

> A hush falls over the crowd at the sight of this magical wisp of a tribute. . . . "I'm very hard to catch," she says in a tremulous voice. "And if they don't catch me, they can't kill me. So don't count me out."[49]

Rue's confident chirpings are framed by the other young Black tribute from District 11, Thresh, and Katniss herself.[50] Yet just as Katniss does not notice Rue at first, she initially forgets all about the mockingjay pin that will eventually be associated with her. It is Cinna who pins it on before she enters the arena on the first day of the competition, saying, "It's your district token, right? It barely cleared the review board. Some thought the pin could be used as a weapon, giving you an unfair advantage. But eventually, they let it through."[51] Ironically enough, the mockingjay is indeed the weapon that Katniss uses throughout the competition.

Although Katniss doesn't think about Rue at the start of the games, she is pleased that the other girl made it through the first day and night.[52] She finds Rue for the first time during the only major moment in the games when they are both alone and in mortal peril. Just before Katniss encounters Rue in the arena, she thinks of her sister Prim and believes that Rue might be an animal:

> The eyes of some animal peer at me from a neighboring tree—a possum maybe—catching the firelight from the Careers' torches. Suddenly, I'm up on one elbow. Those are no possum's eyes, I know their glassy reflection too well. In fact, those are not animal eyes at all. In the last dim rays of light, I make her out, watching me silently from between the branches.[53]

This moment of heightened stress for Katniss manifests three aspects of a dark fantastic spectacle. First, Katniss mistakes Rue for an animal, not a girl like herself. Moreover, the specific animal that Katniss thinks Rue might be is a possum. "Playing possum" in colloquial English means to "play dead." This not only foreshadows Rue's death but also her strategic positioning of her body while she is alive—she is *hiding within plain sight*. African American culture has a long tradition of this kind of hiding, given that escaping from racial oppression has required forms of being present and yet unseen. This association connects Rue within a larger tradition of Black characters in fiction finding means of escape.[54] Later in the scene, as Rue leaps between the trees, Katniss whimsically imagines the little girl in flight, as the inheritor of the People Who Could Fly.[55] Yet Rue is not only a spectacle of both girl *and* bird, she also becomes Katniss's salvation. And she pays for this benevolence with her life.

Hesitation

Within American folk and literary traditions, the primary narrative function of magical Negro characters is to assist White protagonists on their heroic journeys. Although Rue's death is far too tragic for the magical Negro trope, she is part of a long tradition of Black female characters serving as "the help," since her first encounter with Katniss in the arena is to offer aid, pointing to a wasp's nest as both danger and opportunity.[56] At first Katniss feels threatened by the nest, but then she decides to use it as a weapon. Using the tools of oppression to fight back and preserve the self has long been a tactic of the subjugated; with this act, Rue and Katniss elude the cruelty of the Career Tributes and form an alliance in which Rue transfers three distinct survival tools to Katniss—the story of District 11, the skills and traditions Rue inherited from her district, and eventually, her very body as the mockingjay personified.

First, the story of Rue's agricultural District 11 inspires Katniss and reveals that conditions in the neighboring district are harsher than in her own.[57] Although a diverse population inhabits Rue's district, the film reveals what the text implies—that many are of African descent like Rue and Thresh. Rue's people worked in orchards, which is how she learned to "fly" between the trees.[58] Much as in US slavery and debt peonage, the people of District 11 are not allowed to consume the crops they grow. The punishment for eating the crops in District 11 is whipping, which Katniss says is rare in District 12.[59] Even worse, a three-year-old in Rue's district was killed for playing with the night-vision goggles used by the orchard workers' supervisors. When Katniss learns of this violence, she thinks to herself, "Hearing this makes me feel like District 12 is some sort of safe haven. Of course, people keel over from starvation, but I can't imagine the Peacekeepers murdering a simpleminded child."[60] Katniss's own words on the page, along with the evidence on the screen, render a frightening verdict. As unbearable as the conditions of District 12 are, the people of District 11 live under conditions so terrible that Katniss cannot even imagine the incident Rue describes.

The skills and traditions that Rue brings with her from District 11 also play an important role in the story. They not only save the protagonist's life but also provide much of the foundation for the revolution that Katniss will spark. After Katniss is stung by the dangerous hybrid insects known as "tracker jackers," Rue heals the stings using a plant remedy.[61] Grateful, Katniss shares her meat, her burn medicine, and the warmth of her sleeping bag.[62] While a sympathetic reading of Katniss would praise these actions as reciprocal, a critical race counterstory also considers the ending of the tale. Tracker jacker venom is fatal; the burn that Rue suffers from the gamekeeper's forest fire is not fatal. Rue does not ask for the remedy; Katniss volunteers it. And the young girl's reaction to receiving relief is not described in the text, only her praise for Katniss's sponsors, who gave Katniss the burn medicine.

The final gift that Rue gives to Katniss is the very mockingjay represented in the pin that Katniss repeatedly forgets she is wearing. The scene in which Rue speaks of the mockingjay is so significant for understanding the meaning of this gift that I quote it in its entirety:

Rue, who when you ask her what she loves most in the world, replies, of all things, "Music."

"Music?" I say. In our world, I rank music somewhere between hair ribbons and rainbows in terms of usefulness. At least a rainbow gives you a tip about the weather. "You have a lot of time for that?"

"We sing at home. At work, too. That's why I love your pin," she says, pointing to the mockingjay that I've again forgotten about.

"You have mockingjays?" I ask.

"Oh, yes. I have a few that are my special friends. We can sing back and forth for hours. They carry messages for me," she says.

"What do you mean?" I say.

"I'm usually up highest, so I'm the first to see the flag that signals quitting time. There's a special little song I do," says Rue. She opens her mouth and sings a little four-note run in a sweet, clear voice. "And the mockingjays spread it around the orchard. That's how everyone knows to knock off," she continues. "They can be dangerous though, if you get too near their nests. But you can't blame them for that."

I unclasp the pin and hold it out to her. "Here, you take it. It has more meaning for you than me."

"Oh, no," says Rue, closing my fingers back over the pin. "I like to see it on you. That's how I decided I could trust you. Besides, I have this." She pulls a necklace woven out of some kind of grass from her shirt. On it, hangs a roughly carved wooden star. Or maybe it's a flower. "It's a good luck charm."

"Well, it's worked so far," I say, pinning the mockingjay back on my shirt. "Maybe you should just stick with that."[63]

Rue's refusal of the mockingjay pin that she loves so much is a harbinger of her doom. Instead, she chooses a star made of grass, a token of luck from her agricultural district. Along with the biblical association of her name (rue was also known as the herb of grace in the ancient world), grass represents the ephemeral nature of life: "All flesh is grass," declares the writer of Isaiah, "and all the goodliness thereof is as the flower of the field."[64] Secular authors from Christina Rossetti to Margaret Atwood have used this corporeal metaphor to describe the transitory nature of human life. Here, Collins uses the device to mark Rue as a living sacrifice, as innocent and hopeful as the mockingjay's song. She even demonstrates this sweet four-noted song, and teaches it to Katniss. The call, the girl, the moment of friendship within the horrors of the games—they all cause both the protagonist and the narrative to hesitate.

It is this call that Katniss hears when Rue is caught in a Career Tribute's trap.

Violence

In the books, Rue's death and bodily exit from the series recall her entrance: she is trapped and speared much like the animals Katniss used to hunt beyond the District 12 fence. As Katniss observes after her death, "I can't stop looking at Rue, smaller than ever, a baby animal curled up in a nest of netting."[65] Such sacrifices of secondary characters, whether symbolic or actual, are common in children's and young adult literature. One of the more famous examples is the "death" of Wendy in J. M. Barrie's *Peter Pan*, who is mistaken for a bird by the Lost Boys and similarly slain.[66] In the magical Neverland, Wendy-bird is restored with a "kiss." In dystopian Panem things are not as simple. Katniss's kiss on Rue's forehead is but a sad good-bye. There is little textual remorse for Rue being slain because, unlike Wendy, Rue is no lady. Even Katniss, who is sympathetic, is reminded of an animal, not a human girl:

I've stopped for just a moment when I hear it. . . . Rue's four-note tune coming out of a mockingjay's mouth. The one that means she's all right . . .

A mockingjay repeats the melody to me. And that's when I hear the scream.

It's a child's scream, a young girl's scream, there's no one in the arena capable of making that sound except Rue. . . . There's another high-pitched cry, this time my name. "Katniss! Katniss!"

. . . She's on the ground, hopelessly entangled in a net. She just has time to reach her hand through the mesh and say my name before the spear enters her body.[67]

Rue's entrapment seals her textual position as the sacrificial mockingjay. In most ritual sacrifices, the blood of animals is provided as substitute for humans. It is important for Rue to be constructed as both innocent little girl, equated with Prim's purity, and revolutionary bird, provided as a sacrifice. Her innocent life is poured out on behalf of Katniss. Rue is the substitute who purifies Katniss and transforms her from unwilling heroine to revolutionary. "Her hand reaches out and I clutch it like a lifeline. As if it's me who's dying instead of Rue."[68] The little girl's physical pain is not the point of this scene; Katniss's pain at having failed to protect Rue becomes the emotional centerpiece. As she is dying, Rue comforts Katniss and provides encouragement: "You have to win."[69]

As she lies dying, Rue requests that Katniss sing to her. While other critics have focused on the significance of this scene within the context of the Appalachian music tradition,[70] if we focus on the Dark Other in the narrative instead of the protagonist, the song is infused with new meaning:

Deep in the meadow, under the willow
A bed of grass, a soft green pillow
Lay down your head, and close your sleepy eyes
And when again they open, the sun will rise.
Here it's safe, here it's warm
Here the daisies guard you from every harm
Here your dreams are sweet and tomorrow brings them true
Here is the place where I love you.

Katniss's song is very specifically intended for Rue, the innocent flower wearing an amulet made of grass (once again, "all flesh is grass"), who hails from a pastoral district. Katniss decorates Rue's body with flowers, kissing her forehead. In these acts, Katniss honors Rue's life with genuine tenderness and love, and this compassion, as religion scholar Yonah Ringlestein observes, "shows a real person has died."[71] The people of Rue's district respond to Katniss's selfless act by sponsoring her with bread that is shaped like a crescent moon. Just like Rue's star-shaped grass amulet, the crescent-shaped bread is another reminder of the night—darkness.

The death scene and its aftermath unfold a bit differently in the film, and have uncanny resonance within our own culture, as Dubrofsky and Ryalls note:

> After laying Rue to rest, Katniss turns to a camera and makes the hand gesture that is a sign of respect in [District 12]. The next shot is of an uprising in Rue's district, suggesting that Katniss's devotion to Rue leads to the uprising. The scenes of unrest in District 11 are mostly of Black men tipping silos, setting fires, and fighting with troops. *Notably, there is no such scene in the book.* The uprising in the film animates a common racialized trope: Katniss as the great white savior, the person who gives Rue's death meaning, and who inspires an entire district to rebel against its oppressors. These actions highlight Katniss, the white hero, as someone with uncommon integrity and humanity, risking her life for those she loves.[72]

Haunting

In the film, the people of District 11 are so moved by Katniss's devotion to Rue that they rise up against the Capitol. Leaving aside the discomfort that the West has had with Black uprisings from the onset of modernity until now, the visual effect of this scene in the film changes the meaning of Katniss's actions in the text. It diminishes Rue's selflessness as the sacrificial mockingjay and as impetus for revolution, and makes Katniss's unselfish devotion the center of the narrative.

Although we are trained to read texts from the narrator's point of view, when we turn our literature and media upside down, and read it from a dark fantastic perspective, we find the dark girls in the shadows have much to say. If it is, as Atticus Finch famously warns, a sin to kill a mockingbird, how much more of a sin is it to kill a mockingjay—a symbol of triumph over grief, oppression, and adversity that combines the resilience of the blue jay with the mockingbird's sweet song? Within a few pages of Rue's death, Katniss will find new reason to live in Peeta, the male tribute from her district and eventual love interest. Thus, while Rue is the mockingjay who dies, Katniss becomes the mockingjay who *lives* and *loves*. The shedding of Rue's innocent blood, the sacrifice of both girl-bird *and* girl-human, is required for the remission of the sins that Katniss *has* committed, and *will* commit, in the name of Panem's revolution.

As noted previously, the image of a girl, likened to a bird, who is pierced by an arrow recalls Wendy Darling. Like Rue and Katniss, Wendy becomes a slain girl-bird. A "kiss" from Peter revives Wendy, and soon, Katniss will kiss Peeta. But who will resurrect the Rue-bird after she is fatally pierced?

The answer emerges as *The Hunger Games* series unfolds. With her final request for a song, Rue transfers her embodiment of the symbolic mockingjay to Katniss. At first, Katniss cannot stop thinking about Rue's senseless and tragic death. But then she finds Peeta, half dead but not beyond saving. As Katniss shifts her focus to her eventual love interest, Rue fades from the narrative for reasons that I explore next. Yet like all of our dark story-girls, little Rue haunts both the pages of the text and the flickering images on the screen, impossible dark innocence personified.

Sympathy for the Monster:
The Problem with Innocence in the Dark Fantastic

In the collective popular imagination, a dark-skinned child character cannot be innocent. Christina Sharpe notes the impossibility of Black childhood in her tour de force work *In the Wake: On Blackness and Being*. After asking "What is a Black child?" she goes on: "I am thinking of blackness's signifying surprise: the ways that meaning slides, signification slips, when words like *child, girl, mother*, and *boy* abut blackness."[73] Something about Black childhood confounds children's and young adult literature, which is why Black characters are often trapped in narratives about slavery, Civil Rights, ghetto survival, or survival in the White world. While historical fiction and contemporary realism are important genres for Black childhood and teen life, Black children and adolescents are often missing from other kinds of stories, especially stories like *The Hunger Games*.[74] Thus, when a Black child protagonist comes to symbolize innocence in a dystopia, it can confound some in the audience.

Robin Bernstein has traced the origins of racialized innocence in our literature and culture to before the Civil War. As she explains, "Children were innocent: that is, sinless, absent of sexual feelings, and oblivious to worldly concerns. . . . Childhood was then understood not as innocent but as innocence itself; not as a symbol of innocence but as its embodiment. . . . This innocence was raced White."[75] Bernstein traces repertoires of performed racial innocence to the first instances when "angelic white children were contrasted with [black] pickaninnies so grotesque as to suggest that only white children *were* children."[76] Most classic children's and young adult literature has been carefully edited since the 1960s to reflect changing social sensibilities. For instance, the Oompa-Loompas from Roald Dahl's *Charlie and the Chocolate Factory* were originally racist caricatures of the San, the indigenous people of southern Africa. Even Dr. Seuss, as children's literature scholar Philip Nel has pointed out, was not immune.[77]

But no matter how progressive, liberal, or politically and socially astute we think we have become, everyone living in the United States (and elsewhere, for Dahl was certainly not American) has been affected by ideas about *which* children can be—and cannot be—viewed as innocent. Of course, in the Enlightenment, and afterward, there are examples of dark-skinned people depicted as noble savages. But the prevailing cultural script that has been handed down over the generations is that *some children are more innocent than others, and Black children are not innocent at all.* We notice this, but we are not encouraged to voice it aloud, because the construction of childhood innocence on foundations of race is implied but never spoken, lest we offend others. As Robin DiAngelo and Özlem Sensoy note:"When confronted with the history of colonialism and racism and its effects on racialized people, Whites tend to claim racial innocence and take up the role of admirer or moral helper. . . . Challenging White innocence often ignites anger."[78] Other scholars have analyzed how racial innocence (and by extension, racial guilt) has been constructed through discourses of schooling, including Zeus Leonardo and Ronald K. Porter, Michael Dumas, and Dorothea Anagnostopoulos, Sakeena Everett, and Carleen Carey.[79] *The Hunger Games* is a textual example of how our culture's unconscious hierarchies of racial innocence are also embedded in stories.

Narratively, because Rue cannot remain innocent, her innocence is transferred to Katniss, the protagonist. After Katniss finds Peeta injured, and their love story commences, there is a notable shift in her thoughts about Rue.[80] Katniss can't afford to continue to grieve for Rue if she is to survive and save Peeta. Thus, from this point on in the trilogy, Katniss moves from grief to casual gratitude and regret in her thoughts about Rue. Rue is mentioned in a utilitarian sense: she's the one who enhanced Katniss's wilderness survival skills. Katniss also begins thinking about Prim independently from Rue, except for when Clove (one of the professional killer Career Tributes) is about to kill her.[81] Then, almost as if talking and thinking about Rue makes it happen, Thresh, the boy from Rue's district, kills Clove and allows Katniss to live because she tried to help Rue. Although Thresh likens sparing Katniss's life to a debt that he's repaying, it can be argued that Rue, Thresh, and District 11 have more than repaid Katniss's acts of kindness. Rue's place in the narrative is gone, however, and so Thresh's act of mercy does not lead Katniss to think about Rue.[82] It is only when she and Peeta have a moment of misunderstanding that she momentarily feels as if Rue would have understood her better.[83] But Katniss soon returns to the business of survival—and sorting through her feelings about Peeta.

In the balance of the trilogy, Rue further fades from the narrative. She is mentioned twenty-four times in the second book, *Catching Fire*, usually within the context of *regret*, the meaning of her name.[84] Rue is mentioned even less frequently—a mere seven times—in the final book, *Mockingjay*.[85] With another Hunger Games (the Quarter Quell) now under her belt, Katniss's memories of Rue seem more distant, less special. But the final image of Rue in the series is that of a bird, poised to take flight. It is a poignant reminder that Rue's physical presence in the narrative is now unnecessary. Through her sacrifice, her innocence has been transferred to Katniss, who is a survivor, a hunter, and, ultimately, one of the strong girl characters who are so beloved in today's speculative fiction for young adults.

My intention in this section, and the preceding two, is to make the case for Rue being the sacrificial mockingjay in *The Hunger Games*, and to show this by tracing her development, as well as the ways that race, class, and innocence are rendered from text to screen. In the final part of this chapter, I reflect critically on what happens as young people read and view narratives like these in the mainstream fantastic.

When Little Black Girls Become Innocent: Readers' Responses to Rue

In *The Hunger Games* movie, Amandla Stenberg played Rue, the innocent mockingjay. Why were some audiences so unhappy with this casting decision?

Suzanne Collins's deliberate construction of Rue as *the* symbol of innocence meant that some readers automatically imagined her as White. After all, in what universe, fictional or real, is a Black child or teen innocent? Certainly this is not the case in our schools, with their attention-grabbing discipline gaps that anticipate the school-to-prison pipeline.[86] Certainly this is not the case in our parks and playgrounds, where young Tamir Rice of Cleveland was stolen from the world long before his time.[87] And it is certainly not the case in contemporary children's and young adult literature, where Black kids and teens are underrepresented, and when they do appear, are often viewed as "unlikeable" or "unrelatable."[88] Narrative conventions that privilege the first person point of view within young adult literature ensure that young readers' attention will be focused completely on the likeable, relatable, and authentic protagonists—in other words, on the Katnisses of the literary realm.[89] Because of Collins's adept skill at engaging her target audience, teen readers sympathize with Katniss, dismissing the ethical dilemmas she elides as she becomes the mockingjay.

The first movie amplifies sympathy for Katniss. This is done not only through District 11's reaction to her funerary rites for Rue, as described above, but also by diminishing some of Katniss's awareness of the artificial nature of the games. In a film, it is difficult to access the thoughts and feelings of characters without breaking the modal conventions that help to suspend audience disbelief. Even acknowledging the affordances and limitations of translating *The Hunger Games* from page to screen, the choices made by the film lead to Katniss being plunged into a situation in which her critical awareness is superseded by her need to survive. While this makes her relatable and incredibly sympathetic to mass audiences, it also has the effect of obscuring the problems of race and difference in the story.

The odds are ever in Katniss's favor: she is the primary character with whom audiences identify. This is not inherently problematic, as part of the work of literature is to provide mirrors, windows, and doors into other people's experiences.[90] The problem occurs when contemporary literature and media for young people include characters of color who are supposed to provide someone for every reader or viewer to identity with—and yet at the same time construct protagonists who are the only characters worth rooting for. Although the initial authorial intent may have been noble, stories constructed in such a fashion have the pernicious effect of normalizing our existing social hierarchies—including hierarchies of race.

The affordances of the first person perspective for audience engagement also create a significant challenge in that the Dark Other is always focalized through a White protagonist's eyes. Collins does an admirable job on the surface of the story when it comes to Katniss's view of dark-skinned characters. After all, she states from Katniss's point of view that Rue reminds her of her younger sister, Prim. Prim is a much more familiar figure in children's and young adult literature, where a guileless, golden girl-child often is a counterweight to the evil that the protagonist must overcome.[91] The Hunger Games is no exception. What is different is that while trapped in the games, Rue becomes Katniss's Prim, a younger companion who shares in the existential threat until she is overcome by it. Rue's dark skin is not a limitation in Katniss's view; she sees a friend, and someone who is as vulnerable as her little sister would be within the savage games. In a sense, Katniss is colorblind.

The trouble with colorblind ideologies in text and culture is that by not noticing race, writers and other creatives do the work of encoding it as taboo. While silence and evasion around race in dystopian science fiction is "understood to be a graceful, even generous, liberal gesture,"[92] implying the inevitability of a postracial future, this silence also has the effect of confusing readers. Even worse, as noted in chapter 1, is that authors and society have, in Morrison's words, "transferred internal conflicts to a 'blank darkness' consisting of conveniently bound and violently silenced Black bodies," creating a "playground for the imagination."[93] Certainly Rue's body has been conveniently bound and violently silenced in *The Hunger Games*. But because Collins does not overemphasize her dark skin, many readers did not realize she likely had phenotypical African features. The result was that a notable number of viewers did not care for the fact that Rue was a little Black girl.

Dodai Stewart's 2012 article for the feminist blog *Jezebel* features reactions from Twitter users after the casting of Black actors as Rue, Cinna, and Thresh in the first *Hunger Games* movie was announced. Here's a sampling of those Tweets:

> "why does Rue have to be black not gonna lie kinda ruined the movie"
> "cinna and rue weren't suppose to be black"
> "why did the producer make all the good characters black smh"
> "EWW rue is black?? I'm not watching"
> "Kk call me racist but when I found out rue was black her death wasn't as sad #ihatemyself"
> "I was pumped about the Hunger Games. Until I learned that a black girl was playing Rue."
> "And for the record, im still pissed that rue is black. Like you think she might have mentioned that . . . ? Is that just me, or . . ."
> "after watching the hunger games preview 6 times in a row, i realized Rue is black. Whaaaat?! #shocked"
> "I know, rue is too black for what I pictured. But Peeta IS nomworthy #nom"
> "why is Rue a little black girl? #sticktothebookDUDE #TheHungerGames"
> "to all my hunger games readers out there: Did anyone picture Rue as being black? No offense or anything but I just didn't see her like it"
> "HOW IN THE WORLD ARE THEY GOING TO MAKE RUE A FREAKING BLACK BITCH IN THE MOVIE ?!?!?!??! lolol not to be racist buuuut . . . I'm angry now ;o"
> "nah, I just pictured darker skin, didn't really take it all the way to black"
> "Sense when has Rue been a nigger"[94]

During the heat of the fandom debates, Adam, a moderator of the "Hunger Games Tweets" blog, tracked social media responses to Rue, then screen-capped places in *The Hunger Games* books where the physical features of the District 11 tributes (Rue and Thresh) are explicitly described. As Stewart notes, "The posts go on and on and on. It's not just a couple of Tweets, it's not just a coincidence. There's an underlying rage, coming out as overt prejudice and plain old racism."[95] This point is well taken, for as we have seen above, Collins's text makes it clear that she is describing characters of color. But the debate raged on, as shown by the responses to Stewart's article, with commenters expressing anger over the singling out of young fans, defending their position that Rue didn't *have* to be Black, or stating that dark skin didn't necessarily signal a character of African descent.

A person of color—or even *a character of color*—faces dire consequences when he or she steps outside of his or her assigned place, or flips the script in any way. Essential qualities such as goodness, beauty, innocence, and truth have been so often racialized as White in literature and media that ascribing these qualities to other groups is seen as transgressive. Unfortunately, the effects are not just textual. When Collins's Panem moved from page to screen, young Amandla Stenberg and her costars were targets of racist discourse online.[96] It should be noted that the actress playing Rue, Amandla Stenberg, is not *just* Black; she has multiracial ancestry. Her mother is African American, and her father is a White Dutch citizen. Through her father, Amandla also has Greenlandic and Inuit ancestry. Amandla's multiracial and multiethnic background makes her a plausible choice for a character in what we are led to believe is a scenario of a future United States. Yet *any* visible African ancestry means that a character has the potential to become labeled—and rejected—by some parts of the audience.

Why didn't all readers of *The Hunger Games* series realize that Rue was Black? The dark fantastic cycle ensures that characters who are racially marked are rejected by readers. Many authors wishing to diversify their narratives subsume descriptions that are explicitly raced, so that the character just "happens to be" non-White, yet do not have notable cultural differences from the White characters in a story. Collins bucks this tendency by explicitly racializing her characters: throughout the text, the discerning reader can detect the ways that she demonstrates that Rue is plausibly descended from the contemporary Black US population. From her physical description, to the harsher conditions in District 11, and to her tragic end, Rue's Blackness was as familiar and welcome to me as the first bars of a Motown recording. But other readers might not have recognized these subtle signals, rendering the question of Rue's innocence unproblematic until it appeared on the screen, embodied in Amandla Stenberg's light brown skin and natural hair. This likely created a dilemma for some young readers, who might have asked, "Why is Rue a little Black girl?" For where else would they have encountered a similar Black character in popular science fiction who is likeable, relatable—and innocent?[97]

Thus, *hesitation* can be seen in fan responses, as they behold the *spectacle* of a dark innocent bird, sweet as the meadow flower that she is named for, until she is taken away by the *violence* that stalks the Dark Ones of our speculative fiction. In the call of Panem's revolution, and in the memories of Katniss Everdeen, Rue's presence *haunts* the remainder of the text.

Rue.

Regret.

And the dark fantastic cycle continues.

Rue and *Sankofa*:
Counterstories for Real-Life Mockingjays

The idea of Rue as the slain mockingjay—the symbol of purity and innocence—was likely strange, even alien, to some young readers conditioned by the scripts of our society. Yet hope remains. Some of that hope can be found in the best fandom discourse around Rue's Blackness. In "The Revolution Starts with Rue," Antero Garcia and Marcelle Haddix responded to the possibilities of *The Hunger Games*, and the presence of characters of color, through blogging and participating in *The Hunger Games* fandom.[98] Garcia, Haddix, and I are at the trailing end of Generation X and are among the first wave of digital fandom veterans to enter the academy. Garcia and Haddix quote blogger prismatic-bell, who posted on their Tumblr blog a set of six GIF images detailing the scene where Thresh saves Katniss from one of the Career Tributes, and then spares her life for the sake of Rue. It is the scene in the first movie where Thresh says to Katniss, "Just this time, 12! For Rue!" Although GIF image sets like these are very common in Tumblr fandoms, what is significant is prismatic-bell's caption:

Can we just stop and talk about this for a minute?

Thresh doesn't make an alliance. Thresh doesn't waste time liking [Katniss]. Thresh knows that either he must kill her or she must kill him for one of them to win.

But this is the only way he can repay her for protecting Rue when he couldn't. It's the only way he can repay her for honoring Rue when he couldn't. He honors her by sparing her friend, the girl who would have died for her.

The revolution really doesn't start with Katniss.

It starts with *Rue*.[99]

Prismatic-bell, Garcia, Haddix, Suzanne Collins herself, and millions of others heartened by Rue's presence are right. The revolution really *does* begin with Rue, and would have been impossible without her igniting the spark. It must be said, however, that long before *The Hunger Games* was written, there was (and is) another tradition in which counterstories of other dark birds have long been told.

In one of these stories, my favorite folktale of all, retold masterfully by Virginia Hamilton, enslaved Africans sprout wings and fly back home.[100]

In a beloved poem from the nadir of African American history, Paul Laurence Dunbar pleads for the reader to sympathize with the plight of a caged bird;[101] his poem would later inspire the title of the biography of one of the greatest American poets and teachers of the twentieth century, Maya Angelou.[102]

And then there is one of Nina Simone's famous songs from the Civil Rights movement, penned by Billy Taylor during a time of freedom, new hopes, and dreams of peace, which imagined what the bird's-eye view of one who "soars to the sun and looks down at the sea" might be like.[103]

But the progenitor of all these metaphorical birds is the Sankofa bird, originating with the Akan people of Ghana, and today sacred to people of African descent all over the world—a poignant reminder of the link between the past and the future not only for Dark Ones, but for all of humanity. [104]

Thinking about the death of innocent young Rue has particular resonance in the era of the #BlackLivesMatter movement. Just as we have seen notable differences between Rue and Katniss in narrative treatment and fandom response, it must also be acknowledged that such differences are found in the real world, and have profound implications for society and the future. Understanding how race and innocence are constructed in and through texts is vital, for the ways that young people read, write, and think are shaped by the participatory culture associated with stories like *The Hunger Games*.

As education scholars Zeus Leonardo and Ronald Porter write, quoting Japanese philosopher Nishitani Osamu:

> Race dialogue in mixed-race company works to maintain the Western distinction between "anthropos" (the inhuman) and "humanitas" (the human). Osamu points out, "*anthropos* cannot escape the status of being the object of anthropological knowledge, while *humanitas* is never defined from without but rather expresses itself as the subject of all knowledge." Put another way, race dialogues often maintain the status of whiteness as being both natural and unchanging in the white imaginary. . . . Whiteness is the immovable mover, unmarked marker, and unspoken speaker.[105]

If we do not want any of our young people to automatically assume that Rue is White despite a text that states otherwise, and if we find racist Tweets and posts by young people born long after the 1960s to be untenable, then we can no longer shrink away from the project of emancipating the imagination. Moreover, if the death of little Rue is to have any ultimate cultural meaning at all, we must name, deconstruct, and rethink the very meanings of white and black, light and dark, innocence and evil, *anthropos* and *humanitas*, in the depths of our imaginations.

A QUEEN OUT OF PLACE

Dark Fantastic Dreaming and the Spacetime Politics of Gwen in BBC's Merlin

The trouble with magic . . . is that it appears to exist
in realms where only certain children belong.
—Zetta Elliott, *Jeunesse*, 2013

The fantasy vision of a medieval Europe devoid of
people of color isn't realism. It's a different word
that starts with R- and ends in -ism.
—Saladin Ahmed (@saladinahmed), Twitter,
November 8, 2014

I stand amid the roar
Of a surf-tormented shore,
And I hold within my hand
Grains of the golden sand—
How few! yet how they creep
Through my fingers to the deep,
While I weep—while I weep!
O God! Can I not grasp
Them with a tighter clasp?
O God! can I not save
One from the pitiless wave?
Is *all* that we see or seem
But a dream within a dream?
—Edgar Allan Poe, "A Dream within a Dream"

In my imagination, the soundtrack of science fiction, fantasy, and comics is the music of my 1980s childhood. Born in the year that George Lucas debuted *Star Wars* and an avid reader of Bronze Age comics during the era of Marvel Comics' iconic *Dark Phoenix* series and DC Comics' groundbreaking *Crisis on Infinite Earths*, I was influenced by the cultural zeitgeist. The holy trinity of our mid-1980s children's films were *The NeverEnding Story*, *The Dark Crystal*, and—my favorite— *Labyrinth*. The sole collaborative effort between George Lucas and Jim Henson, *Labyrinth* premiered when I was nine years old. For me, the sound of magic was influenced by David Bowie's malevolently naughty and *extremely* inappropriate Goblin King, the fey Jareth. Jennifer Connelly's Sarah served as a stand-in for my generation's growing preteen awareness of our sexuality. The movie sent the message that in order to be an authentic cisgender heterosexual woman, it was important to be desired—and desirable. After all, it was Jareth's desire for Sarah that gave her power over him. The message was clear: becoming the object of desire should be the pinnacle of our dreams.

But where are dreams located? *Who* gets to be desired and desirable, and why? Fairy tales provided answers to those questions. In the 1980s, we gazed at young Sarah in *Labyrinth*, a girl next door caught in a portal-quest fantasy.[1] Unlike previous generations, who had to pay to see movies again and again at the cinema, ours was the first to have VCRs during childhood. My sister and I watched recorded movies like *Labyrinth*, *The Princess Bride*, and Disney's *Sleeping Beauty* until we had every word in each scene memorized. These repeated viewings laminated the message we received from the books that were read to us, and that we later read on our own. As we rewatched, the stories helped to shape our consciousness, so that we knew that it was important to be desired *and* desirable. And these stories were infused with music, laden with promises of happily ever afters with princes both sinister and golden.

Together, my sister and I listened to Jareth, the Goblin King, sing tantalizing promises to young Sarah in what fans would later label the "peach dream scene":

> I'll paint you mornings of gold, I'll spin you Valentine evenings
> Though we're strangers till now, we're choosing the path between the stars
> I'll leave my love between the stars.

Then we would switch our VHS tapes, and sing and dance along with Prince Phillip and Princess Aurora as they made promises to each other to the strains of a famous Tchaikovsky waltz:

> But if I know you, I'll know what you'll do
> You'll love me at once, the way you did once upon a dream.

The lyrics reinforced Disney's lesson that true love is infused with sublime orchestra music, replete with soaring violins and sweetly trilled notes.

But for many of us, especially girls of color, that's not the entire story.

The same year the Disney Channel aired its first broadcast, a popular 1980s Motown family group dropped an album that became an urban classic. DeBarge's *In a Special Way* is one of the most beloved R&B albums of all time. Its songs have been sampled by everyone from Mary J. Blige to Tupac, and from Fifth Harmony to Janelle Monáe.[2] The album was recorded relatively quickly, and part of the instrumental track was lost during the recording process. The result is an album that seems at first listen naively innocent. Influential *Village Voice* critic Robert Christgau called *In a Special Way* "austere lilt and falsetto fantasy . . . pinned to plastic."[3] The title track is a lover's plaint that is spare; the much-covered "Time Will Reveal" is a soft lullaby that promises: "It will all reveal in time." Painting R&B with the tones of jazz, classic soul, gospel, and mid-1980s synthesized pop, *In a Special Way* positions love as sublime but never loses awareness of the ground beneath its feet. Instead of the flowers, crystalline ballrooms, and lilt of sweetly trilling birds found in fairy tale romances, *In a Special Way* evokes the scent of petrichor—perfect for dreaming Black girls of Generation X.

The final track was penned and sung by the eldest sister of the DeBarge family, Etterlene "Bunny" DeBarge. In less than five minutes, her lyrics deconstruct the fairy dreams that George Lucas, Jim Henson, and Walt Disney have sold to billions:

> Then the music stopped—
> In a flash, I was all alone
> It was just a dream
> Haunting me once again . . .

A dream, a simple fantasy
That I wish was reality
That you'd come knocking at my door
And we'd relive this dream once more.

If you grew up anywhere in urban America in the 1980s, I can guarantee you closed your eyes at least once and listened to Bunny DeBarge sing "A Dream." Time and again, I have tried (and failed) to capture that magic from my childhood in my fanfiction as well as in original stories. The 1980s was perhaps the last cultural moment before many of the familiar conveniences of the digital age were commonplace. My childhood was one of the very last in the United States before central air conditioning and computers were present in working-class and middle-class homes. My family didn't even have cable back then. What we had instead were front porches and backyard patios where families, neighbors, and friends would sit in the spring and summer evenings, laughing and talking, playing, braiding hair, and of course dreaming. Often, there would be music from a boombox or stereo. As soon as I had my first Walkmans and Discmans, my music transported me into a world of my own even while in a crowd. Or, if it was later in the evening, my parents would play music on the living room stereo.

And I would press my ear close to the fabric-covered speakers, gaze at the album cover art, close my eyes, and dream.

Throughout *The Dark Fantastic*, I have positioned myself as an interlocutor, reading fantastic worlds as well as some of the unseen work that fantasy does in our world. Black people have always counterstoried the whole of US life, from slave narratives through the contemporary Black Lives Matter movement. Fairy tales are no different. Although my generation of girls of color watched Disney movies and read children's books that promised us so many things, our mothers and our music told a different story. When Bunny DeBarge's sublime soprano warned us in no uncertain terms, "It's just a simple fantasy," we believed her in a way that only reinforced our mothers' distrust of magic. By the time R&B superstar Mary J. Blige revived the song in 1998, I was twenty-one and could only nod along. Like me, she had been a girl when *In a Special Way* first became a cult hit—and like many Black women, she'd lived through many experiences that taught her that dreams and fairy tales were *not* for her.

Lesson learned.

A generation later, I was immersed in TV fandom when several of my friends began talking about a BBC show based on the legends of King Arthur, one of the most famous fantasy stories of all time. If Tolkien's *Lord of the Rings* trilogy represented a modernist attempt to provide the people of England with an origin myth, the oral tales of Arthur and his Knights of the Round Table preceded it. Although Arthuriana is a mythopoeic cycle that is quintessentially English, the story of the noble king who represented post–Roman Britain's last stand against Saxon invaders has been told and retold all over the world. The BBC's *Merlin* was the English answer to the popular US teen show *Smallville*.[4] Just as *Smallville* depicted an iconic cultural hero, Clark Kent, before he became Superman, the creative team behind *Merlin* chose to focus on the years before Arthur becomes king, taking liberties with the source material in order to appeal to audiences. Arthur is no longer an orphan raised in obscurity who must prove that he is worthy to be king of Camelot; here, he is the acknowledged son of King Uther, head of the kingdom's military forces, and heir to the throne. Merlin is not yet an elderly mentor and guide but a teenage boy understood to be an age peer of Arthur—and only just discovering the full extent of his power.

Perhaps one of the greatest liberties that the creators of *Merlin* took with the source material concerns the character of Guinevere, Arthur's fair queen, who has often been depicted over the centuries as the adulterous lover of the Round Table Knight, Sir Lancelot. Instead of making Guinevere the daughter of a lord or king, *Merlin*'s Gwen is is the daughter of a blacksmith and works as the maidservant to the lady Morgana, who is a ward of the crown.

She is also portrayed by mixed-race actress Angel Coulby.

Other than the fan outcry about *The Hunger Games*' Rue, few recent fandom reactions have equaled the objection to Angel Coulby being cast as Gwen, the servant girl who grows up to become Queen Guinevere. Although she is never technically a princess in the series, only queen regent after her marriage to King Arthur and, eventually, queen regnant after his death, the presence of a Black woman as the love interest of the main character was a source of controversy throughout the run of the series (2008–2012). As with Rue in *The Hunger Games*, viewers had a very difficult time suspending their disbelief. This audience difficulty, created through lifetimes of reading and viewing narratives of the fantastic where the Dark Other is locked into place, was complicated because, unlike many other Black female characters, Gwen does *not* die but outlives her king and husband. What, then, should be made of this particular instantiation of the dark fantastic? What happens if a non-White character does *not* go through the cycle of spectacle, hesitation, violence, and haunting? How does the interruption of the cycle complicate the narrative? How might it confuse—and frustrate—audiences?

In this chapter, I first look at the ways that time, space, and emotion shape our experiences in the waking dream of the fantastic. Next, I trace the dark fantastic cycle in *Merlin*, a television series that (unlike *The Hunger Games* or *The Vampire Diaries*) was not based on a single contemporary source text but was a very intentional twenty-first-century take on Victorian retellings of one of the most beloved legends of all time. After that, I look at fan and viewer reactions to Gwen as a princess out of place and their questions about accuracy and authenticity. I conclude by making the case for why Gwen matters in our considerations of the role that race plays in fairy tales, legends, and folklore, given their enduring presence in our culture, and how they ultimately shape the popular imagination.

The Pleasures of Dreaming: How Time, Space, and Emotion Create the Problem of Return

It is perhaps little wonder that some contemporary viewers were jarred by the sight of a dark Guinevere. From ancient Greece and the classical tradition,[5] to the Christianization of the late Roman Empire and Dark Ages Europe, the emergence of Catholic Europe, and the Crusades against the Islamic world,[6] a nameless and lingering fear of dark-skinned people has been normalized in the popular imagination. Darkness—an antagonist born of this primal fear—is the archetypal monster in much of our literature, media, and culture. Thus, the Dark Other becomes monstrous in our collective imaginations, a shadow creature locked into place and time, imbued with a fixity that is difficult to overcome. In my studies of and experiences with the fantastic, I have found that this fixity has led to fan and audience complaints whenever a dark-skinned character moves out of his or her expected place of abjection. Suspension of disbelief becomes difficult, if not impossible, as some readers, viewers, or fans are snapped out of the waking dream of reading, a state that reader response theorist Michael Benton notably called a *secondary world*, thus named for the following passage from J. R. R. Tolkien's essay "On Fairy-Stories":

> Children are capable, of course, of literary belief, when the story-maker's art is good enough to produce it. That state of mind has been called "willing suspension of disbelief." But this does not seem to me a good description of what happens. What really happens is that the story-maker proves a successful "sub-creator." He makes a Secondary World which your mind can enter. Inside it, what he relates is "true": it accords with the laws of that world. You therefore believe it, while you are, as it were, inside. The moment disbelief arises, the spell is broken; the magic, or rather art, has failed. You are then out in the Primary World again, looking at the little abortive Secondary World from outside.[7]

The laws of what Tolkien termed the "Primary World" are those that shape our identities, ideologies, and social subjectivities. When the reader or viewer leaves the primary world and enters the secondary world, these unconscious "laws" are still present. Even in the realms of the imagination, people usually expect certain conditions to be met, or, as Tolkien put it, believe "that a thing exists or can happen in the real (primary) world." Creators of fantastic works, from science fiction to fantasy to comics, have spoken of the internal consistency that must be present in world-building so that audiences can *believe* a secondary fictional world is real.[8] Otherwise, they are shaken out of the waking dream and thrust back into reality.

Yet, as Todorov states, the spirit of the fantastic is *not* unqualified belief. It is *nearly reaching the point of belief*:

> "I nearly reached the point of believing": that is the formula which sums up the spirit of the fantastic. Either total faith or total incredulity would lead us beyond the fantastic: it is hesitation which sustains its life.[9]

Todorov's notion of sustained hesitation is essential for understanding why mainstream audiences looked askance at Gwen being a plausible princess in *Merlin*. This moment of suspended hesitation exists outside of our popular conceptions of spacetime both in our primary world and in the secondary world of stories. This is because the realm of the fantastic is neither real nor unreal, but exists in the liminal space between the primary world of experience and the secondary world as imagined through texts.[10] Homi Bhabha theorizes liminal spaces as providing "terrain for elaborating strategies of selfhood—singular or communal—that initiate new signs of identity, and innovative sites of collaboration, and contestation, in the act of defining the idea of society itself."[11] In my own field of literacy studies, Kris D. Gutiérrez has researched the secondary worlds that students create as they make meaning across words and worlds, deeming them *third spaces*.[12] Because these marginal loci exist in the terrain between the Real and the Unreal, secondary worlds, liminal spaces, and third spaces share qualities that are similar to dreams.

The fantastic is *not* a dream state. When dreaming, one is asleep, and events may or may not make logical sense. In the secondary world of fantasy, the dreamer is wide awake. Yet even though previous fantasists have dismissed dreams as analogous to fantasy, new research that lies at the convergence of quantum physics, psychoanalysis, and the humanities calls for a reconsideration of dreams in the project of emancipating characters like Rue, Gwen, and Bonnie from spatial and temporal fixity in the collective imagination. Psychoanalysts have long positioned dreams as a means whereby the mind reconciles spatiotemporal reality with emotions. Thus, as an article in the *North American Journal of Medical Sciences* has it, "Specific objects exist in waking reality in a definite way in space and time as a definite situation, which provides a certain perception to our consciousness, which provides a certain representation to our imagination and memory, which is connected with a specific emotion."[13] In other words, just as objects (or in this case, people) exist in reality and evoke specific emotions connected to our imagination and memory, this is also the case in dreams—with the added condition that the specific emotions invoked be addressed.

Thinking about the secondary worlds of fantasy as being analogous to dreams (although not quite dream states) provides much insight into why many people sincerely believe that characters of color are out of place in the fantastic: issues of race and difference threaten to shake us out of the waking dream that we inhabit while engaged in the fantastic. The spectacle of the Dark Other in a speculative narrative leads to the hesitation that is the Todorovian hallmark of the fantastic—hesitation that must be addressed. The shared dreams of fantasy and fairy tales move viewers, readers, audiences, and fans out of the fantastic and into the spacetime of our shared, fractured reality in order to face the negative emotions that darkness and dark people evoke. Because our society has traditionally dealt with darkness and difference through violence, this violence is transferred into the waking dream of the secondary world.

When it comes to diversity, the fantastic has a notable spacetime problem. My own experiences led me to seek *why* so many people felt that non-White characters do not belong either in magical medieval settings or in the spaceships of the future. I also observed that some kinds of diverse characters were more readily acceptable in fantasy narratives than others. Author and activist Zetta Elliott, in describing the extreme difficulty in the pre–*Black Panther* era of placing multicultural fantasy for young adults with major publishers, wrote eloquently about the challenge that race presented for her as a mixed-race Black Canadian author:

> I have since made peace with my past self. I accept my own hybridity, which is too often reduced to the fact that I am mixed-race. . . . I am an educator, so I do have a professional obligation to teach others to respect and value difference. As a writer, however, I have a somewhat different mission . . . to expose and explore what Canadian writer Dionne Brand calls "the fissure between the past and the present"; with my writing I aim to reveal "a rupture in history, a rupture in the quality of being . . . a physical rupture, a rupture of geography."[14]

Elliott's 2010 article about decolonizing the imagination introduced me to Dionne Brand's *A Map to the Door of No Return*. Brand describes the "Door of No Return" at the slave castle at Senegal as "that place where our ancestors departed one world for another; the Old World for the New. The place where all names were forgotten and all beginnings recast. In some desolate sense it was the creation place of Blacks in the New World Diaspora at the same time that it signified the end of traceable beginnings."[15] Michelle D. Commander further describes the signal importance of "mapping and examining the myths that Afro-Atlantic communities perpetuate about slavery and their purported retentions from the original Africa—the imagined, pristine landscape from which their ancestors were stripped—despite temporal and geographic separations."[16] If Tolkien famously signaled the impossibility of fantastic return in his evocative phrase "to Cuiviénen there is no returning," descendants of the African diaspora are faced with an even more impossible spacetime chasm to bridge than the Eldar of the *Silmarillion*.[17]

In my own creative writing, I have struggled to depict the challenges of returning to a magical past for Black characters. First, as a fan writer, I used Virginia Hamilton's "The People Could Fly" as the basis of my explanation for how Black secondary characters like Angelina Johnson and Dean Thomas in J. K. Rowling's *Harry Potter* ended up with English first names and surnames. Later, I used the readings from the Black Arts Movement that filled my home as a child and a teen as the basis for my world building in my original fantasy series. Although I went from being taught about the African origins of the classical world as a child, to disbelieving it during graduate school after professors derided the claims of Martin Bernal and others, as a creative writer I was less concerned about accuracy and authenticity and more concerned with the process of myth creation. After all, for the purposes of storytelling, it is less important that myths *are* true than that they *feel* true.

Tolkien's similar longing to construct and create a reparative mythical past led to the creation of the genre of high fantasy.[18] In a 1951 letter, he explains his longing for return:

> An equally basic passion of mine . . . was for myth (not allegory!) and for fairy-story, and above all for heroic legend on the brink of fairy-tale and history, of which there is far too little in the world (accessible to me) for my appetite . . . I was from early days grieved by the poverty of my own beloved country: it had no stories of its own (bound up with its tongue and soil), not of the quality that I sought, and found (as an ingredient) in legends of other lands. There was Greek, and Celtic, and Romance, Germanic, Scandinavian, and Finnish (which greatly affected me); but nothing English, save impoverished chap-book stuff. . . . Myth and fairy-story must, as all art, reflect and contain in solution elements of moral

and religious truth (or error), but not explicit, not in the known form of the primary "real" world.[19]

The search for a past-that-never-was may very well be an expression of the collective longing for return to a time before the ruptures of modernity. The distant past often seems to be a less complicated time and place, one in which the problems that our society faces in the contemporary world are nonexistent. Yet just as the realities of spacetime preclude the possibility of physical time travel, the complexities of space, time, dreaming, and difference complicate and constrain our return to storied pasts-that-never-were in the collective imagination. In *Physics of Blackness*, Michelle M. Wright explains the poignant challenges inherent in the problem of return, specifically for people descended from Africans who had been enslaved:

> The question of returning, whether physically or metaphysically, to the collective's point of origin inevitably arises. . . . Indeed, the problem of return and the paradoxes it entails attend any linear progress narrative: to ground oneself in an origin means that the collective, at any moment, must always be able to define itself through a direct connection to the etiology that first defines and necessarily frames that collective.[20]

Although Wright is particularly concerned with the problem of return created through narrating Blackness primarily through the Middle Passage, this principle can be extended to the problem of return in fantasy. Pulling together these disparate threads of suspended disbelief, secondary worlds, and our collective longing for return to an idealized past, since our narratives of racialized difference in the West have their point of origin at the Door of No Return, it may be the case that the presence of characters whose embodiment hails Atlantic slavery and settler colonialism leads to incredulity on the part of the dreamer. As Toni Morrison noted in *Playing in the Dark*, "The subject of the dream is the dreamer," and, as Tolkien observed, "The moment disbelief arises, the spell is broken; the magic, or rather art, has failed." Seeing a dark-skinned character, particularly one who is of discernible African ancestry, seems to break the spell for many despite the fact that there were people from many different cultures living in England during late antiquity and the early Middle Ages.[21]

Thus, placing characters of color inside magical worlds with a medieval setting is particularly challenging. The field of critical medieval studies provides insight into the reasons why: the past as storied through fantasy literature is itself paradoxical. As Clare Bradford notes, "The medieval is often treated in quite contradictory ways within texts, testifying to the complexity of modern engagements with the past."[22] One such contradiction is the way that race is taken up in stories set in the Middle Ages. Modern racial identities were not fixed in the medieval period but quite fluid and dependent upon the setting.[23] When "race" appears in primary sourced medieval texts, the term could refer to a person's geographical origin, ethnicity, religion, lineage, class, and/or gender.[24] Yet our collective failure to suspend disbelief when dark-skinned characters appear has its origins in this period. From medievalist Dennis Austin Britton:

> Crusade romances play a significant role in constructing white skin as a racial signifier. Through attempting to rid fair Saracen women of aspects of identity that do not fit with the genre's constructions of a white aristocratic race, romance narratives suggest that white skin contains in itself the potentiality of designating that one belongs to a specific racial group.[25]

It was during this period, when chroniclers began recording the Crusader romances and spinning Orientalist tales for popular audiences, that a qualifier for being the object of idealized romantic desire became White skin, although definitive markers of race and desire would not be reified for centuries. Perhaps the most well-known theorist of race in the Middle Ages, Geraldine Heng, observes that "the normativity of Whiteness, and of the White racial body [was] the guarantor of normalcy, aesthetic and moral virtue . . . and full member[ship in] the human community."[26] This was because of the way that medieval Europe imagined people in faraway lands in what Cohen and Steel call "the fantastic expanses of the wonder literature, a Far East that indifferently combines an Africa, China and India all containing monsters, bizarre customs and fabulous wealth."[27] The notion of a Christian Europe was quite precarious indeed throughout the Middle Ages, under continual threat from Others beyond the frontier—the Huns and Vikings during the beginning of the period, and then the Moors and the Ottoman Empire during the end of it. The discernible physical differences between Europeans and potential conquerors, as described by the chroniclers of the Crusades, give us a glimpse of the start of the racialized consciousness of the modern West.

This is why thinking about race as it exists in the secondary world of the reader's imagination matters for understanding how the dark fantastic cycle operates in fantasy and fairy tales. The construct of dreaming-as-reading provides a way to unlock what may be going on as readers, viewers, and fans engage in the fantastic. The presence of the Dark Other amplifies the reader/viewer/fan's sense of *hesitation*. It creates a *spectacle* that hails the monstrous. This leads to textual *violence*, and the Dark Other then *haunts* the text. As in the previous chapter's focus on Rue in *The Hunger Games*, here, focusing on Gwen may provide some context for the troubling reactions that the presence of a Black queen elicited.

The Dark Fantastic Cycle, Interrupted? Arthur's Dark Queen

Spectacle

Spectacle characterizes the early sequences of the *Merlin* series. The opening credits promise that this will be a story set "in a land of myth and magic," but in the first episode, Camelot does not seem to be an ideal locale for anyone searching for a fantastic escape. The pilot is saturated with physical threat and violence, starting with the very first scene in which King Uther orders the execution of a sorcerer for violating a prohibition on magic that has been in effect for twenty years:

> UTHER: Let this serve as a lesson to all. This man, Thomas James Collins, is adjudged guilty of conspiring to use enchantments and magic. And, pursuant to the laws of Camelot, I, Uther Pendragon, have decreed that such practices are banned on penalty of death. I pride myself as a fair and just king, but for the crime of sorcery, there is but one sentence I can pass.
>
> [Uther raises his arm, then lowers it as a signal to the executioner. Thomas Collins is beheaded. People gasp.][28]

Although we do not see any blood (and will rarely see any during the entire run of *Merlin*), the atmosphere in Camelot is ominous. The entire populace is gathered around the scaffold and does not make a sound as their king speaks. After the initial establishing shots, and some back and forth between the king, who is standing on high at his window, and the executioner and condemned on the scaffold, the focus is on the blade of the executioner's axe. The viewer experiences both the dread of its rise, as well as the horror of its fall. Notably, the spectacle in the early episodes has nothing to do with racialized characters; it is that death is the penalty for practicing magic in a television series named for one of the most famous fictional wizards of all time.

Initially, none of the major characters from the Arthurian cycles assumes his or her most familiar form from the legends. King Arthur is not yet a king but is instead an arrogant, entitled, and profoundly unlikeable young crown prince. He bullies his servants and speaks to Merlin as if he is the help. Merlin is not yet the powerful, wizened mage of story and song. Instead, he is an awkward and earnest teenager who must hide his powers to save his life. Morgana experiences prophetic dreams that disturb her sleep but is unaware that she is a witch. The only hint of her future antagonism is the way she frequently challenges Uther's decisions as king, although she is meant to be his obedient ward and foster daughter.

Most notably, the lovely Queen Guinevere is first introduced as the simple and guileless Gwen, maidservant to the Lady Morgana. Traditionally in Arthuriana stories for children and young adults, Guinevere is invariably positioned as a high-born lady or a princess. Often, she is the object of desire not only for the once and future King Arthur but also for his Knights of the Round Table, most notably Sir Lancelot. She is beloved of her parents, particularly her father, and is revered by her people. What has been consistent throughout the centuries since her first appearance in the legends is that Gwen is both fair and faithless, illustrating not only the fundamental treachery of the beautiful, but also the subjugation of Wales, perhaps the agency of the subdued Welsh population in light of English conquest.[29] More recent retellings for children and young adults, including Nancy McKenzie's *Chrysalis Queen Quartet* book series and Robert Mandell's anime television series *Princess Gwenevere and the Jewel Riders*, have focused far less on Guinevere's treachery and faithlessness and more on her agency and power as a young princess.[30]

Before *Merlin*, however, none of these text-based retellings of the narrative have made Guinevere anything other than visibly White. That changed with the nontraditional casting of Guyanese-British actress Angel Coulby as Gwen.[31] There is a long tradition of women of color playing servants in literature and the media.[32] Traditionally, these characters serve in a secondary or tertiary helper capacity, and do not have much interiority that is revealed to audiences. When such characters step out of the background and into the spotlight, that in itself is notable. What is even more significant about Gwen is that she is pushed into the spotlight *while* she is still a servant.

Our first glimpse of the once and future queen in BBC's *Merlin* is fourteen and a half minutes into the pilot episode.[33] At initial glance, there isn't very much to distinguish her from the other extras who serve as castle servants: as she shakes a bedcover out at an upstairs window, she watches Arthur verbally abuse a young servant boy in the tiltyard while he is throwing knives at a wooden shield held by a trembling servant. Uther's son is as cruel and callous to the underprivileged as his father, and Gwen's disgust is apparent. Her disapproval is made explicit when Gwen calls Arthur "a bully" while comforting her fellow servant Merlin, who has been placed into the stocks for defying Arthur.

Throughout the balance of the first season, Gwen's interactions with both Prince Arthur and King Uther continue to be antagonistic despite her status as a servant to Morgana, Uther's foster daughter. Arthur accuses Gwen of being a witch and arrests her after a sorceress uses a magical creature to poison Camelot's water supply and her blacksmith father, Tom, is the only poison victim who recovers.[34] Later in the first season, Tom is killed by King Uther for supposedly harboring a sorcerer, although this time Arthur expresses remorse for what has happened to Gwen's family.[35] This darker Gwen experiences considerably more hardship than the fair princess and queen familiar from the cycles, but her travails are all too familiar to Black characters in fictional narratives: Gwen in *Merlin* is incarcerated, falsely accused, and loses a parent to state violence. Most notably, during the first season, Gwen exists not for herself, but as Morgana's maid, a friend for Merlin, and an unwelcome conscience for Arthur. She is, in effect, one of the many instantiations of a Black servant character in television.

Gwen's tense relationship with Arthur does not change until the final episode of the first season. She nurses Arthur back to health when he is bitten by the Questing Beast, and speaks softly to him while he is unconscious:

> [Gaius is asleep in the chair next to Arthur's sick bed. Gwen enters and knocks on the door to wake Gaius.]
> GWEN: Gaius? You should get some rest.
> GAIUS: He must not be left alone.
> GWEN: I will nurse him.
>
> [Gaius leaves. Gwen takes the towel from Arthur's forehead, dips it in a bowl of water, and sits on the bed to tend to him.]
> GWEN: You're not going to die, Arthur. I'm telling you. Because I know that one day you will be King. A greater king than your father could ever be. It's what keeps me going. You are going to live to be the man I've seen inside you, Arthur. I can see a Camelot that is fair and just. I can see a king that the people will love and be proud to call their sovereign. For the love of Camelot, you have to live.[36]

For the rest of the series, from the second through the fifth seasons, Gwen visibly becomes Arthur's raison d'être. The spectacle of the brown-skinned servant who dares to disapprove of the tyrannical regime of King Uther and the antics of the spoiled Prince Arthur eventually (and inevitably) leads to hesitation on the part of both characters—and, ultimately, the viewers.

Hesitation

Gwen and Arthur's romance begins in the second season episode titled "The Once and Future Queen" and features a great deal of character displacement. While practicing for an upcoming tournament with his knights, Arthur learns that he is being treated more gently than the others and even allowed victories because of his royal status. The thought that his knights are purposefully losing jousts because of his status upsets and offends Arthur greatly. Determined to prove that he can win through merit, he formulates a plan to switch his identity. First, he tells

King Uther that he must hunt a magical beast with "the body of a lion, the wings of an eagle, and the face of a bear" seen in the forest. Next, he enlists the help of Merlin and Gwen. Merlin finds him clothing and a simple farmer to serve as his stand-in, and Gwen offers her home as a place for Arthur to stay and hide. Together, the trio invents the guise of Sir William of Deria so that Arthur can compete in the tournament anonymously.

When he first arrives in Gwen's home, Arthur insults its modest condition:

> [Merlin and Arthur enter, Arthur's hood obscures his face.]
> GWEN: My Lord.
> ARTHUR: Guinevere. It's good of you to let me stay in your home.
> GWEN: I'm happy to help.
> MERLIN (WHISPERING TO GWEN): Food.
> GWEN (TO ARTHUR): I'll prepare some food for you.
>
> [Arthur walks toward the window. Gwen pulls Merlin aside.]
> GWEN (WHISPERING TO MERLIN): I can't believe you talked me
>   into this!
>
> [Gwen goes to prepare the food. Merlin joins Arthur.]
> ARTHUR (WHISPERING TO MERLIN AS HE LOOKS AROUND
>   GWEN'S HOME WITH A FROWN): You can't really expect me to
>   stay here?
> MERLIN (WHISPERING TO ARTHUR): We need to keep you out of
>   sight. We can trust Gwen not to tell anyone you're here.
> ARTHUR (WHISPERING TO MERLIN): I doubt anyone would believe it.[37]

Since hesitation sustains the life of the fantastic, Arthur's observation, "I doubt anyone would believe it," is an apt one. Fantastic hesitation in the scene is signaled through the dialogue as well as the status of the characters. The initial dialogue hails the social distance between Arthur as crown prince and Gwen as a castle servant. She uses the honorific "my lord," his uncharacteristically gracious acknowledgement of her allowing him to stay is answered with her expressing pleasure at helping him, and then she begins to prepare food. Although it is not unusual for a peasant girl in this genre to offer food and shelter to a guest, it is most unusual for Gwen to do so for a prince *while knowing his identity*. The hesitation Gwen and Arthur feel is signaled by the fact that the remaining dialogue is all whispered asides. Merlin's whisper of "food" signals Gwen's servant status, despite the fact that Arthur is a guest in her home wearing the attire of a commoner. Then both Gwen *and* Arthur express their misgivings about the situation to Merlin. Finally, Arthur sums up the challenge of the dark fantastic: "I doubt anyone would believe it." On a scale between belief and unbelief, what Arthur signals to the viewer is that this situation is beyond belief. The handsome royal prince who heretofore has never been seen in anything other than expensive royal garb and knightly armor arrives at Gwen's home in an unadorned cloak and the garb of a peasant—a prince out of place.

During the week that Arthur lives under his assumed identity at Gwen's home, he moves from treating her like a servant to falling in love with her. After he appropriates the sole bed (and she is forced to sleep on the floor), demands water for washing (forcing her to walk to the village well in the middle of the night), and directs her to mend his torn shirt, Gwen finally explodes.

Arthur (pointing to Gwen's bed): Is this where *you* sleep? Where's your bed?

Gwen: You're sleeping in it.

Arthur: Why didn't you say something?

Gwen: How could I? You're Prince Arthur! Besides, you didn't give me the chance. You just assumed the bed was yours.

Arthur: Well, how am I supposed to know if you don't tell me?

Gwen: You shouldn't need to be told to think of someone other than yourself, you're not a child!

Arthur (visibly taken aback): Is there anything else you'd like to say to me? Please, I'd like to hear it. If there's something you want to say to me, don't let me stop you.

Gwen: You don't have any idea, do you?

Arthur: About what?

Gwen: About how rude and arrogant you can be! This is my home and you are my guest in it! I know you are used to more luxurious quarters, but that is not an excuse to be so rude! You claim titles don't matter to you, but you behave like a prince and expect me to wait on you like a servant! Saying it means nothing if your actions betray you! Would it kill you to say please and thank you once in a while?! (THEN, REMEMBERING WHO SHE IS SPEAKING TO) *My Lord.*[38]

Twelve episodes into the series, Gwen finally tells Arthur what she has thought about his arrogance and lack of regard for others since the pilot. Arthur could have rebuked her or even had her arrested for her insolence. Instead he apologizes and offers to make dinner for her. Throughout his stay with Gwen, between his incessant demands, Arthur has shared with Gwen that he wants to be recognized for the knight he is, not because he is the King's son. She is compelled by his desire to be different from the callous father he desperately wishes to impress, while he is drawn to her innate kindness and ability to stand up to him without fear.

Of course, Arthur does not prepare a romantic dinner for Gwen but instead sends Merlin to fetch food from the castle. When Gwen notices that the plates bear the royal seal, she becomes angry. Arthur at first brags that "I can kill a chicken from a thousand paces, just don't ask me to cook it," and says that preparing food is a servant's job until he real- izes he has offended Gwen. After she tells him that "a good king must respect his people, no matter who they are," Arthur confesses that he has much to learn about cooking and "knowing what to say to someone I care about." They share a significant look just before Merlin bursts in with the news that an assassin is after Arthur.

The scene the next morning reveals that Arthur has slept on the floor while Gwen has spent the night in her humble bed. The tournament will have its final match on that day, and Arthur's time undercover will come to an end. Just before he leaves, Gwen shyly offers him her favor to wear, a strip of rough spun cloth. He thanks her, and then leans in; they share their first kiss of true love as violins play in the background and the light from her home's single window floods the scene.

Where, then, lies dark fantastic hesitation after the brown-skinned princess has been marked by true love's first kiss? The series at first side- steps the uncomfortable questions of Arthur's and Gwen's class (and ra- cial) differences by putting a bookmark on their relationship at the end of the episode:

[The courtiers exit into the corridor. Arthur checks that his father isn't looking, then turns to Gwen.]

ARTHUR: Guinevere (clearing his throat). What happened while I was staying with you. . . . I'm afraid my father would never understand.

GWEN: You don't have to explain. Perhaps when you are King, things will be different.[39]

From this point forward, Arthur and Gwen are clearly in love with each other. Throughout the remainder of the second season, they try to hide their feelings but often stare at each other with intense longing. When Gwen is captured by a bandit after she and Morgana switch identities, Arthur insists upon rescuing her against the king's wishes. Before he can arrive at the scene, Lancelot, with whom Gwen had some romantic tension in the first season, comes to the rescue.[40] But unlike in the versions of the Arthurian cycle most familiar to modern audiences, in *Merlin* the legendary affair is never consummated. Lancelot notes to Merlin that Arthur is in love with Gwen, and he will not get in the way. Although later in the series a villainous Morgana will resurrect Lancelot in order to drive a wedge between the royal couple, Gwen remains faithful.[41] After his father, Uther, dies, King Arthur makes Gwen his wife and queen.[42]

Violence

Due to the magical medieval setting, spectacular violence is part and parcel not only of Gwen's storyline but of all the characters' stories. In the preceding chapter, I note how even the normalized violence of fantastic stories is often amplified when and where the Dark Other enters any given narrative. The horror of the futuristic, dystopian *Hunger Games* is crystalized in the spectacle of Rue, the little mockingbird-girl from District 11, being eulogized by the central protagonist, Katniss. The spectacle, the hesitation, and the violence of these stories, when focalized through the perspectives of dark story-girls, seem to tick up a notch precisely because many of these girls have little interiority. Instead, they are two-dimensional foils for the White heroine's storylines.

Gwen does not fall into the same pattern. She begins as a secondary character and a servant, which is common for female characters of color, and her initial narrative purpose is to support the stories of Merlin,

Morgana, and, tangentially, Arthur. After Arthur falls in love with her and makes her the object of his desire, she is elevated to the traditional place of a princess in a fairy tale, although at first she retains her social status as a servant. We are introduced to her blacksmith father, Tom, and her brother, Elyan, who is a knight of Arthur's Round Table. She is positioned as desirable not only by Arthur but also by Lancelot and other characters, and Arthur experiences jealousy because of this. At the end of the fourth season finale, she marries Arthur, and he crowns her Queen.

At first, it seems as if Gwen has broken the dark fantastic cycle. And she would have actually done so if *Merlin* had ended with the fourth season finale. Gwen never becomes a princess, since Uther's disapproval of her means that Arthur has to become king in order to have the power to marry her and make her queen. However, once she is crowned Queen of Camelot, she is expected to live happily ever after. Dark, beautiful, and beloved within the world of her medieval fantasy, Gwen is potentially the heroine that disproves the dark fantastic cycle.

The fifth and final season of *Merlin* puts an end to such emancipatory flights of fancy.

Season five opens two years after Gwen is married to Arthur and has been crowned as his queen. The first five episodes show them in the royal chambers dining together and preparing for the day as they discuss plot events. We do not see the royal couple interacting in overtly romantic ways, however. Now that they are married, the theme of forbidden romantic desire is downplayed, and their kisses, embraces, and touches are less frequent than in previous seasons. Lancelot is dead by this time, so the possibility of the most famous extramarital affair of all is removed from this family-friendly adaptation.[43] Furthermore, the childlessness of Guinevere, significant in Arthuriana, is retained in *Merlin's* fifth season but never remarked upon. It leaves unspoken questions about the state of the royal couple's marriage bed, which were amplified by the fandom, but siring an heir for the realm is not the obsession of *Merlin's* Arthur as it is for the Arthur of myth.

Yet even ensconced in a traditional heterosexual marriage to one of the most powerful legendary kings of all time, this darker Gwen is *still* not safe. Rather than using the infidelity of Gwen to threaten Camelot's stability, *Merlin* departs from other Arthurian legends by invoking the psychological terror of a White woman assuming mastery over a Black one. This terror manifests in the guise of Morgana, no longer the dutiful ward of Uther from season one, in her familiar mythic form as a sorceress in her full power. Although *Merlin* omits the romantic tension between Morgana and Arthur that is present in many of the retellings, it does retain Morgana's unbridled antipathy toward the royal house of Pendragon, which in the series is extended to the realm of Camelot. In order to strike at Arthur, Morgana decides to attack the person who is closest to him—his wife.

The sixth episode of the final season opens with Gwen and her brother, Elyan, visiting their father's gravesite. They are accompanied by several Knights of the Round Table, including Leon, Percival, and Gwaine. On the way back to the castle, their horses are attacked by an ensorcelled snake. They tell the queen to "get to the trees—go!," while Leon and Percival are bitten. The knights return to the castle with their wounded brothers, expecting Gwen to meet them there. Unbeknownst to the royal guard, however, the distraction is a ruse from Morgana. The queen runs straight into the sorceress, who knocks her off her horse and renders her unconscious with an incantation. Morgana's ominous words over Gwen's unconscious body—"Sleep, milady, for it could be some time before you do so again," foreshadow the horror that is waiting for Queen Gwen in the Dark Tower.[44]

When Gwen awakens, Morgana leads her through various kinds of terrain, including forest and desert. Gwen is on foot, tied by a rope and stumbling behind Morgana, who is mounted on a horse. The witch refuses to tell Gwen where they are going and taunts her with an offer of water that she pours on the ground. They eventually arrive at the Dark Tower,[45] where Morgana takes Gwen up a long staircase and locks her inside a room, whispering "Sleep well," much as Gwen used to do when she was servant to the Lady Morgana. The woman Gwen once served has becomes her jailer and torturer.

Within the highest room of the Dark Tower, the spotlight on Gwen's face is the only source of illumination. Screams, high pitched and blood curdling, lead Gwen to plug her ears with her fingers. During the next scene in the Tower, Gwen awakens as a dark, tarlike substance drips onto her face. She walks around the dimly lit room, dodging sinister vines and cringing at random screams. Soon, Gwen encounters a number of mandrake roots hanging from the ceiling, covered with the black substance that fell upon her face. This is an Easter egg for loyal fans among the viewing audience[46]—it is meant to recall the use of mandrake in an episode from two seasons before, "The Tears of Uther Pendragon," to torture, confuse, and twist the mind. Over the next few days, Gwen is haunted by visions of those she loves most in the world—her brother, Elyan, Merlin and his physician mentor, Gaius, and Arthur. All of the hallucinations taunt and laugh sinisterly at her, as ghostly screams of terror fill the air.

Eventually, Gwen is brought down from the Dark Tower to dine with the witch Morgana. In a dining room draped in cobwebs, Morgana tells Gwen that she ought to be grateful for her kindness.

> MORGANA: Eat. Here. Food always makes me feel better. Would you prefer some chicken? You must eat. You are fading away.
> GWEN: I do not know what cruel trick you are playing, but I will not be broken by you.
> MORGANA: I thought this would be nice. I know how lonely you must be. All by yourself in that room. At least you're not shackled. There's daylight. You can move, you can see.
> GWEN: You expect me to be grateful?
> MORGANA: I too have suffered, Gwen. I spent two years living in darkness. I spent two years chained to a wall in the bottom of a pit. . . . [at Gwen's confused look] You did not know?
>
> [Gwen shakes her head.]
> MORGANA: I would have sold my soul for someone to show me kindness such as this. Do you want me to take you back up there?
> [Morgana bites into a grape. Gwen looks fearful.][47]

The cobwebs clearly represent the web that the spiderlike Morgana is weaving around this dark queen trapped inside her dark tower. The uncannily sumptuous feast that Morgana offers nightly is Gwen's temptation, seeking to compel her to join the forces of magic and darkness to end Camelot and bring about the downfall of the king. Morgana is the only source of food, firelight, and companionship within the tower. Arthur, his knights, and Merlin spend the entire episode on a quest to rescue Gwen from the witch. Elyan falls in a battle against an enchanted sword, and as Gaius notes, "The sword that Elyan fell prey to was surely intended for Arthur. Now he's safe, and so is Gwen."[48]

Gwen is indeed rescued, but her time in the Dark Tower has twisted her mind. Whenever she is in Arthur's arms, she has a resentful, angry look, and the smile is gone from her face. The night of Elyan's funeral, she steals off to meet Morgana and pledges her trust.

> GWEN: Arthur thinks he has won. He has no idea.
> MORGANA: Do you understand now who you can trust?
> GWEN: It's you, Morgana. It's only ever been you.
> MORGANA: You are not one of them. And you never will be.
> GWEN: You don't know how much I hate them. All of them.
> MORGANA: You have done well to see past the lies to the real truth. You have an important part to play in the future. Together, we will ensure the destruction of everything that Arthur holds dear.[49]

The next three episodes are the "Evil Gwen" arc of the story, in which the queen attempts to kill Arthur and wrongfully implicates the royal stable boy, Tyr, in the plot. It is here that there is more overt sexual suggestion between the royal couple than in the rest of the series. Gwen uses her sexuality in these scenes to place her husband in danger. The first instance happens at the beginning of the episode, when Gwen walks into the royal bedchamber as Arthur and Merlin are festooning the bed with garlands of flowers.

> [Guinevere enters, removing her cloak and draping it over the back of a chair. She sees Arthur and Merlin arranging garlands around the bed.]
> GWEN: Oh, Arthur, that is so sweet. You've gone to all this trouble. And gillyflowers, my favourite. You remembered.
>
> [Guinevere puts her arms around his neck.]
> ARTHUR: Mm-hmm.
> GWEN: Have you missed me?
> ARTHUR: Mmm.
>
> [Arthur stops, looking up at Merlin.]
> ARTHUR: Merlin, er, it's late. You should probably get some sleep.

[Merlin walks toward the door.]

MERLIN: Thank you, Sire.

GWEN: Oh, Merlin. Before you go, I'd love a hot bath.

[Guinevere squeals and giggles as Arthur sweeps her up in his arms.]

MERLIN: Certainly, my lady.

[Merlin leaves and Arthur carries Guinevere to the bed.][50]

It is when Merlin leaves for the kitchens to draw Gwen's bathwater that he encounters a young boy whom Morgana has hired to draw him out of the castle. Later in the episode, when Merlin is unavailable to help Arthur get dressed, Gwen slowly and sensually dresses her husband, inflicting a little pain by overtightening the leather straps of his shoulder guards. She uses her seductive femininity in a plot to assassinate Arthur, offering a rival king one-third of Camelot for his assistance. It is not until the fourth episode of the arc, "With All My Heart," that Morgana's evil spell is broken and Gwen is restored to normalcy through Arthur's unconditional love and support for her.[51] This comes at a narrative price to Gwen. Although she is forgiven by the king and restored to her position as faithful consort, she becomes incidental for the remainder of the series.[52]

Thus, we see the ways that the violence phase of the dark fantastic cycle unfolds despite following all the conventions of the Arthuriana source material. Unlike Rue's violent death as the necessary sacrifice in the ritual of the sadistic Hunger Games, Gwen's death is symbolic—hers is a social death after being compromised by darkness. After suffering the violence of Morgana's psychological torture in the Dark Tower, *Merlin*'s perfect dark queen becomes the hollow queen, a puppet who exists solely to do the bidding of the series' primary antagonist. Once innocent, Gwen now has the blood of Tyr, the stable boy, on her hands, and although she is forgiven by her magnanimous king, the crimes that she committed while under compulsion are never again addressed in the series. As the witch's puppet, Gwen loses her place as the heart and moral center of the story. The young woman who was once King Arthur's greatest source of strength and hope becomes his great peril. It is only through Arthur's love for her, and Merlin's devotion to his king, that she is saved from the clutches of evil. Most notably, Evil Guinevere is Gwen's very last character arc in the series: from her restoration until the death of Arthur, she is relegated to the background as the story reaches its climax. After Gwen's promising happily-ever-after in season four, her destiny is violence and then obscurity.

Haunting

Even in this family-friendly adaptation, many of the classic elements of Arthuriana are present in *Merlin*. From the Questing Beast to the Round Table, from Morgana's conflicted feelings about Arthur to Mordred's fatal hatred for him, and from the clouded circumstances of Arthur's birth to Lancelot's futile longing for Guinevere—the series covers them all. Furthermore, the authors of many of the most familiar versions of the Arthurian legends appear as guest characters in the series, from Geoffrey of Monmouth to Chretien de Troyes to Thomas Malory.[53]

But perhaps the most notable and resonant element in all versions of the story over the past 1,500 years is that Arthur Pendragon is the once *and* future king. When Britain is once again facing its time of greatest need, her greatest king will return. Both he and Merlin are imbued with an inevitable immortality, as eternal ruler and magical protector of the nation. And so the television series *Merlin* plays the death of Arthur straight. It is orchestrated by Morgana, the witch whose fate is intertwined with his. Arthur falls during the Battle of Camlann, just as in the best-known legends. The killing blow is delivered by Mordred, Arthur dies with the promise of resurrection and return, and the last shot of the series features a wizened, presumably immortal, Merlin, nearly run over by a truck as he surveys the Isle of Avalon, the destination of Arthur's funerary barge, and awaits Arthur's prophesied return.

Given this turn of events, it might seem as if Arthur and Merlin are the characters who haunt the series' ending, and that the dark fantastic cycle has been broken. Recall, however, that the Dark Other is the *engine* of the fantastic. How could any modern-day Arthurian legend be haunted by the very characters that are its source of enduring hope? This timeless story is haunted by neither the messianic once and future king, nor the boy-wizard who saves him (and some viewers would say loves him). Much like the matter of Britain itself, *Merlin* is haunted by the women of the story, tainted irrevocably by dark magic, whose actions against Merlin and Arthur spur the events of the finale. Even more so than Morgana, who is killed by Merlin at the beginning of the final episode, Gwen haunts the text.

During an interview with the *Los Angeles Times* during the final season, showrunner and creator Julian Murphy commented about Guinevere's ending:

> INTERVIEWER: Also in the finale, we discover that the monarch who will lead Camelot in a golden era of peace is Gwen, not Arthur. Was that a decision that came as the result of Arthur's death? Or was it something deliberate you've been planning for a long time?
>
> JULIAN MURPHY: It was, actually. We've had that in our minds for about three series. We felt that with Gwen, to take Gwen from a servant girl to a powerful and strong queen, a person who can bind the kingdom together, was the journey we wanted to do, and I think Angel delivered that brilliantly. And some of the most moving scenes in that last episode are with Gwen as she realizes who Merlin was, and that the king, the love of her life, is going to die, and that she must then take the kingdom forward. And she plays it in no more than three or four scenes, and that whole story is told. It's a real credit to her.[54]

Although Murphy claims that Gwen is destined to be the monarch who will lead Camelot's Golden Age, her scenes lead the viewer to question whether there is something subtler going on. First, she is included at the final War Council of the Knights of the Round Table, where her first line is "She means to take Camelot." While this is certainly referring to Morgana, it is interesting because it bookends a two-part finale where in the end, *she* will take Camelot after Arthur's death. Her other line is "We cannot save everyone, Arthur. No matter how much we may wish it," which foreshadows Arthur's death.

The next time we see Gwen, she insists upon joining Arthur at the Battle of Camlann. Although he protests and tells her that the battlefield is no place for a queen (not *his* queen, but *a* queen), her background as a servant and de facto nurse prove useful as she assists with wounded troops. On the eve of the battle, Gwen assures Arthur about his decision to make his final stand against Morgana and Mordred at Camlann and not Camelot. He tells her, "If you do not doubt me, Guinevere, then I do not doubt myself. That gives me a strength greater than any weapon." This is their final goodbye in the series.

During the battle, Gwen fatally stabs a Saxon who bursts into the medical tent. Before the Evil Gwen sequence, Gwen is a symbol of innocence and mercy in the series, the beloved whom Arthur must save. Here, Gwen saves herself. After she returns to the castle and becomes regent during Arthur's disappearance from the battlefield, Gaius returns Arthur's ring with the royal seal to her. Gwen learns that Arthur is wounded and Merlin is taking him to a place where he might be saved, which most viewers familiar with the legends know is Avalon.

The most chilling scene of *Merlin's* finale occurs during the drama of Merlin and Arthur's journey to Avalon. Eira, Sir Gwaine's love interest, is discovered sending a raven to Morgana disclosing information about Arthur and Merlin's whereabouts. When Gwaine and Gwen confront Eira, she denies it and says that she would never betray the queen or the king. Gwen coldly replies, "And if you didn't, you can go to your death safe in that knowledge." Chillingly, as Eira dies in the courtyard, Gwen, crowned in her royal glory, looks down at the scene as coldly as King Uther does in the pilot. While it is righteous justice that she metes out against this ally of magic, one has to marvel at the changes in Gwen from the first season. With the majority of the audience knowing that if the legends are followed, Arthur is doomed, and Merlin will not return, what will become of the kingdom?

Viewers' final glimpse of Gwen is at her proclamation as queen regnant of Camelot. She sits on her throne in the Great Hall, Arthur's throne beside her conspicuously empty. Sir Leon announces, "The King is dead. Long live the Queen!" And a hall filled with knights shouts, "Long live the Queen!" But the scene is solemn. Other than Gaius, there are no civilians present.

No one is smiling.

In the end, all that is left of magical Camelot is Gwen's tortured, unhappy face with sad brown eyes. Immortal Merlin will walk the earth and wait for the return of his once and future king. Morgana the witch perishes knowing that she succeeded in taking revenge on Arthur and Camelot. But *Merlin's* dark queen remains trapped in the past, alone with a kingdom to run, without father or brother, the prince she loved, or the friends who pulled her into his world. Once a serving girl, and then the queen in a fairy tale, Gwen haunts the text. Just as Bunny De-Barge presaged, her happiness was just a dream.

A Queen out of Place:
Reader and Viewer Questions about Authenticity and Accuracy in Folklore, Fairy Tales, and High Fantasy

As with fan reactions to Rue, there was a range of negative reactions to Gwen in the role of a legendary queen whose dreams come true. Although the fictional time period of Camelot anteceded the time of Atlantic slavery, because we cannot plausibly travel backward in time, only forward, the significance of the enslaved Black body is perhaps unwittingly superimposed on characters like Gwen. Despite Michelle M. Wright's cautions about mapping all human bodies that can be identified as Black onto the single story of the Middle Passage epistemology, because we consume fairy tales and fantasy in the dream space of the secondary world, our emotions lead us to index dark characters primarily within contexts of enslavement, empire, conquest, colonialism, and abiding second-class status. The impossibility of Black heroism, agency, and beauty is the result. Accepting a desirable dark-skinned queen requires not only the suspension of disbelief but also the conscious rethinking of who and what is marked as beautiful and desirable.

It is therefore unsurprising that viewers of the *Merlin* television series had a variety of reactions to the on-screen presence of Angel Coulby as the fair queen of Camelot. These reactions spanned the gamut, but most ranged around the valences of "likeability" and "relatability." Of course, Gwen was seen as more likeable and relatable when she was not a candidate for Arthur's affections. Starting in the second season, when Arthur's interest in Gwen became apparent, fans began to protest. Their offense seemed to fall into three main areas: (1) Gwen is ugly because she is Black, (2) the pairing of Gwen and Arthur is heteronormative and not progressive enough, and (3) Gwen is a character outside of plausible spacetime, thus ruining Arthurian legend. I explore each of these viewer assertions below.

Assertion #1: Gwen Is Ugly

The assertion that the actress Angel Coulby is not pretty enough to play Queen Guinevere pervaded message boards, YouTube videos, and numerous websites both during the run of *Merlin* and afterward. This led to some fans of color writing essays (known in fan communities as "meta") about the phenomenon. One young fan of color, Tassja, had this to say about it:

> Beauty, desire and attraction may be subjective, but 450 plus years of cultural conditioning that elevated Eurocentric beauty standards over all others has left an indelible mark on our collective conscious. We are all implicated in the colonial, white-supremacist gaze. There's a reason that my teenage self could never picture a Black/African descended man as a Prince. There's a reason that same teenage self unthinkingly coded beauty as White.

Tassja notes that a commenter wrote the following about Coulby's Gwen:

> I have no problem with them casting a black woman as Guinevere, but as an artist, my problem is that Guinevere's beauty was legendary (which led to her subsequent "man troubles") and although I find Angel Coulby cute and pretty, she is not captivatingly beautiful! But a huge part of Guinevere's character is her physical beauty (not skin colour!) and that's why I personally feel this particular casting failed, as much as I appreciate the actress' ability.

To which Tassja responds:

> That line "Guinevere's beauty was legendary," has rankled me since I saw that comment. Who gets to decide what is and isn't "legendary"? Aren't codified legends, ultimately, tales that are allowed to flourish because they benefit the status quo? Why do we accept, without question, that all heroes and heroines are physically attractive and why does this seem integral to our cultural capacity to picture those people?. . . . By reducing these historical figures to their beauty, we not only do profound disservice to a history of powerful women, but we also perpetuate narrow understandings of sexuality, desirability, race and gender. [55]

Tassja's blog post generated a string of responses that I found typical within the *Merlin* fandom during my time as a participant. Of the fans who commented in response to Tassja's blog post, three disagreed with her perspectives, two on grounds of the actress's skin color not being appropriate for the time period. One fan, Einylondon, was particularly strident in disagreeing with Tassja:

> I am sorry but your ranting about racism is completely overblown. What I have experienced in my life as an outsider in the country I lived in is that racism definitely goes both ways and that I saw far more racism coming from the blacks than from the whites. For all you bullsh-t political correctness rant, Coulby as Gwen is ABSOLUTELY AWFUL, ruins the show, distracts from the narrative. She is FAR from beautiful, captivating, mesmerizing character we have come to love. I stopped watching Merlin as soon as they started pushing the idea of all these men falling over themselves for her: it was UNREALISTIC, FORCED, UNBELIEVABLE. For me personally its not an issue of race, as I find plenty of female black characters captivating, strong beautiful and well cast for the roles. Coulby as Gwen just doesnt work for multitude of reasons but mostly because how she looks vs the rest of the cast (much older and far less attractive). I am sorry it offends your sensibilities as a POC, but this has nothing to do with race but more to do with believability and attractiveness of the actress. She is NO GWEN, plain and simple.[56]

Such fan attitudes were by no means outliers. As medievalist Jennifer C. Edwards, in an article about the women of Starz's *Camelot* and the BBC's *Merlin*, observes:

> While *Camelot* cast the traditionally blonde, slim, young, and fair-skinned Tamsin Egerton as Guinevere, *Merlin* attracted controversy, especially during the series' move to American television, by casting Angel Coulby as Gwen. . . . Gwen's servile position, combined with Coulby's casting, has polarized viewers and created a vicious backlash among online commentators. Negative fan reactions to Gwen divide into two main camps: those who applaud the selection of a black

actress but criticize the decision to put her in a servile position; and those who reject—often with racist language—the decision to cast a black actress in this position at all, since it alters their expectations of "beauty" for Gwen. The forcefulness of these responses suggests again the power of expectations for portrayals of Arthurian women on screen.[57]

Although some viewers found Gwen's nontraditional casting to be a barrier for their enjoyment of the series, there were other fans, like Tassja, who applauded seeing her on the screen. On LiveJournal, zahrawithaz wrote, "So by casting a black woman as Gwen, the show did a potentially radical thing. It said that the black girl-next-door, who's constantly being overlooked in favor of a glamourous white woman, is going to grow up to become one of the great romance heroines of all time, and the focus of the most legendary love triangle in Western literature."[58] Zahra's response challenges the default viewer position as one of Whiteness. As fairy tales and fantasy become increasingly transmediated and commodified in the digital age, a new generation is responding to Whitewashed media by applauding diverse casting choices like that of Angel Coulby for *Merlin*'s contemporary take on Guinevere. Although it is the case that Gwen is yet another dark girl character trapped by the narrative, going through the cycle of spectacle, hesitation, violence, and haunting, her presence still mattered for girls and women of color all over the world who saw themselves mirrored in her story.

Assertion #2: Gwen and Arthur Are Heteronormative

Given some viewers' objections to the presence of Gwen on *Merlin*, it is perhaps unsurprising that the most popular "ship" (fandom term for relationship) in the fandom is Merthur—the undeniable connection between the young wizard and the monarch he serves so devotedly. Recall that it is not Gwen whom Arthur spends his final moments with in the series, but Merlin, who cares for Arthur devotedly in his futile quest to save him. Series creator Julian Murphy first spoke of Merlin and Arthur's friendship as being the central focus of *Merlin* during the promotion for the finale:

INTERVIEWER: So much of the show is based on relationships between characters. Do you have a favorite pairing?

JULIAN MURPHY: Merlin and Arthur. To me, that's the heart of the program. It's a story of friendship, it's both very funny but very touching and very real. And to go from two characters who in many ways in the first series began hating each other to two characters who profoundly respect and care about each other is a great journey. Those simple journeys are always the best, and the heart of the program is not dragons and swords and myths and legends, it's that story, that friendship.[59]

After the release of the final season DVDs, Murphy amplified his remarks about the importance of Merlin and Arthur's friendship, implying that it was a love story. As reporter Selena Wilken wrote:

> Most notably, the showrunner confirms that Merlin and Arthur did indeed grow to love each other by the end of the series, calling it a "pure" love. "We did, very genuinely, think of the episode as a love story between two men. Which is what I think it is, jokes and innuendo aside," he says. [Morgana's actress, Katie] McGrath adds that, "you can't deny that Merlin and Arthur do love each other, you know? In whatever love way you want to think, there is no denying."
>
> Murphy points to the moment where Arthur finally dies as what the entire series has been building towards. At the "just hold me," Murphy justifies to a shocked McGrath that, "well, he's dying, the man he loves is dying, so he's holding him."[60]

The series creator's reading of *Merlin* as potential gay romance was overwhelmingly supported by the fandom, both during the run of the show, and afterward. A quick glance at the popular fanfiction site, Archive of Our Own, reveals nearly 10,000 fanworks featuring the Merlin and Arthur pairing, compared to only 1,600 for Arthur and Gwen.[61] While there has been some critical work on the role of slash fanfiction in fantasy fandom, most notably by Catherine Tosenberger, there has been less attention paid to the clash between fans who want to see less heteronormative storytelling in media and fans who advocate for racial diversity.[62] This clash is particularly poignant because just as young women of color have spoken up about how important it was to them to see a Gwen in *Merlin* who looked like them, gay viewers have written about how important Merlin's journey was for them. One young man wrote on Reddit about his emotional connection to Merlin growing up:

> As the series went on, Merlin's magic was my sexuality. Arthur was my best friend. . . . Every episode where he felt he had to hide and every episode where he came so close to revealing his secret and every episode where he trusted when it was hard for him to do so, it all resonated with me on a profoundly meaningful level. I started to come out of a dark place, using this show as my therapist, because they understood me and showed me a path. . . . When Merlin ended, I was out to my best friend. It was hard and that fear was there but all my years of escaping into TV led me to this show, which felt like to me, was created to help me move forward in my life. I cried when it ended. Merlin's struggles were mine and when that curtain closed, I closed the curtain on the darkest time in my life. . . . Whenever anyone asks me my coming out story, or asks me how I became as comfortable with myself as I am now, I talk about this show.[63]

The connection between Merlin having to hide his magic for almost the entirety of the show's run and his assumed homosexuality was encouraged by those affiliated with the show. In the DVD commentary for the final season, showrunner and creator Murphy jokes and talks with Morgana's actress, Katie McGrath, about magic within the series as a metaphor for homosexuality.[64] Another viewer and fan notes, "You have to be *blind* to not see at least *some* of the undertones early in the series. Sure, I'd like to have a Merlin/Arthur romance. They've screwed up Arthurian legend as it is, so why not just go and use the ideas of the legends as a springboard for their own ideas?[65] Many applauded Merlin and Arthur's friendship becoming something more, and were disappointed when the show chose to highlight the romance between Arthur and Gwen in the second, third, and fourth seasons.

Due to the popularity of the Merlin and Arthur romantic pairing within the fandom, fans who preferred Arthur and Gwen were characterized by some as homophobic. This was complicated by the fact that the most popular lesbian fan pairing on the show was Gwen and Morgana. On the BBCMerlinConfessions Tumblr, one anonymous post read:

> The way that femslashers are treated in this fandom is disgusting. As a het shipper, I hate to see my femslasher friends getting constant homophobic hatemail from Arwen fans & being condescended by Merthur shippers who think that shipping a M/M pairing qualifies them to tell actual LGBT people how to behave & think, & what they should & shouldn't be offended by. For a fandom who thinks of itself as "gay friendly," we need to take a hard look at ourselves & how we're treating our LGBT peers.[66]

In response to those who noted Morgana's treatment of Gwen throughout the series, another poster said:

> The queering and reclaiming of Morgana and Gwen's relationship by queer fans of the show is in itself an important, subversive process, and whilst it is vital that that process work hand in hand with a rejection of the racism, classism and sexism inherent to Gwen's treatment on the show and by the fandom (or else, frankly, it completely fails to do its job), a rejection of the queering process outright is just as damaging and problematic as the excusal of racist behaviour from fans to begin with. The two MUST happen in tandem, or they might as well not happen at all for all the good they will do in challenging the racist, classist, ablest, misogynist and homophobic narrative tendencies inherent to Merlin, its fandom and the British drama production industry as a whole.[67]

The importance of *Merlin* to gay and lesbian fans, as well as others invested in showing the full range of human sexuality, cannot be understated. Because the Gwen and Arthur romance has its basis in traditional legends and is heterosexual, it was positioned as less progressive than slash and femslash alternatives, although Gwen was played by an actress of color.[68] These points are valid. It must be observed, however, that within the universe of the show, as well as in the fandom, Gwen's race and class matter. While it is the case that fandoms can enforce the homophobia and heteronormativity of the larger culture, fandoms can also reflect racism. As the above-quoted fan aptly noted, "the racist, classist, ablest, misogynist and homophobic narrative tendencies inherent to Merlin, its fandom and the British drama production industry as a whole" must be looked at in tandem.

Assertion #3: Gwen Is a Character outside of a Plausible Spacetime, Thus Ruining Arthurian Legend

As observed above, audiences may reject seeing people of color cast in fantasy and fairy tales because, contrary to most historical evidence, fictional Europe has come to be depicted as all White. Some fans were opposed to Gwen's race on the grounds that it was historically inaccurate. At the beginning of the series, blogger Eurasian Sensation observed in "How Come There's a Black Click in *Merlin*?":

> A quick browse of blogs and forums reveals many viewers who find it ridiculous. Which is understandable. It seems like a blatantly PC move which flouts any notion of historical accuracy. Well, maybe not historical accuracy per se, since Merlin is pure fantasy, but you know what I mean. You wouldn't throw random European actors into *Crouching Tiger Hidden Dragon* to play Chinese noblemen, so why do the equivalent here? Since it is apparently set it Britain circa the 5th Century AD, surely they should try and capture the feel of the era. Back then, ethnic diversity meant the Angles and the Saxons.
>
> But then again, the show has a friggin' dragon in it. And unicorns and fairy-type creatures. And Merlin shoots people with blue fireballs. So if you can accept all those things, why is a black woman too fantastical a creature to fathom in a medieval fantasy series?[69]

Sixty-nine commenters responded to this post between 2009 and 2013 with a range of opinions on the topic. Here are a few that specifically reference the time period:

- The recent BBC series of Robin Hood had various minority characters in it (some ongoing) and much mention of the Crusades and Moors. . . . Perhaps this is how historical Brit shows recuperate some "rainbow" effect in their casting?!
- I find minority characters in Robin Hood easier to accept, since it is set around the time of the crusades and there was some (limited) contact

between England and the Muslim world. Black folks in the Arthurian world is a bit more of a credibility stretch, although I look forward to a Bangladeshi Sir Lancelot.

- The Internet is going crazy over the movie THOR, also. Idris Elba has been cast as Heimdall, and of course, the movie is loosely based on comic books, which are loosely based on Scandinavian myth, and it's killing many white folk, since Heimdall, besides being Scandinavian, is also known as the "white god." I was researching TV tropes and found the Black Viking trope. Black Vikings. And, I did an entire post about token black characters, and how annoying it has become.
- She looks exotic! She's not that dark and might not necessarily be of black ancestry. I think she could pass as a number of European nationalities namely, Spanish, Portuguese, Italian, Greek. I don't know what her ancestry is but I think on Merlin she could represent a variety of nationalities if she wanted to!
- There were few black people back then, some enslaved, some not. Plus, she looks very very mixed, and may be playing a different European ethnicity with darker skin. You never know.
- Guinevere could have had black blood, because she was said to have Roman heritage and Roman people came from all the Empire, not just Italian Peninsula.[70]

As medievalist Andrew B.R. Elliott has noted, "it is most often when the forum of the medieval world does not align with our own image of the period that we are most likely to take exceptions, not to its *accuracy* per se, but its *authenticity*."[71] Academic medievalists such as Geraldine Heng, Dorothy Kim, and Jeffrey Jerome Cohen have written about the anachronistic appropriation of the Middle Ages for contemporary purposes. While much of this has been the province of high fantasy like *Lord of the Rings* and *A Song of Ice and Fire*, Arthurian legend has also been viewed as the province of an all-White Europe. As Kris Swank observes, however, "Recent archeological and historical discoveries suggest Africans occupied a variety of social roles in Roman and medieval Britain."[72] This suggests that *Merlin's* casting choices may be more historically accurate than many viewers believed. But because of the dark fantastic cycle, it is difficult for viewers of fantasy and fairy tales to suspend their disbelief.

In an email interview, Malisha Dewalt, founder of the popular MedievalPOC Tumblr and website, talked further about sociopolitical reasons for audiences' resistance to the nontraditional casting of fantasy and fairy tales, as well as fandom ire over racebent fanwork:

> Emotional investment in the whiteness of fantasy culture, fantasy fandoms, medieval studies, renaissance festivals, you name it, is not something that can be corrected with citations and evidence. This problem was created in the first place by flooding the popular consciousness with a whitewashed version of the past, and that includes but is not limited to medieval Europe (think [about] popular films about Ancient Greece and Rome; Renaissance period films like *Elizabeth*; books and movies set in the 1800s). The only thing that can fight a pervasive cultural assumption that was purposely created is to in turn *purposely* create an accessible, shareable, citable, *visual* counternarrative that can inspire people's imaginations via history in the same way that it has for Whiteness.[73]

The answer for audience objections to Gwen's presence on the grounds of historical accuracy is actually found within the series pilot itself. As Jon Sherman notes, "The opening credits proclaim, 'In a land of myth and a time of magic, the destiny of a great kingdom rests on the shoulders of a young boy. His name: Merlin.' This voice-over, coupled with the episode's title 'The Dragon's Call,' immediately absolves the series from the need for historical accuracy. Merlin is set in a mythic land inhabited by dragons, and it makes no attempt at recreating fifth- or sixth-century Britain."[74] Instead of asking why Angel Coulby was chosen to portray Britain's most famous legendary queen, one might ask why there were no objections to the presence of the talking dragon, Kilgarrah? Why is it easier to believe in talking dragons than in Black princesses and queens? It is because the dark fantastic cycle in our collective imagination makes it difficult to suspend our disbelief that a Black girl can live happily ever after.

Why Gwen Matters for Fairy Tales, Media, and Fan Culture

Diverse fairytale and fantasy characters matter for readers from all backgrounds. Stories set in times long ago continue to capture the collective imagination, and are revisited in every generation to reflect the concerns of the present. In a 2013 essay on the appeal of Arthuriana for all people, Kathryn Wymer writes:

> Modern audiences remain fascinated by the legend of Camelot, and there continues to be a wide variety of adaptations of the Arthurian stories. As the British Empire grew and shared its cultural heritage, the legend of Arthur became part of the legacy that was handed down to the citizens of the Empire's colonies, including those citizens of British ancestry as well as those whose ancestors were enslaved peoples or the indigenous peoples of colonized territories. The fact that current audiences for the legend are made up of a more diverse population may account for the increased diversity in casting for many of the adaptations for film and screen. However, though there are more people of color in Arthurian film and television productions, progress toward inclusivity has not been quick or simple to achieve.[75]

The dark fantastic cycle provides an explanation about why progress toward inclusivity has been difficult and slow. *Merlin*'s Gwen is subjected to the dark fantastic cycle as much as the other dark story girls on screen are. She begins her life in the narrative as a maid for the foster daughter of the king, her presence evidenced at first only by her name and the knowledge of Guinevere's role throughout all the retellings of Arthurian legend. When Gwen and Arthur begin to fall in love, the dialogue and acting are a wink and a nod to audiences, telling us that we are *supposed* to hesitate. In order to subject her to violence after her happily-ever-after, the narrative gets twisted. It is not this dark Guinevere's faithlessness and affair with Lancelot that bring about the downfall of the kingdom, but her inability to withstand torture from the woman she once faithfully served. Finally, despite the social death she has experienced after being tortured out of her mind, Gwen wraps up the story as the sole monarch of Camelot, looking down from a balcony as a practitioner of magic is executed upon her command, mourning her lost love, trapped in the past. There is no happily-ever-after for Gwen—she haunts the narrative even though she lives.

Yet Gwen differs from Rue, and from other dark girls who make the gears of the narrative imagination turn. Our dark Guinevere is part of the national project that is multicultural Britain, which differs from the diversity ideology of the United States. The history of nontraditional casting in England begins with Ira Aldridge, an African American actor who took to the Shakespearean stage as Richard II and Shylock at a time when blackface and minstrelsy reigned as the height of popular entertainment in his homeland.[76] Other Black actors from across the Atlantic, most notably Paul Robeson and Sidney Poitier, would follow during the next century and a half. Since then, the United Kingdom has made efforts to include more Black and Asian minority ethnic actors in their programs. Due to the dominance of the BBC in the British television landscape, as well as the greater prominence of stage performance, efforts to diversify programming have been met with less audience backlash than similar efforts in the United States. Hence, as a subject of multicultural Britain, Angel Coulby could very plausibly be cast as Gwen, a timeless figure in the national legend of King Arthur and his Knights of the Round Table.

As my discussion of fan reactions to Gwen's presence in the series demonstrates, fans from around the world—and not just in the United States but also in Britain and elsewhere—raised objections to this nontraditional casting choice. Viewers questioned Gwen's beauty and worth, her relatability and likeability, and her historical accuracy and authenticity. *Merlin* has been broadcast in 183 countries, both during and after its run.[77] Thus, issues of race in fantasy and fairy tales cannot be said to be exclusive to the United States. Media today circulates globally with increased speed, distance, and intensity, and these questions can reproduce, reinforce, and amplify inequities.[78]

There is much that we can learn from Gwen, a queen out of place—lessons of time and space, reality and dreams, as well as inclusion and exclusion. Gwen matters because she represents the dreams of brown girls who never saw themselves represented in fairy tales growing up. Pegged as a show for the entire family, the BBC's *Merlin* represents how a beloved and familiar legend can become more inclusive, yet still reproduce familiar marginalizations. Unlike *The Hunger Games*, *Merlin* was not anchored by a specific young adult text, but was developed for the screen. David C. Tollerton notes that *Merlin*'s creators did not "explicitly base their series on the writings of one particular author. . . . [*Merlin*] pitches itself as an adaptation of Arthurian legend rather than a specific body of literature."[79] Questions of authenticity and accuracy in choosing a multicultural cast could be answered by the fact that Arthuriana itself has been a mirror of the concerns of the culture retelling the story. Not only does the recurring popularity of Camelot demonstrate the adaptability of a set of tales popular for more than a millennium, it also provides room for those in a multicultural Britain—and, because the program was exported, a multicultural world—to identify with Arthurian legend, instead of feeling excluded and alienated from it.

As analysis through the lens of the dark fantastic cycle has shown, the enterprise of diversifying fantasy and fairy tales always seems to encounter a spacetime problem in the collective imagination. Fans and viewers have insisted that "there weren't Black people in England back then," not based upon the reality of the demographics of the Middle Ages but because popular depictions of the medieval period as exclusively White have shaped the collective imagination—from text to screen. Even *Merlin*'s deliberate resistance to periodization, tagging the setting as "in a land of myth and a time of magic," did not prevent criticisms of nontraditional casting. Although the stated aim of the BBC's Diversity Strategy has been to present "programming which reflects modern Britain accurately and authentically,"[80] the presence of knights in armor and damsels in chemises means that audiences cannot easily suspend their disbelief.

What happens in the imagination as audiences leave the spacetime of the known world and enter the dream-space of fairy tales matters. In her 2005 article, "Seeing White: Children of Color and the Disney Fairy Tale Princess," Dorothy L. Hurley reminds us:

> The fairy tale is one of the longest existing genres of children's literature. Through the ages, children have formed mental images of the princesses and other characters depicted in these tales from their representation in the written text as well as in the illustrations that have often accompanied those texts. Fairy tales, therefore, have an important role to play in shaping the self-image and belief system of children.[81]

Gwen's rise from castle servant to queen, her brother, Elyan's, adventures as a brave Knight of the Round Table, and the presence of her father, Tom, as a skilled blacksmith in the king's household provide a counternarrative to the overwhelmingly White landscape of traditional fantasy and fairy tales. But much like other dark girls, even in a story meant to empower her, Gwen does not live happily ever after. Her sad ending haunts the text, she is trapped in a land less imbued with myth and magic after the passing of the king, and ultimately, her character is eclipsed by the romantic friendship between Merlin and Arthur. While this is a positive and welcome development within the heteronormative landscape of youth fantasy storytelling, it does little to liberate the Dark Other in the collective imagination. It instead labels this dark Guinevere as less desirable and second best—a stereotype that girls, women, and femmes of color, especially those of African descent, have had to fight for centuries.

Fighting for Gwen's place in the narrative of *Merlin* and Arthurian retellings is critical for emancipating the imagination. Due to new narratives of global multiculturalism and postracialism, some may believe that her presence on screen as Arthur's queen is a sign that storytelling has progressed from barring dark people from the fantastic dream. After all, if the province of fantasy and fairy tales is dreaming, then everyone should ostensibly have access. But in order to share the same dreams, perhaps we would have to share the same conceptualizations of spacetime and reality—which even a cursory evaluation of contemporary society shows is not the case. Refusals to acknowledge the realities that people of color experience have been described by anthropologist Johannes Fabian as *allochronism*, or the denial of coevalness—that is, refusing to share the same place and time with those deemed not equal. Education scholar Garrett Albert Duncan has argued that remedying this spacetime gap is a fundamental condition for justice.[82] Denying Gwen as a plausible choice for Arthur's hand and heart is evidence of allochronism of the imagination. Diversity on the screen and in texts is important for the shaping not only of critical consciousness in children and young adults as they view and read stories, but also of common dreams.

Despite the limitations of *Merlin*, Gwen's presence, as well as that of other princesses of color in popular youth transmedia, is a promising development. Girls and women all over the world found Gwen's story inspiring, writing thousands of fanfictions continuing her tale, sharing fanart on Tumblr and DeviantArt, and even cosplaying (that is, role playing, or wearing her costume) her at conventions. This is essential for the goals of motivating and engaging young readers. Restorying our imaginary past—through fantasy and fairy tales, as well as historical fiction—has the potential to help us all imagine better and more inclusive Camelots.

THE CURIOUS CASE OF BONNIE BENNETT

The Vampire Diaries *and the Monstrous Contradiction of the Dark Fantastic*

There is no need today to resort to the devil [or to posthumous reverie] in order to speak of excessive sexual desire, and none to resort to vampires in order to designate the attraction exerted by corpses. . . . The themes of fantastic literature have become, literally, the very themes of the psychological investigations of the last fifty years.
—Howard Kerr, *The Haunted Dusk*, 1983

The fact that of all the characters including several hundred-year-old vampires, adults, and witches, Bonnie must be the "strong" one and moral compass but is rarely given a long-term love interest and certainly not lusted after like Elena and Caroline, who seem to have a steady stream of protectors and admirers, is frustrating.
—Jordan St. John, "Why *The Vampire Diaries'* Treatment of Bonnie Bennett Bites," 2012

Ain't I a woman?
—Sojourner Truth, Speech to the Women's Convention in Akron, Ohio, 1851

The Vampire Diaries was the first fantastic series that my niece Daija and I fangirled together. She is my youngest sister's eldest child and, according to my extended family, my doppelgänger in many ways. An avid reader and aspiring actress growing up in the Detroit suburbs, Daija is as enamored with horror stories as I was with fairy tales when I was her age. The scary elements of dystopias like Margaret Peterson Haddix's *Shadow Children* and supernatural fantasies like the BBC's *Wolfblood* delight her. My sister's daughter is as drawn to creatures foul as I was to creatures fair. Daija loves the smoke of the shadow as much as I am thrilled by the glimmer of magic.

When *The Vampire Diaries* premiered on the teen-focused CW network in 2009, Daija was in kindergarten. But in the digital age, one can find almost any series from any time period. Once she got to middle school, ready access to digital devices and streaming services helped her catch up quickly. Like her mother and aunts, she became an avid marathoner of TV shows, even insisting that I watch the *Wolfblood* series with her. Three months shy of her thirteenth birthday, after viewing the series finale of *The Vampire Diaries*, Daija called me in Philadelphia to tell me that she "cried so hard—it was so sad!" Despite her distress about the series coming to an end, she was thrilled by the return of the series' main protagonist, Elena Gilbert, and Elena's endgame relationship with dark and snarky vampire Damon Salvatore.

Although my niece and I shared a fandom, we "stanned"[1] different favorite characters. Daija, part of the *Twilight* generation and enamored with the love triangle among *Twilight*'s Bella, Edward, and Jacob, immediately fell for the tale of dark desire spun around a similar triangle on *The Vampire Diaries*—Elena, Damon, and Stefan (Stefan is Damon's brother and Elena's first boyfriend on the series). In particular, she favored Elena, a character played by fair-skinned, Bulgarian-Canadian actress Nina Dobrev.

If I had been twelve when I first encountered *The Vampire Diaries*, I might have loved Elena best, too. But a lifetime had passed between my twelve-year-old self and the thirty-six-year-old who first began viewing *The Vampire Diaries*. I began watching another CW show, *Gossip Girl*, at the behest of students in a young adult literature course I taught at Wayne State University. I soon found myself following that show as well as other CW teen television, and it wasn't long before I joined the CW fandom as an active participant. I discussed CW shows like *Gossip Girl*, *The Vampire Diaries*, and *The Originals* on message boards and social media, wrote fanfiction and metatextual essays, and even tried my hand at fanart and GIF-making for the first time ever. By the time that Daija started watching *The Vampire Diaries*, I was a diehard fan of Bonnie Bennett, whose light brown skin marked her as one of the few characters of color in the series and the only one of any narrative prominence.

My allegiance to Bonnie marked the first time in my fanlife that I no longer cared about the fair Elena Gilberts of the fantastic. I did not root for them. I did not long for them to live happily ever after. I did not need them to win.

I didn't need Elena anymore.

I had Bonnie.

* * *

It must be said that Bonnie Bennett is not an easy character for mainstream audiences of teen vampire tales to love. In *The Vampire Diaries* television series, her story often plays out on the sidelines. She rarely attends the big dress-up parties and other events that fill the social calendars of Elena and her other friends. She often judges the vampire characters negatively, as well as the teen girls who are drawn to them. Though she uses her magical powers to bring back Elena's brother from the dead and to come to the rescue of many other characters, she is not seen as a heroine. And in a teen show riven with sexuality, Bonnie remains chaste for close to six seasons.

When considered from this perspective, my niece Daija's preference for Elena over Bonnie makes perfect sense: After all, stories are focalized through the viewpoint protagonist, not characters who are relegated to the side. Those protagonists are aspirational for girls and young women; we read about them, see them on screens big and small, and want to be like them. Stories lead us to want their lives, their social circles, and their boyfriends. Why should demographic differences prevent any young reader from identifying with Elena?

Bonnie presents a curious case for the fantastic, one that originates in her transition from book to screen. *The Vampire Diaries* was originally developed by book packager 17th Street Productions in 1991, before the company became Alloy Entertainment. The creator of *The Vampire Dia-*

ries and author of the first books, Lisa Jane "L. J." Smith, was a writer working on spec.[2] Smith wrote and conceptualized the initial books in the series before other writers took over and had little involvement with the television show, which was greenlit in the wake of the *Twilight* craze.[3] Among teen vampire book narratives, *The Vampire Diaries* has the distinction of both predating *and* following Joss Whedon's cult classic, *Buffy the Vampire Slayer* as well as Stephenie Meyer's blockbuster series, *Twilight*, which spawned E. L. James's erotic fanfiction-turned-bestseller *Fifty Shades of Grey*. Although it was not as critically acclaimed as *Buffy*, nor was it ever as popular as *Twilight*, from 2010 to 2014 *The Vampire Diaries* was the most-viewed show on the teen-focused CW network, which is owned jointly by CBS and Time Warner. Its series finale in March of 2017 was scheduled to coincide with the twentieth anniversary of *Buffy*'s premiere—a nod that bookended two decades of the teen vampire craze in popular culture.

The Vampire Diaries novels focus primarily on the love triangle between high school student Elena Gilbert, a teenage girl who is living in the historic town of Fell's Church, Virginia, and the Salvatore brothers, Stefan and Damon. In the first book, shortly after the untimely death of her parents, Elena meets Stefan, who is purportedly a new student at school. She also meets his older brother, Damon. She falls in love with Stefan, but soon learns that both he and Damon are vampires who were born human in Renaissance-era Italy. The plot of the book series follows Elena's struggles to come to terms with her boyfriend Stefan's darkness—and her inexplicable attraction to his even more dangerous brother, Damon.

Elena's best friend in the novels is Bonnie McCullough, an auburn-haired witch of Irish descent with magical ancestry dating back to the time of the Druids. In the novel series, Bonnie is one of the most significant female characters—second only to Elena herself. She is psychic, can cast spells, and is one of the few characters who can influence vampires using her magic. In the books, as on the television show, Bonnie's magic is a powerful deus ex machina across numerous storylines. Bonnie McCullough's mentor is her Scottish grandmother, with whom she is particularly close. Book Bonnie is described with adjectives of innocence—she is naive, trusting, and femininely petite. Because of her innocence, she is a foil and eventual love interest for the antihero of the series, Damon Salvatore, who is torn between her and his brother's girlfriend, Elena.

When the decision was made to bring the story of *The Vampire Diaries* to the small screen, young actress Kat Graham was cast not as auburn-haired Bonnie McCullough but as raven-haired Bonnie Bennett.[4] Katerina Alexandre Hartford Graham was born on September 5, 1989, to a mother of Russian and Polish Jewish descent and an Americo-Liberian father. Born in Geneva, Switzerland, she was raised primarily in Los Angeles, and had been working in the industry since early childhood. Her casting continued a pattern on the CW of including a single young actor or actress of color among the main players of the ensemble casts. With her light brown skin, Graham could not plausibly pass for a White book character on an American television show. Bonnie's character background was revised to reflect this change.

On the televised version of *The Vampire Diaries*, Bonnie is descended from an unbroken line of magic, the Bennett witches, whose roots go back in time to colonial Salem, and ultimately to Qetsiyah, a powerful witch of the first century BC. Although Qetsiyah, a distant ancestor, is described as Greek (and in played by Janina Gavankar, an Indian American actress), before her introduction in the fourth season, all of the actresses cast in the Bennett family lineage, including Bonnie's mother (Persia White), grandmother (Jasmine Guy), cousin (Natashia Williams), and distant ancestress (Bianca Lawson), are of mixed-race ancestry, and usually cast in Black roles. We do not meet any of the Bennett witches' fathers except Bonnie's, who is portrayed by actor Rick Worthy, who is Black.

Race matters in the real world, and it matters in fiction. In response to calls for greater diversity in media representation, corporations like Alloy, the CW Network, and Marvel Comics occasionally cast an actor of color in a role originally written in the source material as White. Non-traditional casting decisions are laudable, and have been used to great effect, from the stirring performances of Ira Aldridge in nineteenth-century England to the contemporary Broadway smash hit *Hamilton*. In *The Vampire Diaries*, however, instead of Bonnie remaining a viable counterpoint for Elena's journey into the vampire world, nontraditional casting relegated televised Bonnie to the shadows, from the beginning to the end of the eight seasons of *The Vampire Diaries*. TV Bonnie's characterization, plot, and eventual fate bear little resemblance to Book Bonnie's.

Just as it is impossible for *The Hunger Games'* Rue to be innocent, and just as a happy ending to the waking dream is impossible for Gwen in the BBC's *Merlin*, it is also impossible for TV Bonnie—a character who, as a witch, is responsible for restoring balance to an off-kilter storyworld riven with the undead—to be appreciated by audiences for her fundamental goodness. Just as Black girl characters cannot be *innocent* or *loved*, they also cannot be *good*. If, as children's literature scholar Philip Nel noted, "genre is the new Jim Crow,"[5] then the mere inclusion of characters of color is not enough to emancipate the dark fantastic. Jeffrey Jerome Cohen's monster theory, as well as Black feminist readings of contemporary vampire fiction, can help us understand why.

Sistas versus Vampires: Race, Desire, and the Monstrous Contradiction of the Dark Fantastic

The sixth thesis of Jeffrey Jerome Cohen's monster culture (see chapter 1), "fear of the monster is really a kind of desire," applies both to vampires themselves *and* to Dark Others trapped in vampire narratives. Although it is rare that Black characters are transformed into vampires instead of being killed by them (Tara Thornton from HBO's *True Blood* being one of the exceptions that proves the rule), it is indeed the case that "the monster awakens one to the pleasures of the body, to the simple and fleeting joys of being frightened, or frightening—to the experience of mortality and corporality."[6] This embodied connection between *eros* and *thanatos*—desire and death—invoked by monsters and Dark Others is emblematic of this very "simultaneity of anxiety and desire."[7] Characters (and by extension, audiences) being anxious *and* aroused at the same time is a signal feature of vampire narratives, one that is complicated by race, gender, and sexuality.

Reading Bonnie Bennett through a Black feminist lens is essential for understanding the interplay of race, gender, and sexuality in *The Vampire Diaries*, as well as the contemporary vampire genre more generally. Not only do vampire stories shed light on society's gender paradigms and sexual politics, as Agata Łuksza has argued, but they also bring racial politics into sharp relief. [8] The geographies of recent vampiric desire seem to inhabit the margins of the known world, with the most popular of these stories set in places with significant populations of people of color and/or Native peoples who are necessary to the narrative, yet not always vampires themselves—from the Quileute people of the Olympic peninsula in *Twilight*, to enslaved Africans in *The Vampire Chronicles'* New Orleans, to contemporary Black Americans in Bon Temps, Louisiana, in the *True Blood* series. In these stories, not all of which are intended for young adult audiences, the vampire often brings the fair fantastic into the contact zone with perilous Dark Others.

While vampire narratives tease the threat and allure of bloodlust, horror theorist Kinitra Brooks envisions the possibilities of liberation. Reading vampire stories for the adult market by Black women authors Tananarive Due and L. A. Banks, Brooks argues that in these kinds of narratives, "Black women's bodies [are] sites of reality-changing power, and that their characters occupy multiple positions as complexly constructed lovers, and as both protector and protected."[9] Unlike most vampire stories, where women of color are marginalized and subjugated by the narrative, in the work of Due, Banks, and other notable Black women writers like Octavia Butler and Sherri L. Smith, vampirism is reimagined as a location for humanization.[10] The margins between pleasure and pain that are evoked by the vampire are also evoked by the Black female body in our culture. Thus within these narratives of death and unnatural longevity, characters like Bonnie have the potential to form counternarratives of nature and fertility, life and renewed hope.

As a witch, Bonnie is one of the few non-vampires on *The Vampire Diaries*. This is significant for theorizing a dark fantastic, for vampires are one of the few malevolent creatures that can be difficult to map onto characters of African descent.[11] In Luise White's *Speaking with Vampires: Rumor and History in Colonial Africa*, terrified people in colonized Central and East Africa told tales of vampires as analogues of European bloodlust:

> The power and uncertainty of these [vampire] stories—no one knew exactly what Europeans did with African blood, but people were convinced that they took it—makes them an especially rich historical source, I think. They report the aggressive carelessness of colonial extractions and

ascribe potent and intimate meanings to them . . . . . . The inaccuracies in these stories make them exceptionally reliable historical sources as well: they offer historians a way to see the world the way the storytellers did, as a world of vulnerability and unreasonable relationships. These stories of bloodsucking firemen or game rangers, pits and injections, allow historians a vision of colonial worlds replete with all the messy categories and meandering epistemologies many Africans used to describe the extractions and invasions with which they lived.[12]

Charting the terrain of the dark fantastic requires taking seriously the perspectives of those heretofore categorized as monstrous. What does the fantastic look like from the point of view of the monster? Although the claims of the supernatural by those suffering under colonization may not have been accurate from a Western point of view, White argues that they are meaningful as a metaphor for understanding the way that race and power functioned within colonialism. I would further argue that this has import for the ways that dark people and darkness have functioned in recent vampire stories. Although the way that the fantastic is typically narrated in the Anglo-American tradition causes the reader or viewer to slot the Dark Other into the role of the monster, in a vampire narrative, the monster is the object not only of submerged desire but also of *overt* desire; in other words, the vampire is a lightning rod that channels forbidden sexual power. While taboo sexual desire is the crux of the problem with the inclusion of the monster in the fantastic (and by extension, the inclusion of Black girlhood and womanhood), the vampire's power is *extractive*. Through consumption of lifeblood, a vampire sustains its existence. This taboo consumption is quite conspicuous—the erotic nature of the extraction of blood being the very focus of vampire stories—and brings to mind the ways that dark bodies are subjected to extraction, consumption, and death beyond the fantastic.

Just as vampires are sites of consumption and desire, so is contemporary teen television itself. Supernatural shows like *The Vampire Diaries* feature superhuman characters facing extraordinary circumstances, throwing societal and cultural debates into sharp relief.[13] Television viewing is associated with pleasure and community, as well as memory and identity formation.[14] Teen television is participatory as well. Teens view shows, discuss them online using social media, and create fanwork that an increasing number of companies are finding quite valuable. When, in the spring of 2013, Alloy made international headlines with its ground-breaking deal with Amazon's Kindle division to publish fan fiction based on three of its book series for young adults—*The Vampire Diaries*, *Gossip Girl*, and *Pretty Little Liars*—there was much discussion within digital fan communities about intellectual property, authorship, and the changing nature of textual production in a digitally networked, social media age.[15] Yet within the fan cultures being commodified, vigorous debates about race and visual representation in multimedia continued to rage.[16] In her award-winning 2013 essay in the *Journal of Popular Culture* about problematic subjects in *The Vampire Diaries*, Mary Bridgeman notes:

> In the case of *The Vampire Diaries*, the mode of viewing established both by network television and the CW channel specifically is one targeting young women [who are] young, female, feminine, middle-class, white, and heterosexual. . . . . If the dominant ideology informing the production of *The Vampire Diaries* is neo-liberal consumer capitalism, then the text engages with the anxieties thrown up by the acceptance of difference and the increasingly niche-market driven focus of 21st century consumerism.[17]

For all her careful attention to problematic subjects in her essay (especially protagonist Elena Gilbert), Bridgeman does not mention Bonnie at all. This is unfortunate. If Elena is an instantiation of White female anxiety about conspicuous consumption and hyper-commodification, then Black female subjects like *The Vampire Diaries'* Bonnie Bennett are possible sites of reconciliation simply because they are not allowed to consume. While Elena's journey from human to vampire allows her to move from the consumed to a consumer, Bonnie remains in the role of the consumed from the first episode until the last. And although she is consumed, the narrative positions this as her own fault due to her disposition and anti-vampire ideologies. Where Elena is uncertain, Bonnie is resolved. Where Elena is ambivalent, Bonnie is assured. In a vampire story that defines morality for its own purposes within the world, any character positioned as a paragon of human morality—any character who dares to question the escapist, seductive temptation presented by vampirism, and who actively works to maintain balance between the natural and the supernatural—is presented as the monster anyway.

This brings us to a monstrous contradiction within the dark fantastic, and the setting for Bonnie Bennett's curious case. Instead of being admired by her friends within the story and by viewers for providing a counterbalance for the undead, Bonnie is judged as a killjoy and relegated to the margins of the narrative. While Black skeptics of supernatural phenomena are almost commonplace within speculative fiction, Bonnie is not among these. It isn't that she questions the existence of magic or vampirism—after all, she is a magical character herself. Rather, her skepticism about the pleasures offered by the vampires, as well as her occasional opposition to their agenda, is presented as a recurring problem.

But is Bonnie inextricably trapped in the dark fantastic cycle? Or are there possibilities for emancipation?

And, perhaps more importantly, will a new diverse generation of readers and viewers embrace characters like her?

Bonnie Bennett as Archetypal Dark Other: The Dark Fantastic, Televised

Spectacle

To understand Bonnie Bennett's story, it is critical to walk through her scenes on *The Vampire Diaries*, focusing on Bonnie herself instead of Elena or the Salvatore brothers. One of the earliest scenes establishing Bonnie as an important character occurs in the first season, when she tells Elena that she is a witch. Visually, this is perhaps one of the most stunning scenes featuring a young Black actress in recent teen TV. In it, Bonnie floats a series of white feathers telekinetically as Elena gazes on in wonder. The lighting is soft, and the effect illuminates Bonnie's dark skin so that she looks angelic. Signaling the gentle and kind nature that is the hallmark of her book counterpart (who is affectionately nicknamed "little bird"), Bonnie smiles beatifically as white feathers float around her face:

> [Bonnie closes the window and grabs one of Elena's pillows. She tears it
>   open and empties it of the feathers.]
> ELENA: Hey!
> BONNIE: Be patient.

ELENA: OK.

BONNIE: I need to swear you to secrecy.

ELENA: It's kind of a bad week for that kind of stuff.

BONNIE: Swear, 'cause I'm not supposed to be showing you this.

ELENA: OK, I swear.

BONNIE: There's no windows open, right?

ELENA: Right.

BONNIE: There's no fan. No air conditioning.

ELENA: None. What are you doing?

BONNIE: Grams just showed me this. You're gonna love it. You ready?

ELENA: Bonnie what's going on?

[Bonnie levitates a feather in front of Elena. Then she levitates several more. Elena watches on with shock and amazement.]

BONNIE: It's true Elena. Everything my Grams told me. It's impossible and it's true. I'm a witch.

ELENA: I believe you.[18]

While Bonnie is made up and perfectly coiffed, Elena, who had been sleeping, is wearing very little makeup and her hair is tousled. When I first viewed this episode, I tried to remember a corresponding scene in teen television featuring a character of African descent in the same frame as White girl characters, appearing in quite the same way—and came up short. How often on television does the darkest girl in the room get to be the fairest of all? I couldn't help but contrast Bonnie's agency with the most visible Black girl character on a majority White show during my teen years, *Saved by the Bell*'s Lisa Turtle.[19] When I watched Bonnie during those first few episodes of *The Vampire Diaries*, I felt hopeful. Perhaps the genre of horror could liberate Black teenage girl characters in a way that comedy, drama, and reality TV could not.

But after those initial episodes, the gears of the dark fantastic cycle started to turn.

The first principle of the dark fantastic in Bonnie's narrative is, of course, *spectacle*. The presence of the Dark Other in a text of speculative fiction (across genre and mode) creates a profound dilemma for readers, hearers, and/or viewers—a dilemma that viewers of *The Vampire Diaries* face when Bonnie Bennett floated white feathers around Elena

Gilbert's room. While witches like Bonnie are powerful, and vampires were created by witches, witches in this story universe have generally been subservient to vampires. Bonnie's ancestress, Emily Bennett, was the handmaiden of Katerina Petrova, an ancient vampire who turned the Salvatore brothers into the undead more than 150 years before the start of the series, when she was posing as Katherine Pierce (an identity she retained through contemporary times). It is unclear on the show whether Emily had been Katherine's slave or a freedwoman servant, even though we see Emily and Katherine in several flashbacks. In an early scene, Emily literally *haunts* Bonnie, and then possesses her, foreshadowing Bonnie's later position in the series as a ghost who haunts her friends.[20] This haunting of the text by an Africanist presence is a key principle of the dark fantastic—in fact, the series finale featured the return of Bonnie's *entire* ancestral lineage in order to violently save Mystic Falls and the world. Yet since Emily is only a minor character, and not the major Dark Other in this series, her eerie presence on the screen functions as part of the spectacle of the dark body.

Hesitation

The presence of the Dark Other interrupts the waking dream of the fantastic. Few kinds of characters make readers, viewers, and hearers of a fantastic story hesitate faster than Dark Others. In early seasons, because Bonnie was not originally written as Black, she is not the source of the hesitation; instead, it is notably Bonnie's Black woman ancestor, Emily Bennett, handmaid to the vampire Katherine whose seductive bite turned Stefan and Damon Salvatore. While Katherine, who is portrayed by Nina Dobrev, is perhaps the most dangerous character of the first two seasons, she is also positioned as a wisecracking and desirable badass who seduced both Salvatore brothers during the Civil War. In contrast, her servant, Emily, looms at the side of the frame during flashbacks, which makes the viewer hesitate. What is Emily's story? In *The Vampire Diaries*' internal mythology, witches can inflict damaging migraines on vampires. If they are willing to pay the price for a powerful spell (more on that later), they can destroy the undead altogether. If this is the case, why does Emily choose to serve

Katherine? Answers are never given, and Emily remains at the margins of the narrative, referred to more than seen.

The Dark Other also causes hesitation for the powers that be—that is, the corporations that stand to make the most money from a commodified dark fantastic. One point of hesitation on the part of the CW Network has been whether to replicate the books' relationship between Damon and Bonnie on the show. In both the books and the TV show, Damon is obsessed with Elena, who looks exactly like his first love, Katherine. But in the books conceived by the original writer, L. J. Smith, Damon ultimately falls for Bonnie McCullough. On the TV series, this presents a problem. The CW's target audience is young, middle-class White women between the ages of sixteen and thirty-four. Perhaps the network felt that its audience wanted to identify either with the female protagonist, Elena, who is caught in a love triangle between Stefan and Damon, or with Elena's quirky blonde sidekick, Caroline Forbes, who has dated or had romantic storylines with several regular and recurring characters (unlike her book counterpart, who is a secondary character). The CW is noted for the love triangles that generate interest for young audiences, who then engage in conversations on social media about "shipping," a fan term for relationships. The fervor of shippers and other interested fans drives social media buzz, which is a means of marketing shows.

The network was purportedly uninterested in bringing the relationship between Damon and Bonnie to the small screen. According to actor Ian Somerhalder, who plays Damon, "We had some scenes in season two where Damon and Bonnie had a f—ing awesome connection and the studio and the network and producers were like, 'No more, no. This is about Damon, Elena and Stefan and that's why you never see Bonnie and Damon."[21] One scene where this connection is evident is in an episode in season two when the characters are attending the Decade Dance, an annual event at the local high school. A new menace, original vampire Klaus Mikaelson, threatens Elena. Bonnie believes she can use her magic to destroy him, although other characters are skeptical. One of the skeptics is Damon, who is madly in love with Elena, although she is still dating Stefan. He cuts into Bonnie's dance with Elena's younger brother, Jeremy Gilbert (more on him below), to question her about whether she knows what she is doing:

DAMON: May I?

[Jeremy looks at him and leaves. Damon dances with Bonnie.]
BONNIE: You heard Jeremy and me talking, didn't you?
DAMON: Is it true?
BONNIE: Yes.
DAMON: The part about you having a 50-50 shot of surviving? Is that
    true?
BONNIE: He was upset. I didn't want him to worry.
DAMON: So you'd lay it out on the line for Elena, no matter what?
BONNIE: No matter what.
DAMON: Good.
BONNIE: You can't tell her.
DAMON: Your secret's safe with me, but I mean . . . with all that power,
    isn't there a way to increase your odds?
BONNIE: Careful, Damon. I might start to think you actually care.

[Damon quirks his eyebrows upward as he looks at her.]
DAMON: We wouldn't want that.

[Damon and Bonnie continue to dance. Elena joins Jeremy, who is
    standing across the dance floor looking at Bonnie and Damon.]
ELENA: What are they up to?
JEREMY: Who knows?[22]

The show resolves the dark fantastic hesitation around the dilemma
of having an alpha male vampire hook up with the protagonist's Black
best friend by making TV Bonnie hate Damon—the very character that
her book series counterpart most uniquely understands. To avoid protests from avid book fans using social media to advocate for a Damon
and Bonnie romance, the show has Bonnie first dating a minor character
named Luka, a Black teenage warlock who is quickly killed off in the
initial seasons and who (very disappointingly) served as a plot device for
the story of the original vampires. Bonnie then engages in an on-again,
off-again romance with Elena's younger brother, Jeremy Gilbert.[23] It is
a romantic relationship that lasts several seasons, ending only when the
actor leaves the series.

Jeremy presents several challenges for Bonnie's character development. First, he is one of the few mortal human beings on a supernatural show, so his death (or the threat of his death) is a recurring plot point.[24] To save Jeremy from his fate, or to bring him back from the dead, Bonnie has to repeatedly break the rules of magic, for which the universe punishes her with death.[25] A representative scene in the second season shows the physical price that Bonnie pays for resurrecting Jeremy and upsetting the natural balance her witch ancestors valued. Alaric, a friend of the family, urges Bonnie to use her magic anyway:

[Bonnie and Alaric and Jeremy's body are in an abandoned house, said
    to be haunted by the spirits of Bonnie's deceased witch ancestors.]
ALARIC: Is this even possible?
BONNIE: There's a spell for it if they'll give me the power to use it.

[Jeremy's head rests on Bonnie's legs. She begins to cast a spell. Voices
    whisper around them.]
BONNIE: No.
ALARIC: What? What is it?
BONNIE: They're angry at me for coming back here. They don't want to
    help!
ALARIC: Well, they have to!
BONNIE: They said there'll be consequences . . .
ALARIC: Well, he's just a kid. Tell 'em to shut up!

[Bonnie continues to cast the spell. Her nose bleeds. She cries.]
BONNIE: Emily! Emily! I know you're there. Please help me. I love him.

[The whispering stops.]
BONNIE: No!

[She cries. Jeremy opens his eyes.]
BONNIE: Oh my God.[26]

Alaric's urging to Bonnie to push her magical limits to the point of self-harm is typical of the ways that Bonnie is often positioned in *The Vampire Diaries* television show.

Also notable is that Elena is central to the romance between Bonnie and Jeremy. In the second season, the two dread Elena's reaction to their relationship, though they also want her approval. In the fourth season, Bonnie states that she has to resurrect Jeremy for Elena's sake—it is clearly not enough that she, Bonnie, is in love with him. Repeatedly, Bonnie Bennett's magical ability and sexual agency are used to further Elena's character development at the expense of her own.

Further challenging Bonnie's character development is Jeremy's flagrant unfaithfulness. Shortly after he begins dating Bonnie, for instance, he chooses to be with his dead ex-girlfriend Anna—now a ghost whom only Jeremy can see—instead of Bonnie.[27] This strains credulity—for a young teenaged boy-next-door type, would an ephemeral spectral being *really* be more alluring than a beautiful flesh-and-blood girlfriend? Moreover, on a show (and on a network) that is marketed as being sexy and where all of the other main female characters are sexually active and positioned as desirable, it is not until halfway through the fifth season that Jeremy and Bonnie are physically intimate.[28] This is significant, as other female characters not only hook up with the series leads but also with attractive guest stars. Jeremy also sleeps with all his previous girlfriends within a few episodes of their initial encounter. Given the way sex and sexuality are positioned in *The Vampire Diaries*, Jeremy's treatment of Bonnie marks her as the least desirable girl on the show, and uncomfortably underscores societal views of the desirability of young Black women.

Violence

Bonnie's attempts to resurrect Jeremy and help her friends at her own expense lead to the third principle of the dark fantastic cycle: the dilemma created by the presence of the Dark Other in the fantastic must be inevitably resolved with *violence*. This violence often ends in the death of the dark presence, whether it is a character, force, or merely symbolic. The containment and destruction of dark bodies in the real world has been noted by Black feminist scholars.[29] The fantastic is driven by the same imperatives at the symbolic level. Postcolonial critics argue that this mortal violence occurs because we cannot deal with the fear, desire, and longing that the Dark Other elicits in us.[30] Consequently, we must eradicate the Dark Other to set everything right in the universe. Although this may seem to be an overstatement, it is part and parcel of the fantastic, and is quite evident in Bonnie's story. Moreover, the violence is not just arbitrary; the Dark Other has to be positioned as *deserving* of it. *The Vampire Diaries* uses Bonnie's magical powers, her greatest gift, as a way to indict her—much as dark-skinned young people are indicted in the real world.

In order to resurrect her reluctant boyfriend and her friends, Bonnie begins delving deeper into a kind of dark magic called "Expression."[31] Through characters' dialogue, the show repeatedly reminds us that Expression is the *darkest* magic there is, and so Bonnie Bennett is (of course) incredibly good at it. The practice of Expression involves blood sacrifice and takes a dangerous physical toll on the practitioner, yet the power rush is like a narcotic. Bonnie's grandmother and others warn her not to use this dangerous magic, but, tempted by the enigmatic ancient warlock Silas, she disregards them in order to save Jeremy's life:

SILAS: All right. Look. You invited me into your home, right? Why? Why'd you lie to your friends and tell them everything was fine? Why did you convince your dad that you needed Professor Shane's help to control your magic? What am I doing here?

BONNIE: You're in my head. You're making me see things and do things.

SILAS: Hey, now. See? Look. I'm strong, but you're a witch, and I can't force you to do anything that you don't already want to do. You care about Jeremy, right?

BONNIE: I do.

SILAS: Yeah. You were with him, and you promised to protect him, but you failed. And now, in order to bring him back . . .

BONNIE: I need to get rid of the Other Side.

SILAS: You are descended from Qetsiyah, one of the most powerful witches of all time. Only you can complete the triangle and cast the spell.

BONNIE: Completing the triangle means killing twelve people.

[Bonnie turns and walks away.]

SILAS: Twelve people you can bring back.

[Bonnie turns and faces Silas again.]

SILAS: Bonnie, you can do this—for Jeremy.[32]

Within a season of starting to use Expression, Bonnie pays for this transgression with her life.[33] This is because even a Dark Other who is transcendentally beautiful, beloved, and self-sacrificing—one who has, to borrow a term from the uber-popular *Game of Thrones* TV series, "skin changed" or "warged" a White character—even that Dark Other *must* be sacrificed, and her death *must* be positioned as deserved. On a vampire show where most of the main characters are technically "dead," Bonnie is the first major character who has an official funeral.[34] Even within a fictional milieu peopled with undead characters, where death is the norm, it has to be underscored that the Dark Other is dead.

Haunting

But Bonnie Bennett is not *really* dead. This brings us to the fourth dark fantastic principle, *haunting*. When the Dark Other is defeated and catharsis is reached, his or her (or its) present-absence nonetheless haunts the story. Bonnie spends the rest of the fifth season first haunting her own friends and then being returned to her body, only to serve as the anchor for the mythical Other Side, with her second and ultimate death presented as an inevitability. Yet through dangers untold, from the first episode until the last, traversing death and hell itself, Bonnie Bennett continues to exist.

Emancipation?

The final principle of the dark fantastic is that of emancipation. At the end of *The Vampire Diaries'* fifth season in the spring of 2014, Bonnie Bennett does not walk into oblivion alone. When she goes to face her second death, fan favorite Damon Salvatore is right there with her:

[Jeremy runs through the woods, screaming Bonnie's name over and over again, while Elena, Alaric, and the rest of the group try to sort out what's going on.]

TYLER: What's going on?
JEREMY: Bonnie! Bonnie! *Bonnie!*

[Jeremy sees Bonnie standing across the graveyard, but before he can
   reach her, the Other Side's disintegration comes to a head.]
DAMON: This place is going down, isn't it?

[Huge holes of light poke through to the other side, while the winds
   blow all around them.]
BONNIE: It is. I'm sure there are a million people we'd rather be with
   right now, but . . .

[Bonnie takes Damon's hand and their fingers entwine.]
DAMON: A couple thousand, at most.

[A huge orb of light rips through the treetops.]
BONNIE: Do you think it'll hurt?

[The fabric of reality itself starts to shatter, leaving nothing but light.]
DAMON: I don't kn—
[Before Damon can finish his sentence, the light engulfs them both, and
   the season ends.][35]

This episode sparked a range of reactions from fans of the show.[36]
Some viewers were thrilled, believing *The Vampire Diaries* would finally
explore the book series' relationship between Damon and Bonnie, even
if that relationship would be an interracial one. Others were horrified
by this development—Damon and Bonnie were holding hands as they
walked into oblivion! How could Damon end the season (or the series)
with Bonnie, and not with Elena, whom the television series had positioned as his true love?

It was as if the feather scene from the first season had been repeated
all over again.

But the balance of the show does not fulfill Bonnie's potential as written in the book series. In her post-series analysis of Bonnie's ending,
author and *Vampire Diaries* fan Kristen Carter narrates what happens
in the sixth season:

Bonnie's biggest story arc was escaping the 1994 prison world (that she
was transported to with Damon after the fifth season). Her relationship

with Damon grew and deepened, and we saw a dynamic that we haven't seen in a long time. Unfortunately, this was also the same season where Bonnie unwillingly had her life tethered to Elena's. While Elena was in a magically induced coma, a la Sleeping Beauty, she would only awaken when Bonnie died and stayed dead.[37]

The promise of Bonnie's emancipation in the fifth season finale is thwarted in the final three seasons. Much as Rue dies so that Katniss can live in *The Hunger Games*, Bonnie's life is tethered to the fate of a beloved White protagonist. This means that Bonnie must lead a suspended existence until she fulfills her role as a dark sacrifice. With the promise of a final and lasting death hanging over her head, Bonnie begins dating a new vampire, Enzo. She briefly becomes a vampire huntress, but unlike the sympathetic and nuanced portrayal of hunters in series like *Buffy*, on *The Vampire Diaries*, the new storyline simply serves as yet another way to show Bonnie antagonizing the vampires who are the central focus of the narrative. After that, she once again loses her magic.

Although the latter part of the series represents an attempt to provide Bonnie with the potential of love and intimacy, fans were still dissatisfied. Kristen continues:

> I felt as though the writers put her in last minute relationships that nobody cared about because the writers never made us care (except Jeremy). And if anyone was ever interested in Bonnie, in the end, they were only using her for their own devices (see her relationships with Ben, Luka, and Shane). The Bonnie/Jeremy relationship introduced in the second season was supposed to mark a new path for Bonnie, but it didn't. . . .
>
> Throughout the final season, everything that Bonnie did was for someone else (except Enzo). It wasn't until Enzo died that Bonnie's magic resurfaced. From that point on she was determined to find a way to bring Enzo back to life. And if she couldn't do it, she would gladly die to be with him.[38]

When book Damon's "little red bird" Bonnie McCullough became the dark bird Bonnie Bennett on the television series, her fate was sealed. Mainstream literature and popular culture demand this positioning of the Dark Other as an antagonist. Tracing the development of Bonnie from page to screen, considering the way that horror narratives like *The Vampire Diaries* typically position Black girls and women characters, and situating her tale as a dark fantastic counternarrative within the broader story, we can see that the imperatives of commercial teen television and fan response limit the liberating possibilities of characters of color.

Although *The Vampire Diaries* does not end with Bonnie's physical death, after she saves everyone, she alone of the surviving characters decides to leave Mystic Falls for "Africa." Of course, Bonnie has never expressed any interest in visiting the continent throughout the eight seasons, and no specific nation, city, or region is mentioned. Separated from her end-of-series love interest, Enzo, by his death, she has no outlet—other than to be sent back over the Black Atlantic, through the Door of No Return through which her witch ancestors came—far beyond the sweet seduction of a vampiric happily-ever-after.

Can This Black Girl Be Saved? The Rise of Black Girl Fandom, Social Media Activism, and Representation in the Fantastic

Bonnie's run as the dark witch of *The Vampire Diaries* spanned a time of tremendous social change. When the show premiered in September 2009, Facebook, Twitter, YouTube, and Tumblr were exploding onto the digital landscape, expanding the scope of nearly fifteen years' worth of platforms for communicating quickly and easily online beyond anything previously possible. During the show's run, platforms like Instagram, Vine, and Snapchat further transformed the way that people communicated. In 2015, well past the midpoint of *The Vampire Diaries'* run, Pew Research Center's Teens, Social Media, and Technology overview found that 92 percent of teens went online daily, with 24 percent indicating they were online "almost constantly."[39] By the time the final episode aired in March 2017, social media platforms dominated the way that young people received news and entertainment.

The ways that audiences view television shows also changed. In the previous chapter, I note how fans of the BBC's *Merlin* debated issues of race, gender, and culture in order to support or refute Gwen's place within fantastic spacetime. *Merlin* ran from 2008 until 2012 on the BBC, just before the phenomenon of live-tweeting shows became central to networks' marketing strategies. *The Hunger Games* movie debuted in the same year that *Merlin* finished; although the treatment of Rue and her actress was discussed on Twitter and Tumblr, the racist commentary surrounding her death did not (in general) lead audiences to question whether alternate ways of depicting Rue might have been possible or desirable. Rue's heart was pierced on the big screen more than a year before another Black female character of the fantastic debuted, racked up ratings, and stole audience hearts—Abbie Mills of *Sleepy Hollow*, who for three seasons would tease the possibility of an emancipated dark fantastic heroine, all before sacrificing her life for her White male lead. But instead of audience attention being focused on the racist commentary over even the very appearance of a Black character, critics, fans, and even the general audience were flabbergasted over Abbie's death. Viewership for *Sleepy Hollow* fell, and never fully recovered.

The world that Bonnie Bennett emerged into in 2009 was not the same world that she left in 2017.

If social media transformed the ways that teen audiences were able to interact, then Black teens, youth, and young adults both transformed and were transformed by the social media age as well. By 2015, according to Pew's survey on teen internet and social media use, "African-American teens [were] the most likely of any group of teens to have a smartphone, with 85% having access to one, compared with 71% of both white and Hispanic teens." Additionally, "African-American and Hispanic youth report[ed] more frequent internet use than white teens. Among African-American teens, 34% reported going online 'almost constantly' as [did] 32% of Hispanic teens, while 19% of white teens said they [went] online that often." Discourses about the digital divide do little to describe the zeitgeist of the era: Black youth and young adults increasingly began driving the tenor of the conversations on social media. The phenomenon of Black Twitter, Black children and teens joyfully declaring "Do it for the Vine!," the contested digital circulation of Black bodies through GIFs, memes, and viral videos, and the rise of Black digital activism dominated social media platforms through the 2010s.[40]

After the explosion of the RaceFail controversies of 2009,[41] the 2010s have seen the rise of Black girls and women using social media to connect with other fans, advocating for more and better representation, and even creating their own alternatives to popular culture. Sites like Black

Girl Nerds (founded in 2011), Graveyard Shift Sisters (founded in 2013), and others have helped fans find each other across fandoms, and created visibility and awareness about different Black girl and woman characters in books, television shows, and movies. By 2015, periodicals like *Black Enterprise* were noting the power of Black girls and women in fandom.[42] They were among the first media outlets to acknowledge rising audience investments in characters like those from Shonda Rimes's popular #TGIT (Thank God It's Thursday) lineup of shows, *Scandal* and *How to Get Away with Murder*, teen genre shows like *The Flash* and *Riverdale*, and adult genre shows like *The Walking Dead* and *Sleepy Hollow*.

At the same time, powerful new movements were changing the way that people of color and from other marginalized groups were harnessing the power of social media—especially Twitter—to raise public awareness about injustice. Perhaps the most salient activist function of Black Twitter has been the #BlackLivesMatter movement, founded by Patrisse Cullors, Opal Tometi, and Alicia Garza after the shooting death of Trayvon Martin by his neighbor George Zimmerman.[43] As a decentralized but coordinated movement that has called attention to "racialized policing, the vulnerability of black bodies, and the problematic ways in which blackness is perceived as a constant threat,"[44] #BlackLivesMatter was initially driven forward by young people talking about and taking pictures of themselves in hoodies or putting their hands in the air to signal solidarity with unarmed young Black men killed unjustly. Since the early 2010s, hashtag activism has transformed politics, media, and culture around the world.

The rise of social media activism has created a way for Black fans to carry the movement for Black lives right into the realm of the fantastic. Campaigns like #AbbieMillsDeservesBetter raised awareness of the mistreatment of Black girl characters that paralleled misogynoir (Moya Bailey's term for mistreatment on the basis of both race and gender) in the real world. By the time *The Vampire Diaries* went off the air in 2017, movements from #WeNeedDiverseBooks to #OscarsSoWhite to #StarringJohnCho had begun to influence popular conversations about media and literature. The "Every Single Word" Tumblr was chronicling the how characters of color lacked voice in films, while the #ownvoices hashtag, created by young adult author Corrine Duyvis, mainstreamed conversations about author identity, positioning, and privilege.

Throughout *The Vampire Diaries*' eight-season run, articles, blogs, and Tumblr metaessays chronicled Black fans' hopes and dreams for Bonnie as a character, as well as their anger and frustration. After Elena's actress, Nina Dobrev, left the show, these calls expanded beyond the fandom to pop culture and television critics. Here's a sampler of titles that aptly illustrate the consistency in demands for justice in storytelling when it came to Bonnie's curious case:

Loving *Vampire Diaries*: Why History, Slavery, and Race in Fandom Matters (The AntiJemimaLife, 2011)[45]

The Vampire Diaries: What People of Colour Do When They're Not Snack Food (*Fangs for the Fantasy*, 2011)[46]

Why Can't *The Vampire Diaries* Just Let Bonnie Bennett Be Awesome? (*iO9*, 2014)[47]

What Would *The Vampire Diaries* Have Been Like without Bonnie Bennett? (*Wetpaint*, 2015)[48]

7 Reasons Bonnie Bennett Deserves to be the Leading Lady on *The Vampire Diaries* (*Bustle*, 2015)[49]

21 Problems that Only Bonnie Bennett from *The Vampire Diaries* Understands (*Buzzfeed*, 2015)[50]

How *The Vampire Diaries* Wronged Bonnie Bennett (*Black Girl Nerds*, 2017)[51]

The final post in the timeline of fan and media support for increasing Bonnie's visibility and importance in *The Vampire Diaries* is worth examining in greater detail. Posting one month after the series finale, Kristen Carter expresses the angst of Black Girl Nerds over the ultimate meaning of Bonnie Bennett as a character:

She never was treated the same as Elena or Caroline. We never got to see what her home life was like or the full extent of her dynamic with her parents. We didn't get to see her dress up and attend the same events Elena and Caroline attended—such as the Mikaelson's Ball or participate in Miss Mystic Falls pageant—even though young ladies who aren't a part of the founding families are allowed to participate. From the beginning, they desexualized her, and no one desired her like Elena or Caroline. The show waited entirely too long to present her with people who cared for her as she cared for them. I found Bonnie Bennett's treatment telling. Especially, when you compare Bonnie's treatment to that of her peers, Elena and Caroline.[52]

Kristen's views were shared by other fans of the character. Using Tumblr and Twitter, I invited Bonnie fans to share their thoughts about the character's treatment by the show in 2015 and 2016.[53] The first to respond was Selah Mitchell, who had watched *The Vampire Diaries* since the first season aired. Describing herself as very active in *Vampire Diaries* fandom, and a writer of both fanfiction and metatextual essays, Selah's words echo what my niece told me: she didn't care for Bonnie at first. Our exchange sheds light on why even Black viewers are positioned to sympathize with protagonist Elena instead of "judgey" witch Bonnie:

> I became a fan of Bonnie through the show. I haven't read the books but do know how vital of a character Bonnie McCullough is in the series. Honestly, I've been watching the show since 2009 and Bonnie wasn't my favorite. It took a second rewatch of the series and a lot of internal work on myself to figure out why I didn't like Bonnie. A viewer who doesn't think critical[ly] wants what the protagonist [in this case, Elena] wants. Because Bonnie was often contrary to what Elena wanted even when Elena didn't know what she wanted, Bonnie was framed as an antagonist. Bonnie Bennett was written to be unlikable. Instead of being the moral center of the show, which she is, the narrative told us she was judgmental. So my stanning for Bonnie didn't happen until 2011.[54]

Selah's words attest to the problematic way that Bonnie came to be positioned as an antagonist blocking the access of her White female friends to the allure of the vampire's seduction. Interestingly, Bonnie herself was rarely positioned the same way in the story: whenever she was threatened by a vampire, with the exception of secondary characters Kol and Kai, the implicit promise was death, not sex. Fangirls were frustrated by the way that Bonnie was excluded from the promise of intimacy, and Selah was no exception. After reading an earlier draft of this chapter, and assuring me that I had accurately characterized many Black fangirls' feelings about Bonnie, she continued:

There is a real problem with the show's desexualization of Bonnie—that in 5, 6 seasons I, as a viewer, am supposed to believe Jeremy Gilbert is the *only* person in this large cast of characters that finds Bonnie attractive—I am of the opinion that Bonnie should have all these male characters worshipping at her altar. They're all alive because of her, after all. So, yes, I ship Bamon [Bonnie x Damon], but I also love the idea of Bonkai (Bonnie x Kai) as completely problematic as that ship is. I'm late to the party, but I like Kennett (Bonnie x Kol), which makes watching The Originals uncomfortable because Kaleb (Kol 2.0) is dating Davina, a witch, but [showrunner Julie] Plec refused to let Kennett happen because why would I want "beautiful, strong Bonnie to be with a murderous vampire like Kol"?[55]

Selah gives voice to the frustration of Black girls and women who are elevated by platitudes attesting to beauty and strength while facing racism, sexism, and colorism in both the real world and the fantastic. Arguments that Bonnie deserves better than to date the vampires in a vampire series fall short when we consider that dating vampires does little to detract from Elena's and Caroline's beauty and strength (or their popularity among viewers). Instead, the fact that Bonnie does not date vampires implies that there was something wrong with her and, by extension, all girls and women who look like her.

In contrast to Selah, who needed a few seasons to warm up to Bonnie, Natandy Thomas was drawn into Bonnie's curious case right away. She was active in *The Vampire Diaries* fandom, shipping Bonnie with Damon, hosting the first Bamon Fan Fiction Awards on LiveJournal, and participating in the Bamon Shippers Club Google Hangouts live chats. Much like me, she was intrigued by witch characters, so Bonnie quickly became her favorite. She told me:

> I started watching TVD [*The Vampire Diaries*] at the behest of one of my best friends who absolutely adored it. I bought S1 on DVD and ended up marathoning the show in 2 weeks. I wasn't attached to any particular character but I have always been obsessed with witches and I was intrigued with Bonnie and her relationship with Elena and Grams. Especially with the way the show wrote her awakening into her powers as this story that was completely hers and was focused on this amazing black

heritage she inherited. Then Grams died and Kat Graham completely blew me away so I became a stan. Her anti vamp attitude and growing powers were the best scenes of S1 and S2 for me.[56]

Much like Selah, Natandy felt that *The Vampire Diaries* responded to Bonnie's growing popularity and potential by sidelining her in the third season:

> She started out as this girl who was completely in the dark about her power and we got to watch her discover her ancestors and herself. They had built so much with her and the Bennett line but then S3 happened and it became more about Bonnie losing people she loved through betrayal or murder while she willingly put her life on the line for this white woman without consideration for herself. It was frustrating. . . .
>
> I know a lot of Bonnie fans stopped watching from S3–mid S5 for this very reason and I totally got it. A lot of the story telling was hard to swallow. It was glaringly obvious that the show only included her for what she could do for others. She was constantly excluded from fancy parties where the white female characters could shine. Her male love interests ranged from the main character's little brother who cheated on her with a ghost to her mother's stepson who replaced her in her mother's life.
>
> Then . . . the showrunners decided to put her with Enzo in one of the most random and underwritten romances on the series. I wouldn't have been so against it had it not been for the fact that they had an entire season to write this and only used around 3 episodes to really show why they got together. One moment really stood out to me and solidified my feelings on Bonnie/Enzo. Julie Plec (EP) posted that someone on set had cried during a romantic scene between Enzo and Bonnie because they were so happy that Bonnie was loved and Julie seemed to think this was a reason to pat herself on the back. It left a bad taste in my mouth because it took 7 bloody seasons for you to show that Bonnie was a) a woman and b) worthy of being romanced. . . . There was no growth, no stakes, no development, just pain and sadness and sacrifice.[57]

If dark girls are destined to die in the fantastic (as a famous Anita Baker song, "Fairy Tales," attests[58]), Black fangirls are entitled to express their frustration with this fact, to counterstory and restory Bonnie's possibilities through fanwork, and to advocate for better representation. Fans like Kristen, Selah, and Natandy embraced Kat Graham's portrayal of Bonnie on the television series.[59] An active contingent on social media calling themselves the "Bonnie Bennett Brigade" avidly create Bonnie-centric fanworks and advocate for her characterization by the show. They frequently complain that many of Bonnie McCullough's best storylines from the book series were given to Caroline Forbes, a minor character in the books who is played by a White actress in the show.

It should be said that Bonnie was by no means favored by all in the audience. Most viewers outside of the self-proclaimed Bonnie Brigade did not pay much attention to Bonnie until her character interfered with or defied the fan favorites on the show—Elena, Damon, Stefan, Caroline, and Klaus (the latter is now the protagonist of the spinoff show, *The Originals*). Others felt as if she added nothing to the show, and might as well have been killed off.[60] A small group of book fans resented Bonnie Bennett or were not happy that she was cast and written very differently from the way the books described her counterpart—petite, red-haired, sweet, and naive—and in response, drew fan art that is specifically for Bonnie McCullough.[61] By the end of the series, Caroline had emerged as the second most important female character, and arguably the fan favorite.

As for Bonnie, despite her portrayer's best efforts and her fans' advocacy, she exited the landscape of teen TV and vampire narratives much as she entered it: destined to be the undesired monster in a series where the monstrous was desirable. For dark girls like her, she remains a symbol of thwarted potential due to the monstrous contradiction of the dark fantastic.

Conclusion: Why the Emancipation of Bonnie Bennett Matters

The principles I sketch above are found not only in the characterization of Bonnie Bennett in *The Vampire Diaries*, but throughout the horror genre. The rules of the dark fantastic seem so ingrained in our collective consciousness that when the expected pattern is subverted, much of the audience cannot suspend their disbelief. As we have seen with Gwen, some readers and viewers complain that dark heroic protagonists are not *likable*. Critics may observe that diverse characters, settings, circumstances, and resolutions in fantastic settings are *unbelievable*. Television networks like the CW tell production teams that diverse stories are not *marketable*. Thus, the Dark Other remains locked in place.

In the televised characterization of Black teen Bonnie Bennett, we see the first four elements of the dark fantastic cycle: *spectacle, hesitation, violence*, and *haunting*. Although many vestiges of her White book counterpart's characterization were retained, some elements simply could not be, for both intimacy and agency for a Black teen seemed beyond writers' and showrunners' imaginations. Thus, the monstrous contradiction of Bonnie Bennett is that she is rendered incomprehensible by the narrative. As a Black girl character, she *must be* both abject and monstrous. But as the witch in a vampire story, she must also reconnect the other characters to a world rendered unnatural by the supernatural. Furthermore, in a narrative where White male vampires are the ultimate focus of teen sexuality, Bonnie must be neutered and kept far away, although her dark beauty visually indexes *centuries* of taboo desire for Black bodies. An unwelcome intrusion into even a horror fantasy (much as Gwen is unwelcome in a magical medieval world), Bonnie jerks viewers out of the fantastic dream and back into reality.

Bonnie's self-sacrificing use of her magical powers is positioned differently across fan bases. Bonnie fans, especially Black women, have expressed the view that she has been stripped of agency. Elena fans believe that as her best friend, Bonnie should sacrifice herself—that is the very least she should do. No matter which side the viewer falls upon, it is clear that White Bonnie McCullough's naiveté, innocence, and sweetness in *The Vampire Diaries* novel series, transmediated so beautifully on the TV show in scenes like those with the white feathers, were ultimately not retained for Black Bonnie Bennett. These character traits were replaced by TV Bonnie's constant self-sacrifice and self-righteousness—traits that are not favorably viewed by characters inside of the story universe or viewers of the series. Bonnie's characterization indexes stereotypes of African American women. Persistent taboos about showing positive interracial relationships onscreen are also evident in the televised version of *The Vampire Diaries*. Instead of being the love interest of the dangerous alpha vampire, as her White book counterpart is, TV Bonnie is a secondary character and an afterthought. Instead of being central to the narrative, TV Bonnie is marginalized.

The limits of the collective imagination that show up on screen have their genesis early in the production process. Diversity among television writers is important, as veteran television writer and producer Felicia D. Henderson confirms:

> The writers' room is . . . creative ground zero. It is here that a process of collective decision making that I call "situational authorship" exists. Inside this ground zero, quasi-familial and organizational rules structure conventionalized socio-professional activities that overdetermine the manner by which television's on-screen texts are authored. In this space, ideas are negotiated, consensus is formed, and issues of gender, race, and class identities play out and complicate the on-screen narratives that eventually air on network and cable television.[62]

Casting matters for dark fantastic emancipation as well. One observation that I have made from watching and analyzing today's teen television is that actor aesthetics seem to have changed since the turn of the millennium. While actors and actresses on youth programming have always been good looking, today, most teen show characters are uniformly attractive, thin if female, and strong and athletic if male. It isn't just that these young actors (usually in their twenties through early thirties) are most often White. It's that many seem to be selected specifically for their physical perfection—not even most *White* teens would be able to relate to them aesthetically, except in an aspirational way. And for all their marginalization on their respective shows, most of the actors and actresses of African descent with speaking roles on teen television are of mixed-race and relatively light skinned. When these actors' and actresses' multiracial backgrounds are acknowledged on the shows and reflected in the writing for their characters, it is refreshing. But dark-skinned Black teenagers need to see themselves visually represented on teen television and films, too.[63]

Young people who are neither Black nor White also deserve to be represented in teen television and movies—the number of Latinx, Asian, Arab, and Native American youth on television certainly does not reflect their numbers in United States schools, neighborhoods, and society. Not only should the stories being published reflect who today's youth are, so should the television programming that is being marketed to them. Television in the United States has historically not only served as entertainment for children and youth but has also been expected to contribute to their growth and development, and so advocating that on-screen characters reflect the rich diversity young people experience in their everyday lives is far from unreasonable.[64]

Ultimately, what youth and young adults watch on television, on their computers, on their tablets, and on their smartphones matters for learning and teaching young adult literature, media, and culture in schools. Bonnie Bennett and other teens of color matter in our convergence culture of transmedia storytelling, where youth and young adults are making fantastic worlds and shaping our collective consciousness. Teen fans of stories like *The Vampire Diaries* will not only read the books but also watch the associated television shows and movies, peruse comics and graphic novels, participate in social media, and create fanwork online.[65] Expanding the visual representation of Bonnie and other characters like her, instead of locking her into the centuries-old place of the Dark Other, has the potential to help young people from all racial backgrounds close the imagination gap. In such a rich and vibrant participatory television culture, race and visual representation matter for the dark fantastic.

One Last Drop of Blood: Bonnie, Daija, and Me

I close this chapter not on a note of hope, but on a note of trepidation, and in doing so, return to my opening anecdote about my niece. During the winter and spring of 2017, a number of young adult novels featuring Black girl protagonists debuted, and one, Angie Thomas's *The Hate U Give*, topped the *New York Times* bestseller list for the majority of the year. After many decades of advocacy, the landscape was starting to shift toward diversifying literature and media.

Of course, I was excited to share *The Hate U Give*, along with Ibi Zoboi's *American Street* and Renee Watson's *This Side of Home*, with Daija during a visit to my mother's home in Detroit. My excitement turned to dismay when I saw her reaction.

"Auntie," she explained patiently, "just because I'm Black doesn't mean that I only like to read about Black girls."

(Like I said, she's my doppelgänger in many ways.)

Unfortunately for Daija, both her mother and grandmother were within earshot. They both began to fuss at her, explain that "your auntie is an *expert* on children's books!," and tell her that she ought to be grateful to have so many stories with girls like her in them. Her father was called, and he echoed this message of racial uplift that is common in Black families in the United States: *You need to learn about your history, and your people. You need to support stories with Black characters, and you need to root for the Black character in the story.* I'd had the same messages drummed into my mind by parents, teachers, and librarians many years before.

As Daija reminded me that day, it isn't just White audiences who sometimes reject Black characters. All readers and viewers want characters with whom they can identify, dream alongside, and perhaps aspire to be like. Characters in the fantastic represent our hopes, our aspirations, and our dreams. The limitless possibilities of their fictional lives stretch our minds and imaginations.

But messages of racial responsibility and respectability like those Daija heard from her elders can only go so far. Black girl characters are always an instantiation of Blackness in the fantastic, and carry with them all of the weight of Blackness in the real world. Many children and teens seek the fantastic as a means of escape; as we have seen, Black girl characters in mainstream science fiction and fantasy do not offer agency but are marked by the narrative for death and haunting. This may be why even Black girls might find themselves drawn toward White protagonists instead of Black sidekicks; overidentification with Black story-girls often leads to heartbreak that is not unlike the pain found beyond the page and the screen.

Jared Sexton, a leading theorist of anti-Blackness and Afropessimism, elaborates:

> In a world structured by the twin axioms of white superiority and black inferiority, of white existence and black nonexistence, a world structured by a negative categorical imperative—"above all, don't be black"—in this world, the zero degree of world transformation is the turn toward blackness, a turn toward the shame, as it were, that "resides in the idea that 'I am thought of as less than human.'"[66]

The crux of the matter in the fantastic and in the real world is, as Sexton notes, "Don't be Black." The afterlife of slavery, as best articulated in the work of Saidiya Hartman, is ever present not only in the dark fantastic cycle, but also in the minds and imaginations of audiences.[67] The spacetime conundrum created by the Door of No Return (described in chapter 3) is superimposed on Black bodies, and by extension, on dark characters and darkness in the fantastic, rendering the very existence of *Blackness itself* problematic.

Young readers learn early that they are *the* problem in the story. Some reject speculative fiction as a result. Others internalize the sense of being existentially problematic.

In *The Souls of Black Folk*, published in 1903, W. E. B. DuBois recounts the crux of always already being a problem, both in reality and imagination:

> Between me and the other world there is ever an unasked question: unasked by some through feelings of delicacy; by others through the difficulty of rightly framing it. All, nevertheless, flutter round it. . . .
> To the real question, *How does it feel to be a problem?*
> I answer seldom a word.[68]

The monstrous contradiction that forms the curious case of Bonnie Bennett is the monstrous contradiction of the dark fantastic: the Dark Other is both the resolution to the problem, and *the* problem to be solved. Dark girls like Bonnie are the problem *and* the solution, always. Dark girls and women reading the narrative see their real-world social status mirrored in the purported escapist realm of the fantastic, while others complain that dark characters are neither likable nor relatable. Worse still, in vampire narratives, comic series like Marvel's *Thor*, and throughout the commodified fantastic, the position of darkness is coopted by not only desirable vampires like the *Diaries'* Salvatore brothers, but also by "dark gray" yet sympathetic antagonists like *Thor's* Loki.[69] Somehow, these well-rounded villains are not subjected to the full dark fantastic cycle, yet are positioned as "dark," rendering sympathy for characters who hail racial darkness impossible.

Even as many push for more diversity in science fiction, fantasy, comics, fairy tales, and horror, anti-Blackness in the real world inhibits the acceptance of protagonists of color. Much like Benjamin Button in the classic tale and movie aged backward, *The Vampire Diaries* similarly pulls Bonnie Bennett backward into the inescapable cycle of the dark fantastic. The conclusion of the series requires not only her willingness to sacrifice herself, but the return from the dead of all her Bennett ancestors—Black witches still laboring for White liberation beyond the grave, their emancipation elusive even in death. Given the fact that some of Bonnie's ancestors, including Emily, lived and died entirely during the period of Atlantic slavery, this resolution of her story is outrageous. It sends a clear message that Black women and girls, no matter how beautiful, strong, and magical, must always labor for others—even in the fantastic.

As Natandy told me during our interview, summing up the ultimate meaning of Bonnie:

> Kat [Graham, the actor who played Bonnie] said something that stuck with me once. She pointed out that she and Bonnie are not the same, but then said: "And there are people in this world who sometimes do get taken advantage of and they do get the short end of the stick sometimes."
>
> Which was sort of a jolt to hear because I think [while] we, as fans, focus a lot on ideals instead of honest storytelling . . . what Kat said still holds value. Bonnie's character is every black woman who has given and given without getting anything back in return. Bonnie is our mothers and grandmothers who worked as cleaners or maids for white people. Bonnie was no more than a modern-day slave to the white characters on this show. Bonnie *is* realistic but [she's] just one page in the book of what it means to be a female from the African diaspora. She's not what we want to see anymore. We are more. We've always been more. It's white people who have kept shoehorning us into those roles.[70]

After viewing the conclusion of *The Vampire Diaries*, and thinking it through with other fans, I understood perfectly why my niece was incredulous where Bonnie and dark fantastic girls were concerned. When I was her age, I turned away from the dark possibilities in the looking-glass, too.

Live-Tweeting with other fans, I wrote after the final episode:

Honestly? *flips locs* Don't trust these writers w/ Black girls' dreams, fantasies or our hearts. Let Bonnie's ultimate endgame be up to us. For 8 seasons, the people who brought us The Vampire Diaries were utterly confused about how to write Bonnie. They took us through it. . . . The very least they could have done was keep Bon alive & give her an open ending. Some young Black girl out there will do the rest.

There are young girls who watched all of TVD. My 12-going-on-13 year old niece is among them. And Bonnie's presence has inspired them. They will see the wisp of Bonnie's story, the ghost of it. What could have been. What might have been. They'll give birth to new stories. One day, some- one will ask them where they got the idea for their amazing story. And they'll talk about Bonnie, and Kat, and what was lost.

That is the spirit of fandom. But most importantly, that's what our people do, and have always done—we make the dry bones *live.*

I'm glad they didn't write an endgame for her. After the way they made Bonnie Bennett suffer, and serve, and strive, *leave us her heart.*[71]

While many of us loved Bonnie, and Kat's portrayal of her, being the engine of the dark fantastic is no longer enough.

We dark girls want more.

Because we *are* more.

HERMIONE IS BLACK

*A Postscript to Harry Potter and the Crisis
of Infinite Dark Fantastic Worlds*

Books belong to their readers.
—John Green

As a biracial girl growing up in a very white city,
I found myself especially attaching to the allegory
of Harry Potter's blood politics. . . . I related to her
deeply, but like with so much of what I watched
and read, I couldn't see myself in Hermione.
—Alanna Bennett, "What a Racebent Hermione
Really Represents," *The Root*

Words can't express how elated I am that it's common knowledge in 2015 that Hermione is Black. . . .
This is so beautiful and idk what started it, if it was a
text post, a racebent fancast, or ppl just collectively
coming out and saying "hey, I thought that while
reading the books, too" but I am forever grateful.
—Breianna Harvey, "Hermione is Black," Tumblr

Canon: brown eyes, frizzy hair and very clever.
White skin was never specified. Rowling loves
black Hermione.
—J. K. Rowling, about the casting of Noma
Dumezweni as Hermione in *Harry Potter and the
Cursed Child*

My immersion in Harry Potter fandom now seems like it was a lifetime ago. As I write these words, it has been almost twenty years since I opened my first Harry Potter novel, a hardcover copy of *Harry Potter and the Chamber of Secrets* that one of my fifth graders left in the classroom. After failing to uncover its original owner, I took the book home over the weekend and immediately fell in love with the wizarding world. I devoured everything about Harry Potter that I could find online and then discovered Fanfiction.net later that spring. By the time the fourth novel in the series, *Harry Potter and the Goblet of Fire*, was released in the summer of 2000, I had discovered the Harry Potter for Grownups Yahoo! Group (HP4GU for short). From July 2000 until August 2006, I was a highly visible member of Harry Potter fandom. Online and in person, I openly used my real life professional name, Ebony Elizabeth Thomas, as well as the alias AngieJ (short for Angelina Johnson, a Black British witch in the novels).

Digital Pottermania in the early 2000s was an intimate online community that consisted of less than a thousand members and perhaps fewer than one hundred regular posters across several websites, forums, and listservs. Within that small community, I was among the first—and during its earliest days, one of the most prominent—Black fans.[1] My fandom participation was a daily event, as I logged on eagerly after teaching and classes in the final few years before smartphones became ubiquitous. I volunteered for a number of Potter websites, including the Harry Potter for Grownups Yahoo! Group, FictionAlley, and the now-defunct PumpkinPie.org. I worked on the first Harry Potter fan-initiated conference—Nimbus-2003 in Orlando, Florida—co-chairing one of two programming committees. And between 2000 and 2004, I wrote and posted a popular post-Hogwarts fanfiction duology, *Trouble in Paradise* and *Paradise Lost*, which had beta readers from Britain to Brazil and enjoyed a broad international readership.[2]

Written between December 2000 and August 2001, *Trouble in Paradise* is narrated from the first-person perspective of Angelina Johnson, a witch who is described in *Harry Potter and the Goblet of Fire* as "a tall black girl who played Chaser on the Gryffindor Quidditch team." Those twelve words introducing the only Black girl character in the story launched this dark fantastic journey of mine. Set ten years after the Battle of Hogwarts, but written before the last three books in the series were published, *Trouble in Paradise* was the beginning of my recognition of the dark fantastic cycle. Since this was many years before the emergence of the expanded universe platform, Pottermore, and controversies like #MagicInNorthAmerica about Rowling's representation of Native and Indigenous peoples, I wondered how wizards and witches of color like Angelina ended up in the Western world, let alone England.[3] At the time, Rowling hadn't left us much to go on. Wrapping my head around a magical theory for Black characters in high fantasy was something for which I had no precedent. I'd avidly read Octavia Butler, Tananarive Due, and Nalo Hopkinson in high school and college, but this was different.

In contrast to Black authors who wrote emancipatory Black fantastic and Afrofuturistic tales and centered Black characters in their narratives, J. K. Rowling's treatment of race in the *Harry Potter* series almost seemed like an afterthought. I thought it odd that the Black witches and wizards had British surnames. I didn't understand how that could be possible. How could anyone subject a magical person in Rowling's legendarium to chattel slavery? Wouldn't their magic prevent it? These echoes from the afterlife of slavery seemed inconsistent with the rules of the otherwise compelling wizarding world that J. K. Rowling had built. In a series featuring a boarding school where magical children and adolescents are learning how to defy the laws of physics, I had trouble imagining the origin stories for *Harry Potter*'s characters of color—most of whom were relegated to the background.

In order to come up with a good explanation for Angelina's magical ancestry, I revisited folklore of the African Diaspora, just as fantasy writers of European descent revisit their own ancestral folkloric traditions. African and Caribbean folklore, while foundational for much contemporary Black speculative fiction, did not sufficiently account for why the character would be surnamed "Johnson." In the process of this research, I rediscovered one of my favorite stories from childhood, Virginia Hamilton's "The People Could Fly," which is the final story in the book of Black American folktales of the same name and is her rendering of a classic Black folktale in African American English. I had heard it read aloud as a child, and I had read it aloud to younger family members and students. In the story, I wanted Angelina to engage in the same kind of loving storytelling with her daughter. In a sense, I was inscribing myself into multiple beloved narratives at the same time.

In chapter 6 of *Trouble in Paradise*, I created a scene in which Angelina tells her daughter Malinda, a character original to my fanfiction, about the origins of magical people of African descent who were enslaved. For that origin story, I used long passages from "The People Could Fly," putting Virginia Hamilton's words into Angelina's mouth. The file on my computer is dated February 1, 2001. The disclaimer on the chapter read as follows:

> I'm emphatically not JKR—she owns Harry and company, and the fact that I'm writing about them doesn't mean that I want to infringe her copyright, it simply means that I'm obsessed with the fictional world she has created. Certain elements of this chapter were inspired by Virginia Hamilton's award-winning folklore collection *The People Could Fly* and Zora Neale Hurston's *excellent* anthropological study of magic, superstition, and voodoo in the Caribbean, *Tell My Horse*.

But in reality, the passage was more than just "inspired." I had my fanfictional version of Angelina Johnson-Weasley treat "The People Could Fly" as if it were oral folklore, leaving it unclear where my words ended and Hamilton's began. Here's a brief excerpt from the long scene between my fanfictional Angelina and her daughter:

"Tell me a story, will you?"

I kissed her cheek impulsively. "All right, I will. This is a story that my father heard when he was a little boy growing up around Muggles."

"Oh, good! I love Grandpa's Muggle stories!"

"I know you do, darling. Which one do you want to hear?"

Malinda whipped her head out of my hand to beam at me. "Tell me the one about the people who could fly!"

She would choose *that* one. The only one that was real.

They say the people could fly. Say that long ago in Africa, some of the people knew magic. And they would walk up on air like climbin' up on a gate. And they flew like blackbirds over the fields. Black, shiny wings flappin' against the blue up there.

Then, many of the Blackbird people were captured for slavery. The ones that could fly shed their wings. They couldn't take their wings across the water on the slave ships. Too crowded, don't you know.

The folks were full of misery, then. Got sick with the up and down of the sea. So they nearly forgot about flyin' when they could no longer breathe the sweet scent of Africa.

Say the people who could fly kept their power, although they shed their wings. They kept their secret magic in the lands of slavery. They looked the same as the other people from Africa who had been coming over, who had dark skin. Say you couldn't tell anymore one who could fly from one who couldn't.

My father told my mother this folktale long before they were married. Although she was full-blooded Society, she'd never heard of it before. She was astonished to learn that it is by far the most cherished and treasured tale in all of black Muggle lore. The story has several variations, but the main points of the narrative are universal amongst Muggle descendants of the black Diaspora. Mum was also stunned by how accurate the details were.[4]

The italicized portion of the excerpt is Virginia Hamilton's retelling of the African American folktale. They are her words, not mine. The part that I quoted was also italicized in the original posted chapter on Fanfiction.net. In the balance of that scene, I went on to have Angelina reflect at some length upon "The People Could Fly" in her own words, filling out more of the details, and positioning it as an origin story for Black Atlantic peoples within Rowling's wizarding world—a legend within a legend. I ended the section with Angelina snapping out of her reflections, using another long quotation from Hamilton as she wrapped up the folktale for her daughter. In all, about one-seventh of the scene is from "The People Could Fly," and the chapter itself was fifty-two pages long. (I was infamous for my long chapters back in those days.)

Five years after completing *Trouble in Paradise*, in August 2006, I was accused of plagiarism in a post on bad_penny, an anonymous Live-Journal dedicated to exposing bad fan behavior. In the post, passages from "The People Could Fly" were placed side-by-side with verbatim passages from chapter 6 of *Trouble in Paradise*. I had intentionally used Hamilton's story within that fanfiction, and the accusation of plagiarism surprised me. There's no question that I was naive in thinking it was okay to use Hamilton's writing without formal attribution, even in fanfiction, but during the time that I wrote the story—December 2000 to

August 2001—there were few fandom conventions for digital citation. Fan authors regularly quoted phrases, sentences, and passages from the *Harry Potter* series with only vague attributions. For many of us, it was our first time in any kind of fandom, writing fanfiction. Fanfiction was seen as a place of freedom, where we could play, borrow and blend, and practice creative writing skills for our own original work. There was also the thrill of the forbidden and the taboo, of taking a popular work that was swiftly becoming part of the cultural landscape and appropriating it for our own purposes.

Hidden behind anonymous internet handles, people were quite nasty, saying that I was always so self-righteous, that a teacher should have known better than to *steal* a Black writer's story, and that I had deceived the fandom. My position as a prominent supporter of the Harry/Hermione ship was also noted, as *Trouble in Paradise* and *Paradise Lost* were written to support my preferred pairing.[5] Several prominent Potter fans stopped speaking to me altogether. There were other repercussions as well. Prior to the controversy, I had received an invitation to be a featured guest speaker at Phoenix Rising 2007, a Harry Potter fan conference in New Orleans, and to review proposals for the event, much as I had during Nimbus-2003. It was mutually agreed that I should excuse myself from the conference as well as any further involvement in Potter fandom, including my own HP_Paradise Yahoo! Group and the Fiction-Alley website. After posting a message of apology to the LiveJournal community Blackfolk, which was discussing the scandal, I posted a good-bye message to my LiveJournal on August 16, 2006.[6] Within a week of my apology, I decided to pull *Trouble in Paradise* and *Paradise Lost* from all the websites where I could control access to them. Thus, my years in Harry Potter fandom came to an ignoble end.

In retrospect, the fandom provided many lasting benefits for me. It was at Nimbus-2003 that I met children's literature scholars Philip Nel and Karin Westman, who were among those who encouraged me to pursue a PhD. Later that fall, I joined the Child_Lit listserv, hosted by Rutgers University and moderated for more than two decades by Michael Joseph before coming to an end in September 2017. These experiences put me on the path to becoming a tenured professor of education specializing in children's and young adult literature. Many of the ideas in this book germinated during my time in Harry Potter fandom, and in the years immediately afterward, when I tried (and failed) to publish my original fantasy novel series featuring Black characters. (I gave up in 2007, when I had to choose between revising my novel manuscript or completing my doctoral exams.)

But in the wake of the plagiarism accusation and my ensuing self-imposed exile, I began to recognize a not-so-idyllic side of Harry Potter fandom that I had largely ignored while I was in it, a side that led me to seek LiveJournal communities like Blackfolk to converse with geeks of color before the dawn of the social media age. I had only glimpsed that side before, but it was always there. It was there in the way that I was taunted in an otherwise fun AOL chat when I code-switched into African American English. It was in the argument I had over Dean Thomas's name signaling his Welshness, one in which I retorted that *my* last name is Thomas, and I've never been to Wales. It was in being unaware that my special status within the early fandom as *the* Black fan was a form of tokenization as much as my chosen name in fandom—Ebony AKA AngieJ—signaled the presence of the only named Black girl character. It was in my inability to see that I was hypervisible while inside Harry Potter fandom but still marginalized in ways that surfaced only after I withdrew from the community that defined my twenties.

For many of us, fandom is as much about the community and the friendships we make as it is about the source material. After the plagiarism scandal, few of my friends in Potter fandom reached out to me. Heidi Tandy, Flourish Klink, Clare Worley, and Josh Aronovitch were notable exceptions to that rule, as were most of the regulars on the Harry Potter for Grownups Yahoo! Listserv who'd been around during the genesis of *Trouble in Paradise*. In recent years, I have been asked to sit on the Harry Potter fandom panel at San Diego Comic-Con International as an academic and fandom old-timer. However, the scandal ended some of my newer friendships and distanced me from others I thought would be there through thick and thin. Some of the people in question were those I'd invited to my home, traveled with, attended *Potter* movie premieres with, and thought would be there for a lifetime. In short, the fandom scandal marked the start of my exile from a digital community that I'd loved.

When I saw others who had been involved in similar plagiarism exposés defended vigorously by the community, and then reconciled and restored to fandom while I remained at the margins, I couldn't help but wonder what happened. I was far from innocent, but the fact that I remained ostracized while others remained in the fold bothered me greatly. The exile—*social death*—that I suffered both hurt and puzzled me at first. Was it because I was still seen by some as a shameless plagiarist, although my intentions for including a slice of my own childhood—and solving the dark fantastic dilemma at the heart of the *Potter* series—were noble? Was it because I was associated with the Big Name Fan clique in early Harry Potter fandom, and thus a mean girl? Was it because I was open about being religious at times?

Or was my race ever a factor?

Was any of it because I was Black?

In the Wake:
What Does It Mean to Defend the Dead?

In her introduction to *In the Wake: On Blackness and Being*, Christina Sharpe asks a poignant question, which she then answers:

> What does it mean to defend the dead? To tend to the Black dead and dying, to tend to the Black person, to Black people, always living in the push toward our death. It means work. It is work: hard emotional, physical, and intellectual work that demands vigilant attendance to the needs of the dying, to each their way, and also to the needs of the living.[7]

This question is not limited to humans who have been labeled as Black in the past and present, both quick and dead, but extends to Black *characters*, and to the very idea of Blackness itself. As the title of Sharpe's book suggests, this is an ontological question that every Black child, woman, and man is confronted with throughout the course of a lifetime. It is a question that demands an answer.

The wake, according to Sharpe, is the path behind a ship, keeping watch with the dead, coming to consciousness, all at once. Throughout *The Dark Fantastic*, we have witnessed Black girl characters caught in the wake within the storied realms of the collective imagination. These girls-that-never-were, but who nonetheless remain with us due to their very fictionality, are dying and *not* dead, present and *not* present, inconsequential to speculative narratives yet vital to their functioning. Rue's impossible dark innocence, Gwen's impossible dark beauty, and Bonnie's impossible dark virtue are signs that Black girls in speculative fiction are the *real* "impossible girls" (with due respect to Doctor Who). Yet the conundrum is that these Black girl characters (like Black girls in the real world) are both impossible *and* necessary at the same time.

I am by no means the only one who has observed the myriad ways that the fantastic, the speculative, and the collective imagination have rendered Black presence impossible and Black nonexistence compulsory. Most Black fans and other fans of color have thought quite a bit about our precarious state even within realms of supposedly infinite possibilities. During a Twitter chat, an observer by the handle @relicUA noted that "I think poor nonwhite people are in a state of quantum super-position, such that they only exist when the narrative requires."[8] Indeed, young Black women and girls exist in a state of quantum super-position in the fantastic.[9] They cannot exist, and yet, they must: when it comes to the fantastic, Schrödinger's cat is a young Black girl.[10]

Due to the quantum problem created by the Door of No Return, a profound crisis is created for stories fantastic and real. This crisis is one found in infinite fantastic worlds. As Michelle M. Wright observed in *The Physics of Blackness*, when all of Blackness is refracted through the Middle Passage, dilemmas of space and time result (discussed in chapter 3). These dilemmas are resolved through both progress (calls toward greater diversity in the fantastic) and regress (doubling down on the violence and erasure of the Dark Other). To note but one example among many, in the same year N. K. Jemisin and Nnedi Okorafor won the prestigious Hugo Award for their emancipatory fantastic stories, detective Abbie Mills (portrayed magnificently by actress Nicole Beharie) in the genre television show *Sleepy Hollow* was caught in the gears of the dark fantastic cycle and killed. Showrunners were unmoved by the outcry from Black fans and audiences over the trauma of losing a beloved Black woman lead in a horror show, perhaps unwittingly echoing painful long-ago words of Thomas Jefferson about people of African descent: "Their griefs are transient."[11] Even as a growing number of Black authors, artists, screenwriters, and showrunners are producing extraordinarily creative work to endarken the popular imagination, the shadows of the past remain in mainstream speculative fiction created by others.

In the wake of these shadows and echoes, it seems vital to examine the ways that Black writers, fans, and audiences are narrating the self into existence in the face of narrative erasure—and have *always* had to read themselves into fantastic canons that excluded them. The traditional fantastic has historically assumed a White audience, and, in turn, those who are endarkened and Othered have had to read those stories to understand the cartographies of the imagination. In contrast to histories of fandom and audiences that portray audiences for the speculative and the fantastic as predominantly White, new work from scholars like Rebecca Wanzo and Andre Carrington sheds light on the ways that Black fans and audiences have always engaged in interpreting fantastic media even though such media does not imagine us as part of the audience—a view that I share.[12] It is my hope that future scholars and researchers will extend Sharpe's call for wake work into the dark fantastic.

How Hermione Became Black:
Black Girls' Emancipatory Readings

When I finished *Trouble in Paradise* in the summer of 2001, it was such a hit in the fandom that, like many fan writers, I penned a sequel. Posting the first chapter just before 9/11, I centered the second half of my Potter fanfiction duology on Hermione Granger, one of the "Golden Trio" of central characters in the series. But instead of taking the first-person perspective as I did with Angelina in *Trouble in Paradise*, I wrote my alternate-universe-Hermione's story in the third person:

> Hermione Granger sat bolt upright in bed. Her heart was pounding at a frenetic rate and her teeth clattered. Underneath the covers that she'd clutched with trembling fingers, her chest heaved with her quickened breathing. She felt rather as if she'd just finished flying at a fantastic 250 m.p.h . . . but there, she wasn't supposed to be thinking about flying anymore, was she?[13]

While I loved Hermione Granger, perhaps too much for a young adult needing to leave childhood behind, she wasn't a mirror for my experiences. Because I did not look like her, I knew that I could never view the wizarding world through her eyes, but only peer over her shoulder.

Even after writing half a million words about what I imagined Rowling's most beloved character might be like as a young adult, I never imagined Hermione Granger as Black. Reading the first few *Harry Potter* novels as a twenty-two-year-old schoolteacher, it never occurred to me to unmake my reality to read Hermione as anything except White. That is why it never occurred to me to dress up and cosplay her, although in the early 2000s I owned everything from magic wands, to figurines, to editions of Harry Potter from multiple countries. Instead, as with *Anne of Green Gables* and *Alice in Wonderland*, I could only directly experience Hermione's inner world by donning my Invisibility Cloak.

Unlike my own and previous generations, today's young readers are choosing to read characters as mirrors of their own experiences. After a viral *Buzzfeed* article by Alanna Bennett, "What a Racebent Hermione Really Represents," was shared among Harry Potter fans online in early 2015, a new movement on social media formed insisting that Hermione's description in the popular novels means that she is really Black.[14] One young adult author of several "Hermione is Black" Tumblr posts, Breianna Harvey, talked with me about growing up with the *Harry Potter* book series as a child and reading the uber-popular girl protagonist of the series as a mirror of the self:

> Prior to Tumblr, I had thought Hermione was like me and it was my first experience at being upset with deviations from the book, specifically casting. But like many other Black girls in my situation, I kept my mouth shut. It wasn't until Tumblr that I started to speak up about it. I saw drawings of Hermione . . . where the artists would subconsciously draw Hermione darker than everyone else. Then my friend started posting fancasts of [Welsh actress] Jessica Sula as Hermione and I really loved it. Then I started to see fanart where she was darker than Jessica and followers were engaging in conversation with me about how much a black Hermione would make sense along with speculation of her origins.[15]

Breianna's reading of Hermione as a Black girl may seem quite radical, yet she is in good company. Posts in the "Hermione Is Black" Tumblr tags have been shared thousands of times by Tumblr users. It is clear that some dark girls and women today are choosing to enter their reading experiences, to quote Audre Lorde, "Blackened and whole."[16] Their interpretive agency brings to mind a reader of Chimamanda Ngozi Adichie's books, who loved one of the stories so much that she excitedly told Adichie how the story should continue.[17] In my work with digital literacies scholar Amy Stornaiuolo, I have examined how readers use digital literary affinity spaces, such as fan communities, to restory their worlds and subvert traditional expectations about relationships between readers, authors, and texts.[18] As readers and viewers begin to claim interpretive agency, they not only imagine themselves into stories but also *reimagine the very stories themselves.* This imaginative restorying work is often viewed as transgressive, as authors fight for the official word, cultural pundits trivialize readers' efforts, and the general public positions authors as "under attack" by wayward readers. But there are signs of change.

Shifting cultural attitudes toward texts—and the contemporary struggle for interpretive authority over them—characterize meaning-making. While theorists from Roland Barthes to Michel Foucault would point out the historical nature of this struggle (and the longtime absence of the author), the question of reader-author relationships must be revisited, given that in this digital age, more people than ever before are writing for work and during leisure, readers connect with one another in powerful networks, lines between readers and writers blur, definitions of what counts as text are negotiated and reconfigured in hybrid multimodal and multilingual constellations, and texts and people circulate across asymmetrical trajectories.

It should be noted that long before Rowling left Hermione's racial and ethnic identities up for reader interpretation in a Tweet,[19] she'd established a propensity toward providing details for the vast wizarding world outside the official books and movies. Years earlier, she had revealed to fans that Dumbledore was gay. In "Oh My God, the Fanfiction! Dumbledore's Outing and the Online Harry Potter Fandom," Catherine Tosenberger notes:

> Among participatory fans, one contingent was unsurprised when Rowling, during an appearance at Carnegie Hall, announced that Hogwarts headmaster Albus Dumbledore was gay: readers and writers of "slash" fanfiction. Slash—fanfiction that concerns a romantic and/or sexual re-

lationship between characters of the same gender—is one of the most popular forms of Potter fanfiction. Slash fans are always on the lookout for hints of homoeroticism in the source text that can be spun into a story, and the description of the relationship between Dumbledore and his boyhood friend-turned-enemy Gellert Grindelwald proved especially fruitful in this respect; fans began creating stories, art, and critical essays concerning their relationship immediately following the release of Harry Potter and the Deathly Hallows—anticipating Rowling's announcement by three months. Immediately after her revelation, Rowling laughed, "Oh my god, the *fanfiction*." Over the years, Rowling has proven to be not simply aware, but actively supportive, of fanfiction; her confirmation of Dumbledore's sexuality lends support to Sarah Gwenllian Jones's articulation of slash not as a perverse "resistance" to a given text's presumed heteronormativity but rather "an actualization of latent textual elements."[20]

More recently, Rowling expressed doubts about the way she tied up the main characters' romances in the epilogue of the final book, *Harry Potter and the Deathly Hallows*. Within twenty-four hours of the interview, readers around the world who grew up with Harry and his friends responded with passion. Using social media, youth and young adults wrote numerous articles, columns, essays, and fanfictions responding to Rowling's uncertainty. Some defended the series epilogue, while others preferred Rowling's statement about Harry and Hermione that "it could have gone that way."[21] (As a one-time Harry and Hermione supporter, I admit that her remarks vindicated our long-suffering ship!)[22]

What Rowling's statements and the ensuing backlash revealed was the extent to which readers felt ownership over *Potter*'s narrative landscape. Some in Harry Potter fandom asserted that the reader's role was to imagine possible futures for the story, a role threatened by Rowling's apparent efforts to wrest control of the narrative from fans. Perhaps the best summary of this reading rebellion belonged to popular young adult author John Green when he wrote on Twitter at the height of the controversy, "Books belong to their readers."[23] Green's statement, reposted by Twitter and Tumblr users over 45,000 times within six weeks of its initial posting, demonstrated the role of contemporary audiences in determining narrative meaning.[24] Today's readers are using the tools of social media to make meanings that are not just independent of authorial intent but that can also deliberately *contradict* it—which is to say that meaning itself is in the process of becoming crowdsourced and jointly imagined.

As we have seen throughout *The Dark Fantastic*, constructing new meanings in a speculative fiction landscape where the Dark Other remains trapped within the narrative is potentially quite challenging. Most readers, viewers, and fans have not responded to Bonnie, Rue, or Gwen by moving them to the center of their respective stories. Yet from *Harry Potter* to *Hamilton*, previously White cisgender heterosexual characters (and in *Hamilton*, historical figures) have begun to be imagined as Others. The rising generation is not only inscribing themselves into the narrative but also demanding to be the center of all their worlds, textual, visual, fannish, and otherwise. Thus, in a textual landscape where the author of *Harry Potter* has told us that Dumbledore is gay, where Harry and Hermione *could have* ended up together, and where Hermione's appearance is left up to the readers' imagination, we are left with the possibility of infinite storyworlds. Though this plurality of possible worlds might represent a crisis for some audiences, it may provide an answer for emancipating the imagination for readers and fans who have for too long inhabited the margins—real and imagined.

Reading and Restorying after Hermione: Reconciling the Dark Fantastic Crisis on Infinite Storyworlds

In the 1980s, the two major US comic houses, Marvel and DC, reconciled years of discontinuities and alterities in their canons with two series that are now legendary: DC's *Crisis on Infinite Earths*, and Marvel's *Secret Wars*. In both cases, several decades of changes in the writing staff as well as changes in the audience meant that each of the top superheroes had different story arcs, many of which contradicted each other. For instance, in one series, Superman aged and became elderly, while in another, he was still young. Multiverse series like *Crisis on Infinite Earths* answered the question "Which Superman is the real Superman?" by presenting the possibility of parallel worlds. But multiple storyworlds featuring different outcomes for the same character may be difficult to process, as comics scholar Karin Kukkonen notes:

Cognitive-psychological research on mental models, that is, scenarios we mentally develop in order to reason, also stresses that situations triggering the creation of multiple mental models are difficult to process . . . and that we construct mental models in order to eliminate alternatives and create coherence. Thus, when reading fiction, interpreters construct a "three-dimensional model akin to an actual model of the scene" in order to locate the characters, monitor the events, and project the narrative's progress.[25]

Given that multiple worlds are notably difficult for readers to process, encountering the racial Other within a narrative presents even more difficulty for some mainstream audiences. While Kukkonen rightly notes that readers and fans of contemporary superhero comics are far more comfortable with alterity than most because of canon discontinuities,[26] the comics readership is not notably better on race than others. While the production of transformative fanwork and vigorous discussion show that fans are invested in alternate worlds, there is a vast gulf between the acceptance of slash celebrating homosexual relationships between White cisgender male characters and the disdain for racial and ethnic diversity in many fan communities. This shows that not all alterities are created equal, and creates an ontological dilemma that must be reconciled.

This dilemma can be reconciled by accepting all storyworlds as possible. Rowling's comments since finishing the *Harry Potter* series—"it could have gone that way" and "never specified"—open up narrative space for difference. Changing the mode of storytelling also opens up this narrative space. When the books were transmediated to the screen, Potter fans noted many changes, and yet the eight-movie series was still wildly successful. The play makes further changes, not only to Hermione's race and ethnicity, but also in time, for the Golden Trio of Harry, Ron, and Hermione are now middle-aged adults. Changes like these ask audience participants to reimagine the narrative. But as I have demonstrated throughout the dark fantastic cycle, some changes are more acceptable than others. Given the examples of Bonnie in *The Vampire Diaries* and Gwen in *Merlin*, it is evident that differentiating a character's race seems to be more difficult than other kinds of changes.[27]

How, then, can creators of stories and worlds assist audiences in opening up their imaginations to racial difference in the fantastic? Returning to Kukkonen, readers of superhero comics are able to accept multiple versions of the same characters because writers and artists provide two aids to assist in the reconciliation of multiple storyworlds: iconography and reader/viewer/audience surrogates. Iconography such as costuming, shields, and logos "provide shortcuts into readers' knowledge structures, enabling them to keep different character versions distinct and connect them to their original storyworlds."[28] For example, Superman's iconic "S" logo has undergone multiple makeovers from his original appearance in 1938's *Action Comics #1* up through his more recent appearances in movies such as *Man of Steel* and *Batman vs. Superman*. No matter what *Superman's* situation is in the comics, no matter what he looks like, as long as he has his logo, he is recognizable.[29] These icons exist beyond comics. Returning to *Harry Potter*, wands from Ollivanders, brooms from Quality Quidditch Supplies, and even Harry's scar are iconographic in nature, and help orient readers within the wizarding world.

Surrogates, in contrast, are secondary characters with whom the audience can identify as the narrative unfolds.[30] One of the best and most enduring examples of a surrogate comes not from books or comics, but from television—Doctor Who's traveling companions are ordinary people whose purpose is to react to the time traveling, eponymous Gallifreyan alien as the audience might. Although the Doctor has regenerated (changed actors) more than a dozen times, no matter what he looks like, each generation of companions marvels in turn that the TARDIS, Doctor Who's flying police box phone booth of a spaceship, is "bigger on the inside" and "smaller on the outside."[31] Surrogates thus provide important narrative continuity. As surrogates provide explanations for in-universe phenomena, "readers acquire by proxy the mental model that the surrogates construct at the [narrative] level."[32] Within *Harry Potter*, his best friends, Ron Weasley and Hermione Granger, provide perspectives on the wizarding world from both the inside (Ron, born to a wizarding family) and outside (Hermione, raised by nonmagical parents). Characters of color, like Cho Chang, Viktor Krum, Fleur Delacour, Dean Thomas, and my own favorite Angelina Johnson, provide tantalizing yet fleeting glimpses of diverse possibilities for fantastic worlds, and serve as even more surrogates in the series.

The challenge of the dark fantastic comes when neither iconography nor reader surrogates suffice to diversify and decolonize the baseline world. This has been evident throughout our journey in *The Dark Fantastic*. Neither the power of a witch, nor the trappings of girlish innocence, and not even the accouterments of more than a millennium of tales about the fair but treacherous Guinevere prevent audiences from rejecting Bonnie, Rue, and Gwen. Even Angelina, who survives canon, is fated to marry her boyfriend's twin brother once the dust clears, as if her fate was an afterthought.

Yet not all hope is lost. Recently, I have argued that how we make sense of reader response, audience, and transactions between creators and audiences must be revisited in a global digital age where diversity and social change are no longer at the margins of life but, increasingly, at the center.[33] In an era of struggle and contestation over narrative and meaning, young people today are, in the words of literacy scholar Vivian Vasquez, "reading and writing the self into existence,"[34] using fan communities and other digital affinity groups to *restory* the popular imagination by making it into their own image.[35] Restorying describes the complex ways that contemporary young people narrate the word and the world, analyze their lived experiences, and then synthesize and recontextualize a multiplicity of stories in forming new narratives. In other words, as young readers imagine themselves into stories, they *reimagine the very stories themselves*. Now more than ever before, people of all ages are collectively reimagining time, place, identity, perspective, mode, and metanarratives through retold stories, as represented in figure 5.1 and described in greater detail below.

RESTORYING TIME AND PLACE. One of the most common forms of restorying involves readers changing the location of narratives to alternate times and places. In classrooms, this practice might include shifting canonical works into current settings, as actor, director, and playwright Ricardo Pitts-Wiley did with a group of incarcerated youth in Rhode Island when they restoried *Moby Dick* and made Ahab a powerful drug dealer.[36] This act of taking characters and situations to new locations is prevalent in theater (just one example comes from *Romeo and Juliet* and *West Side Story*). Similarly, the speculative fiction genre known as *alternate history* features stories that have an identifiable point of divergence from the history of our present reality, although some alternate histories also feature anachronism, magic, or advanced technology. Within fan communities, a phenomenon known as *alternate*

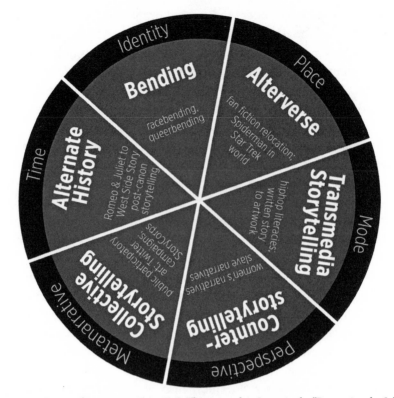

Figure 5.1. Forms of Restorying. From E. E. Thomas and A. Stornaiuolo, "Restorying the Self: Bending toward Textual Justice," *Harvard Educational Review* 86, no. 3 (2016): 313–338.

universe (AU) fanwork—fanart, fanfiction, fan videos, and fan "meta" essays—explores divergences from source texts. For instance, young fanfiction authors imagine the young adult lives of the characters between the final chapter of *Harry Potter and the Deathly Hallows* and the epilogue that takes place many years later, moving Rowling's narrative forward in time.[37] Some of this fanfiction imagines the wizarding world in other locations, and during other periods of history. This is important work that disrupts predominant metanarratives and epistemologies that lock people into a single story.[38]

RESTORYING PERSPECTIVE. From *Wide Sargasso Sea* to *Grendel*, and the more recent *The Wind Done Gone*, telling stories from a non-protagonist's point of view has long been the province of parallel novels and avant-garde Hollywood movies. Playing with perspective has also been a hallmark of storytelling in comics and graphic novels,[39] as well as in popular television series like *The Wire* and *Game of Thrones*. But people from nondominant groups—people of color, women, religious and sexual minorities, and the disabled—have always had alternate stories to tell and have used many different means of telling them. Young people in digital communities who sympathize with unsympathetic characters, like Draco Malfoy in the *Harry Potter* series,[40] or want to know more about characters in the margins, like Rue in *The Hunger Games*,[41] are participating in an age-old tradition of restorying from different points of view. Retelling the same story through a number of different perspectives has the power to build empathy and understanding. For, as postcolonial theorist Shaobo Xie notes, "To speak from an other's thought is to redefine and renarrativize the world."[42]

RESTORYING ACROSS MODES. In addition to digital media, whenever young people retell stories through, for instance, hip-hop, the visual arts, dance, or slam poetry, they are engaging in yet another kind of narrative transformation. In 2013 Thomas Philip and Antero Garcia noted that "traditional texts can be transformed by ease of access as well as by their availability through new modalities. Students' experiences outside of the classroom, encapsulated by images, video, sound, notes, and GPS tags, can ever more easily become texts for study. New technologies have also multiplied the prospects for students to create and exchange multimodal texts."[43] While Philip and Garcia rightly note that it is ultimately the job of teachers to facilitate discussions about cultural relevance and power during multimodal lessons in the classroom so that multimodality is connected to academic literacies, Amy Stornaiuolo and I have observed youth and young adults engaged in multimodal restorying in out-of-school spaces as well. A growing body of literature, including the work of Ernest Morrell, Valerie Kinloch, and Maisha Winn, is talking about the potential of out-of-school literacies to inform effective classroom practice, and some of these spaces include virtual affinity communities online.

RESTORYING TOGETHER. Today's teens and young adults are increasingly using new forms of communication to engage in textual and visual production that is collaborative, made up of pastiche and allusions, and shared in what has been characterized as environments of "digital intimacy."[44] Digitally intimate virtual communities have their own ever-evolving rules, norms, and assumptions about meaning-making processes, authorship, and composing. As young people participate with one another across these affinity spaces and networked publics, they engage in participatory cultures "in which everyday citizens have an expanded capacity to communicate and circulate their ideas . . . [and] networked communities can shape our collective agendas."[45] Some scholars have noted that the digital age is merely facilitating a return to a previous era before the advent of the printing press and the rise of the novel, when stories belonged not to individual authors but to the collective and evolved according to the needs of the times.[46] If, as literacy scholar Peter Smagorinsky observes, the reader's construction of new texts is truly the source of meaning in reading,[47] today's readers are using the tools of social media to collectively make meanings that are not just independent of authorial intent but that can deliberately *contradict* it—in other words, meaning itself is in the process of becoming crowdsourced and jointly imagined. Twitter campaigns such as #WeNeedDiverseBooks offer a compelling example of this restorying work, as people together challenge the predominantly White world of children's and young adult fiction by offering alternate readings of "normal" families portrayed in most published books for youth. These collective forms of restorying can challenge metanarratives through collective action, offering an alternate "reading" of the mainstream.

RESTORYING IDENTITY. One of the most compelling forms of reclaiming narrative is restorying of identity, as young people change the identities of characters to more accurately reflect the diversity of the world, to play with identities to blur boundaries between traditional categories, or to create characters whose identities more closely mirror their own. Young readers' restorying of identity seems to be particularly visible in the fandom practice of bending characters to make them more diverse. In online spaces, racebending occurs when artists, fanfiction writers, video makers, and others create fanworks about popular, usually White, characters but change their racial or ethnic makeup. Although there has been some significant backlash to racebending (and analogous forms of bending, such as genderbending and queerbending), it is clear that young people are not only writing themselves into existence,[48] but also *reading* themselves into existence within what has been characterized as the "all-White world of children's literature" and youth media.[49]

Transmediated racebending of characters from popular children's and young adult stories within fan communities has the potential to be culturally transformative.

RESTORYING THE IMAGINATION ITSELF. Today's literary and media landscapes, mediated by digital communication, increasingly require audiences to restory imagination itself. In the past, reading, viewing, and participating required people who were marginalized and minoritized to acquire the dominant reader position—a position that was all too often White, male, ablebodied, cisgender, and middle class or wealthy. In literacy and English education, we often talk about culturally relevant, culturally responsive, and culturally sustaining pedagogy as a way to bridge these gaps for diverse students, families, and communities.[50] However, teaching *all* people to coexist with contradictions between their lived experiences and the lifeworlds of others while maintaining a core self that one can live with is an even greater challenge. Literature, media, and the popular imagination continue to be weighed with dilemmas of race, ethnicity, and other aspects of identity for which there is little productive discourse.

How, then, can readers and audiences of youth literature, media, and culture navigate the multiple worlds that one must exist in during this century?

One solution, when iconography and surrogacy are ineffective in breaking the dark fantastic cycle, may be to provide audiences with little choice but to accept diversity and racial difference. *Hamilton*, the revolutionary Broadway musical by Lin-Manuel Miranda, is a case in point. In his staged adaptation of Ron Chernow's biography of US Founding Father Alexander Hamilton, Miranda chose to use nontraditional casting. The only visibly White actor with a speaking role is Jonathan Groff, who plays a comical yet ominous King George III. The rest of the characters, including Alexander Hamilton, Aaron Burr, George Washington, Thomas Jefferson, and the Schuyler sisters, are all magnificently played by actors of color.

When asked about the impact of *Hamilton* on society, Miranda said:

What I can tell you is that works of art are the only silver bullet we have against racism and sexism and hatred. [Vice President] Joe Biden happened to see *Hamilton* on the same day James Burrows was here. James

Burrows directed every episode of *Will & Grace*, and remember when Biden went on *Meet the Press* and essentially said, "Yeah, gay people should get married"? He very openly credited *Will & Grace* with changing the temperature on how we discuss gays and lesbians in this country. It was great to see Jim Burrows and Joe Biden talk about that, and Jim thanked Biden and Biden thanked Jim because that was a piece of art changing the temperature of how we talked about a divisive issue. It sounds silly. It's a sitcom, but that doesn't make it not true. Art engenders empathy in a way that politics doesn't, and in a way that nothing else really does. Art creates change in people's hearts. But it happens slowly.[51]

The reception to *Hamilton* provides hope that change is coming faster than even Miranda might have imagined. The rising generation is moving toward a kind of collective restorying—what Chinua Achebe has referred to as a "balance of stories"[52]—to begin to address the crisis of infinite storyworlds. In our current landscape of persistent inequality, the efforts of marginalized people to author themselves in order to be heard, seen, and noticed—to assert that their lives matter—contribute to emancipating the imagination. If overcoming these inequities requires that, collectively, we must enter an exciting new Wonderland where we imagine seven impossible things, and words mean what we want them to mean, so be it. Today, when Alexander Hamilton can be Puerto Rican and the "smartest witch of her age," Hermione Granger, can be Black, there are infinite narrative possibilities.[53] As Alanna Bennett, the author of *Buzzfeed's* viral article, "What a Racebent Hermione Really Represents," put it:

> Hermione will always be an icon, no matter what color her skin. The least we can do is provide her with more room to be that icon. Maybe along the way more people will be able to see themselves reflected back at them.[54]

From the Dark Fantastic to the Black Fantastic: Toward Terra Incognita

I have spent the entirety of *The Dark Fantastic* exploring the way that race works in the popular fantastic traditions of the West, primarily within mainstream speculative transmedia that is produced in the United States and England and is marketed to youth and young adults all over the world. In turn, these young people have created rich, dynamic, and creative digital media communities (including fandom) in the first two decades of the twenty-first century. Although decolonizing and emancipating the dark fantastic is a laudable goal, although signs like Black Hermione and racebent *Hamilton* are promising, our journey into these story worlds-that-never-were must continue. In order to achieve true justice, exploring the perspectives of those interpellated by the fantastic as the *monstrous*, the *invisible*, and the *always dying* is essential. In order to do so, we must move beyond the charted territory of known fantastic worlds to what the writers of fantasy have thought of as terra incognita, "the undiscovered country," to the places in the waking dream where the lines disappear on the maps and we step out into places unknown.

This requires rethinking the cartographies of our imaginations. In a passage from *Peter Pan*, J. M. Barrie invites the audience to think about the territory of the dream-world created in fantasy:

> I don't know whether you have ever seen a map of a person's mind. Doctors sometimes draw maps of other parts of you, and your own map can become intensely interesting, but catch them trying to draw a map of a child's mind, which is not only confused, but keeps going round all the time. There are zigzag lines on it, just like your temperature on a card, and these are probably roads in the island, for the Neverland is always more or less an island, with astonishing splashes of colour here and there, and coral reefs and rakish-looking craft in the offing, and savages and lonely lairs, and gnomes who are mostly tailors, and caves through which a river runs, and princes with six elder brothers, and a hut fast going to decay, and one very small old lady with a hooked nose. . . .
>
> On the whole the Neverlands have a family resemblance, and if they stood still in a row you could say of them that they have each other's nose, and so forth. On these magic shores children at play are for ever beaching their coracles [simple boats]. We too have been there; we can still hear the sound of the surf, though we shall land no more.[55]

Although as adults, we lose access to Neverland, it is a place that we know all too well. We cannot land, but we hear the sound of the surf because we have been there, and our journeys have shaped the waking world that we know. Yet as we have seen throughout *The Dark Fantastic*, Neverland can be problematic when not all children, youth, and young adults can land on its shore.

The narrative imagination is shaped and reshaped through what Claudia Rankine has termed "the racial imaginary."[56] As she writes with collaborator Beth Loffreda:

> Many writers of all backgrounds see the imagination as ahistorical, as a generative place where race doesn't and shouldn't enter, a space for bodies to transcend the legislative, the economic—transcend the stuff that doesn't lend itself much [to] poetry. . . .
>
> Transcendence is unevenly distributed and experienced, however. White writers often begin from a place where transcendence is a given— one already has access to all, one already is permitted to inhabit all, to address all. . . . For writers of color, transcendence can feel like a distant and elusive thing, because writers of color often begin from the place of being addressed, and accessed. To be a person of color in a racist culture is to be always addressable, and to be addressable means one is always within stigma's reach. So one's imagination is influenced by the recognition of the need to account for this situation—even in the imagination, one feels accountable, one feels one must counter. . . .
>
> . . . This is what we mean by a racial imaginary, an unlyrical term, but then its lack of music is fitting. One way to know you're in the presence of—in possession of, possessed by—a racial imaginary is to see if the boundaries of one's imaginative sympathy line up, again and again, with the lines drawn by power. [57]

While the laudable project of the racial imaginary is concerned about how *writers* interact with race and the imagination, here, I have been concerned about how *readers* as well as viewers and audiences do. How does reading the word and the world shape the imagination? We already know that the White reader imagination is vast and contains multitudes; it has been imagined and reimagined by generations of storytellers for centuries, and directly addressed whenever a speculative tale-spinner breaks the fourth wall, as in the Barrie example.

But what about the rest of our imaginations?

What about our fantasies?

What about our dreams?

What happens to the fantastic when the implied reader is White, but the *actual* reader is not? Can all points of view be taken into account in the waking dream of the fantastic? If, as Toni Morrison asserted, "the subject of the dream is the dreamer," what happens to dark subjectivities in a fantastic encounter? (As Kevin Young wrote: "Forget cosmopolitanism: let's explore the trapped Black mind as cosmos.")

And what happens if that encounter happens in childhood, as experiences great and small shape the maps in children's minds?

It is easy to dismiss this as terra incognita, as territory heretofore undiscovered. However, this has been the work of *generations* of Black women scholars, librarians, and teachers before me. From Augusta Baker and Charlamae Rollins nearly a century ago, to recent work by Rudine Sims Bishop, Dorothy Strickland, Violet Harris, Wanda Brooks, and Jonda McNair on Black children's literature, along with many others, there have always been those who have been concerned about what young people read, and how it shapes not only their development but also how they see and are seen in the world. From Rudine Sims Bishop:

> It is true, of course, that good literature reaches across cultural and ethnic borders to touch us all as humans. . . . However, for those children who historically had been ignored—or worse, ridiculed—in children's books, seeing themselves portrayed visually and textually as realistically human was essential to letting them know that they are valued in the social context in which they are growing up. Near invisibility suggested that books and literature, while often pleasurable, were in some sense apart from them. At the same time . . . children whose images were reflected in most American children's literature were being deprived of books as windows into the realities of the multicultural world in which they are living, and were in danger of developing a false sense of their own importance in the world.
>
> My assessment was that historically, children from parallel cultures had been offered mainly books as windows into lives that were different from their own, and children from the dominant culture had been offered mainly fiction that mirrored their own lives. All children need both.[58]

Bishop's metaphor of the mirrors, windows, and doors of children's literature also applies to what is necessary to reconcile dark fantastic crises in infinite storyworlds. Restorying fantastic traditions is one solution; an emancipatory dark fantastic is another.

What would that look like?

We already know.

It looks like the groundbreaking, singular vision of the late great Mac-Arthur genius Octavia Butler in novels from *Kindred* to *Dawn* and *The Parable of the Sower.*

It looks like the work of Sheree Renee Thomas in her landmark anthology, *Dark Matter*, Adrienne Maree Brown's *Octavia's Brood* a generation later, and Nisi Shawl's short stories in a field that, according to a 2016 Fireside Fiction report, almost completely excludes authors of color.[59]

It looks like the dreams of Black women poets from Maya Angelou to Alice Walker, from Gwendolyn Brooks to Nikki Giovanni, from Lucille Clifton to June Jordan, and from Sonia Sanchez to Ntozake Shange, who once said, "I write for young girls of color, for girls who don't even exist yet, so that there is something there for them when they arrive."[60]

It looks like Virginia Hamilton's fantastic tales and folklore being a harbinger for those who would follow, from Sherri L. Smith, to Alaya Dawn Johnson, to Zetta Elliott.

It looks like the Black Southern magical realism from Zora Neale Hurston to Tina McElroy Ansa and Jewell Parker Rhodes.

It looks like Black Atlantic and Caribbean fantastic traditions from Tananarive Due to Nalo Hopkinson, from Rosa Guy to Maryse Condé, and from Edwidge Danticat to Malorie Blackman.

It looks like the Hugo Award–winning fantastic dreams of N. K. Jemisin and Nnedi Okorafor.

It looks like the #BlackGirlMagic found in the lyrical contemporary realism of Jacqueline Woodson, Sharon Flake, Sharon Draper, Renee Watson, Nikki Grimes, Tanita S. Davis, Brandy Colbert, and all the authors of the Brown Bookshelf.

It looks like a rising generation of stars from Ibi Zoboi to Tracey Baptiste, Dhonielle Clayton to Tomi Adeyemi, Justina Ireland to L. L. McKinney, and so many other Black fantastic visions waiting in the wings.

It looks like Daija's generation of Black girls, and the generation after her, and the generation after that . . .

It looks like stories told and retold in the wake, dancing in Schrödinger's pernicious box, shapeshifting beyond the gaps of the collective imagination.

An emancipatory Black fantastic requires interrupting the dark fantastic cycle in order to create new paradigms. It requires mentoring diverse talent, actively acquiring new stories, and then moving toward culturally sustaining visions of editorship, marketing, reviewing, librarianship, book retailing, and literacy education. It requires publishing, Hollywood, education, libraries, and merchandising to acknowledge the ways that they have been complicit in reproducing the known world for every generation in the stories that we tell our children, teens, and young adults.

But, ultimately, emancipating the dark fantastic requires decolonizing our fantasies and our dreams. It means liberating magic itself. For resolving the crisis of race in our storied imagination has the potential to make our world anew.

ACKNOWLEDGMENTS

What an incredible journey *The Dark Fantastic* has been from start to finish! Here are some of the people who made this book possible.

Series editors Henry Jenkins and Karen Tongson believed in *The Dark Fantastic* from my first incredibly lengthy email pitch in March 2014. I am so thrilled to be part of their Postmillennial Pop series, and to join conversations about diversity in media within and beyond literacy education. I would also like to thank press director Ellen Chodosh for her belief in this project's potential, editor-in-chief Eric Zinner for his brilliance and vision, acquisitions editor Lisha Nadkarni for her patience and grace in shepherding a scholar from an "article field" through the process, as well as Dolma Ombadykow, Alexia Traganas, Sarah Bode, adam b. bohannon, Charles B. Hames, and the rest of the NYU Press team for getting me over the finish line. And I am *beyond* thrilled to have the extraordinary art of Paul Lewin grace my cover—"The Tree Spirits" is akin to the fantastic dreams of my childhood!

Black women scholars of children's and young adult literature inspired and encouraged this labor of love, both in word and deed: Michelle H. Martin, Dianne Johnson-Feelings, Cynthia Tyson, Violet Harris, Jonda McNair, Wanda Brooks, KaaVonia Hinton, Cheryl Willis Hudson (along with her husband, Just Us Books co-founder Wade), Nancy Toldson, Detra Price-Dennis, Sybil Durand, Vanessa Irvin, Kafi Kumasi, and Stephanie Toliver. I am proud to be within this sister circle, and hope to continue to build together in the years to come. I also send my love to authors and illustrators of children's and young adult literature, as well as my academic colleagues, especially those whose life's calling is focused on Black children, teens, and young adults both here in the United States and around the world. In lieu of a long list of names, I have cited and acknowledged your good works throughout the pages of this book.

When I first decided to write *The Dark Fantastic* before tenure in a field where monographs from junior faculty are discouraged, I knew I was taking a risk. At the University of Pennsylvania Graduate School of Education (Penn GSE), my mentor Vivian Gadsden and chair Gerald Campano supported me every step of the way. Amy Stornaiuolo has been an amazing writing and research collaborator, and Diane Waff's connections were essential during my move from Detroit to Philadelphia. And Lorraine Hightower, Penny Creedon, and Paula Rogers keep our Reading/Writing/Literacy program humming right along. Truly, all of them have become like family.

Penn GSE Dean Pam Grossman and former Literacy, Culture, and International Education Division Chair Kathleen Hall both deserve special note—as does former Penn GSE Dean Andrew Porter, who encouraged me to apply for the National Academy of Education/Spencer Postdoctoral Fellowship in the fall of 2013. My 2014–2015 fellowship provided time and funding for me not only to conduct empirical research on reader responses to slavery in children's literature, but also to begin drafting *The Dark Fantastic*.

Although dozens among the Penn GSE faculty, staff, and students encouraged me throughout the writing of *The Dark Fantastic*, the one person who travailed with me, persisting through its many drafts, and patiently providing her wisdom, expertise, and good humor, was our GSE editor (and fellow Michigander!), Jennifer Moore. There just aren't enough words to thank her for everything she's done to assist with the process from start to finish.

Philip Nel and Karin Westman have mentored me since the time they approached me at Nimbus–2003 and asked, "Ever thought about becoming a professor?" Phil, Farah Mendlesohn, and Katharine Capshaw read my first drafts of the proposal, and then read *subsequent* drafts of this book, giving me substantive feedback. Robin Bernstein and Heather Love provided valuable advice about publication, encouraging me to think broadly about potential audiences for my work. David Low and Nora Peterman read and gave feedback on the earliest drafts of the proposal, and Kinitra Brooks, Andre Carrington, Crystal Fleming, and Sarah Hamburg suggested resources that greatly enriched my theory.

Deborah Roberts, Karin Westman, Anne Jamison, Julia Mickenberg, Stephanie Toliver, and Maya West invited me to present my dark fantastic cycle at Haverford College, Kansas State University, the University of Utah, the University of Texas at Austin, the University of Georgia, and the University of Michigan, respectively. The opportunity to present on this topic to academic audiences around the country helped me refine my ideas, and led to an article in the University of Georgia's *Journal of Language and Literacy Education* (JoLLE), edited by Peter Smagorinsky and his students. Special acknowledgment must be given to the Children's Literature Association (ChLA) and the now-defunct Rutgers Child_Lit listserv, and all their many members. Flourish Klink and Elizabeth Minkel's *Fansplaining* podcast connected me to the burgeoning acafan community inside and outside of academia.

My academic BFF, Kya Mangrum, listened to me when *The Dark Fantastic* was barely an idea. She continues to challenge me, both intellectually and ethically, and has shaped me into a better scholar and writer. Some friends are for a reason, a season, or an entire lifetime—Kya has proven to be the latter kind since our doctoral student days at the University of Michigan.

Speaking of friends, where would I have been without my fandom friendships? Of the many I've gotten to know over the years, Heidi Tandy, Clare Worley, and Josh Aronovitch have been the ones who've stuck with me through thick and thin, transcending our youthful infatuation with J. K. Rowling's wizarding world. There are so many others—especially the original crew of the Harry Potter for Grownups Yahoo! Group—as well as those from dozens of other fandoms and conventions. (You know who you are!) Librarians Kathleen T. Horning of the University of Wisconsin's Cooperative Children's Book Center, and Deborah Taylor, newly retired from Baltimore's Enoch Pratt library, also deserve mention for their tireless work on diversity in children's books over many decades, and their unfailing support, as do the librarians of my childhood at the Detroit Public Library. Finally, sending all my love to three special Philadelphia spaces for diverse geek community—Amalgam Comics and Coffeehouse (Ariell Johnson), Uncle Bobbie's Coffee and Books (Marc Lamont Hill), and the East Coast Black Age of Comics Convention – as well as the Source Booksellers (Janet Jones) in Detroit, where I meet my sage friends Gloria Mills and Dale Rich every time I visit home.

Engaging on social media has helped me become a better writer. When I first began using my @Ebonyteach account on a daily basis in the winter of 2014, I had only a few hundred followers; today, I follow over 3,500 accounts and have more than 20,000 followers. There are so many whom I could name, but some of the most important during the writing of this book have been the #DiversityJedi collective of authors, critics, educators, and librarians (Debbie Reese, Zetta Elliott, Edith "Edi" Campbell, Sarah Park Dahlen, Jennifer Baker, Sarah Hamburg, Sarah Hannah Gomez, Deborah Menkart, Laura Jimenez, Sarah McCarry, Kristin McIlhagga, Alia Jones, Marilisa Jimenez Garcia, Anne Ursu, Cynthia Leitich Smith, so many others) and Black feminist Twitter (I'Nasah Crockett, Trudy of Gradient Lair, Mikki Kendall, Sydette Harry, Mariame Kaba, Eve Ewing, many others). During my bleakest moments, all I'd have to do is log on and get lifted by my sisters in virtual spaces. I am ever grateful.

My students past and present, near and far, also make my work possible. Besides the early encouragement I received from my former students Nora Peterman and David Low, this book wouldn't have been possible without my graduate student assistants James Joshua Coleman, Jacqueline Dawson, Sherea Mosley, and Christopher Rogers, as well as my @HealingFictions social media managers, Kanitra Alston, Amy Brown, and Rabani Garg. The gift that they provide is time for me to write, revise, and edit, in exchange for a mentor who can be like trying to catch a Bandersnatch! I'd like to also give a special shout to another former student, Rebecca Kuss, who encouraged me not to give up on my dreams of publishing my fiction—and introduced me to my agent, Brooks Sherman.

Saving the best for last, this book is especially for my family of origin—a deeply rooted, ever-growing tree that I am thankful for. Since the 2012 passing of my grandmother Elizabeth and her sister Naomi one year later, my beautiful mother, Susan Caldwell, has become our family matriarch, and the person whose words open this book. My sisters, Danielle Carter and Lorri "Lady L" Thomas, are my forever friends, as is the best brother-in-law on the planet, Alexzander Carter.

When I first attempted the transition from fanfiction to original stories, I dreamed about dedicating my first book for children to my eldest niece and nephew, who were then toddlers. Now, there are six—Jalen, Daija, Alexzis, Kellen, Danielle, and Dylon. My cousins also have children of their own, and I am reminded of the wisdom of Mildred Taylor, author of *Roll of Thunder, Hear My Cry*: "Let the circle be unbroken."

While this isn't the kind of book that I thought I'd write when I first set pen to paper, I trust that *The Dark Fantastic*, and other books like it, will provide insight into the struggle for more and better representation in all our imaginative worlds.

As always, everything I do is for the love of my God, my family, and my city – #ThomasGirlsRock, I'll always be a Detroiter, and I'll always adore the One who sent me on this journey—the One who loves us all. This has been such a strange and unexpected trip so far, but I thank God for my travels *and* my travails on this scenic route . . . always.

NOTES

INTRODUCTION

1 Here and throughout *The Dark Fantastic*, I use the terms "Black" and "African American" interchangeably to refer to the racial/ethnic group from which I hail—that is, the descendants of West and Central African peoples who were captured, sold, enslaved in the British colonies and then in the United States prior to the Civil War. In the United States, "Black" predominates in intracommunity usage, and is experiencing a resurgence in criticism, journalism, and popular culture. I also acknowledge that Native, Indigenous, First Nations, and Alaska Native nations and peoples were the original inhabitants of this continent, and that the Americas extend from the Aleutian Islands to Tierra del Fuego, although as of this writing, "American," a contested name, is still in broad academic and general usage.

2 I acknowledge that there is a gender spectrum and that myriad pronouns exist. Here and throughout *The Dark Fantastic*, I use pronouns that correspond with the pronouns that individuals use to refer to themselves. For fictional characters, I use pronouns that are used by each character's creators, while acknowledging that audiences may read and/or refer to these characters differently than I do.

3 Riggs, *Ethnic Notions*.

4 Jenkins, *Convergence Culture*, 21.

5 Thompson, "I'm So Totally, Digitally Close to You."

6 Gee and Hayes, *Language and Learning in the Digital Age*; danah boyd, "Why Youth ♥ Social Network Sites," 119–142.

7 Jenkins and Ford, *Spreadable Media*, 7.

8 Adichie, "The Danger of a Single Story."

9 Walter Dean Myers, "Where Are the People of Color in Children's Books?" See also Christopher Myers, "The Apartheid of Children's Literature."

10 Cooperative Children's Book Center, A Few Observations on Publishing in 2013.

11 We Need Diverse Books, "About WNDB." BookCon is an annual fan convention established by ReedPOP in 2014. It seeks to combine popular culture with the publishing industry. It was founded to support BookExpo America, the most important book trade fair in the United States.

12 Some of the notable voices in children's and young adult publishing that amplified the efforts of authors Ellen Oh and Aisha Saeed during the initial #WeNeedDiverseBooks campaign include Jason Low, founder and CEO of the multicultural publisher Lee and Low Books, Stacy Whitman, publisher and editorial director

of the diverse science fiction and fantasy imprint Tu Books, independent scholar Debbie Reese of American Indians in Children's Literature, librarian Edith Campbell, and booksellers Wade and Cheryl Hudson of Just Us Books.

13 Schoenberg, "Slavery in Children's Books."

14 For an excellent treatment of the history of racism in children's literatures and cultures in the United States, see MacCann, *White Supremacy in Children's Literature*. See also Bradford, *Reading Race*; McGillis, *Voices of the Other*; and Forest, Garrison, and Kimmel, "'The University for the Poor.'"

15 Cooperative Children's Book Center, "A Few Observations on Publishing in 2013."

16 Older, "Diversity Is Not Enough."

17 Elliott, "Decolonizing the Imagination."

18 For critiques of the educational achievement gap that highlight gaps between diverse students, see Irvine, *Educating Teachers for Diversity*; Ladson-Billings, "From the Achievement Gap to the Education Debt"; and Milner, "Rethinking Achievement Gap Talk in Urban Education."

19 Thomas, "The Imagination Gap in #Kidlit and #YAlit."

20 Bishop, "Mirrors, Windows, and Sliding Glass Doors"; Adichie, "The Danger of a Single Story."

21 Lee and Low Books, "Why Hasn't the Number of Multicultural Books Increased In Eighteen Years?."

22 Holmes, "White until Proven Black."

23 James and St. John, "Why The Vampire Diaries' Treatment of Bonnie Bennett—and Her Fans—Bites."

24 Eddo-Lodge, "Call Out Culture."

25 Reese, "Patricia Wrede's Thinking as She Wrote The Thirteenth Child." Shapiro, "Can You Revise a Novel to Make It More Woke?"

26 Stephens, "Between Imagined Signs and Social Realities"; Attebery, *Stories about Stories*, 169–185; Nevins, "The Black Fantastic."

27 Key titles on Afrofuturism, Black comics, and Black speculative fiction published between 2000 and 2014 include Brown, *Black Superheroes*; Howard and Jackson, *Black Comics*, which won the 2015 Eisner Award at Comic-Con International; Jackson and Moody-Freeman, *The Black Imagination*; and Womack, *Afrofuturism*.

28 See also Brooks, *Searching for Sycorax*; Commander, *Afro-Atlantic Flight*; Howard and Jackson, *Black Comics*; Mafe, *Where No Black Woman Has Gone Before*; and Schalk, *Bodyminds Reimagined*.

29 Young, *Race and Popular Fantasy Literature*.

30 Solórzano and Yosso, "Critical Race Methodology."

31 Cook and Dixson, "Writing Critical Race Theory and Method."

32 Wright, *Physics of Blackness*.

33 Hellekson and Busse, *Fan Fiction and Fan Communities in the Age of the Internet*, 24–25.

CHAPTER 1. TOWARD A THEORY OF THE DARK FANTASTIC

1 Morrison, *Playing in the Dark*, 9.

2 "Shipping," short for "relationshipping," is the fan culture practice of advocating for two characters in a fictional narrative to engage in a romantic relationship. The term first appeared in the *X-Files* fandom, and was used to describe advocates of a relationship between male and female leads Fox Mulder and Dana Scully. Shipping is often the source of the greatest fan devotion—as well as the root cause of the greatest level of discord and conflict. (For more information on this phenomenon, I recommend the articles on shipping at TVTropes.com.)

3 An important recent account of Black American fantastic longing for Brazil—specifically Bahia—can be found in Commander, *Afro-Atlantic Flight*, chap. 3, "We Love to be Africans: Saudade and Affective Performances in Bahia, Brazil."

4 Macunaima, "Why Myth-Making Is Dangerous for Subordinate Peoples"; my emphasis.

5 In response to an early draft of this chapter, children's literature scholar Katharine Capshaw made a fascinating observation in a personal communication: "This version of African American children's literature has been facilitated by the educational system and big corporate publishing. That is to say, there are black-authored children's texts that employ poetry, for instance, and are experimental—those are not the ones that get taught in schools or sold by Scholastic. The texts by canonical writers like Virginia Hamilton that stay in print are not the experimental *Arilla Sun Down*, for instance, or *Sweet Whispers, Brother Rush*, which involves history but its mode is fantastic—it's a ghost story."

6 Attebery, *Stories About Stories*, 9.

7 Mendlesohn, *Rhetorics of Fantasy*.

8 Todorov, *The Fantastic*, 25.

9 Adichie, "The Danger of a Single Story."

10 African American scholars and thinkers have been noting similar issues around reader identification in Black children's culture since at least the early 1970s. Those studying girls' reading practices have noted this as well. See, for example, Blackford, *Out of This World*.

11 Christopoulos, Karakantza, and Levaniouk, *Light and Darkness in Ancient Greek Myth and Religion*. See also Guerlac, "Can There Be Colors in the Dark?"

12 Painter, *The History of White People*.

13 When I first began to theorize the role of darkness and Dark Others in fantasy, I asked colleagues and mentors for critical antecedents to inform my work. Children's literature scholars and educational researchers are among some of the most generous faculty in the academy, and soon many different titles poured into my mailbox. I immediately began immersing myself in the critical work of Maria Nikolajeva, Farah Mendlesohn, Brian Attebery, and others. I also returned to Todorov, whose volume on the fantastic I first encountered as a graduate student. Toward the end of this journey through theory, friends on social media men-

tioned work on color theory and monster theory, authored primarily by medievalists. Through this process, I became ever more convinced that the origins of endarkened Otherness predate the modern world.

14 Cohen, "Monster Culture: Seven Theses," 4.

15 Cohen, "Monster Culture," 5.

16 Gates, *The Signifying Monkey*. See also Lee, "Signifying as a Scaffold."

17 Cohen, "Monster Culture," 6.

18 Cohen, "Monster Culture," 7.

19 Cohen, "Monster Culture," 12.

20 Cohen, "Monster Culture," 16–17.

21 Cohen, "Monster Culture," 20.

22 Cohen, "Monster Culture," 20. As Kevin Young notes: "Forget cosmopolitanism: let's explore the trapped Black mind as a cosmos."

23 Elizabeth Young suggested the metaphor of the monster as a means to recast the study of race in United States literature and culture. "The black Frankenstein monster also converges, at moments, with other politicized monster figures, including the many-headed hydra, the golem, King Kong, and Caliban" (*Black Frankenstein*, 13).

24 Young, *The Grey Album*, 11.

25 My reference to marble halls is intentional. "I Dreamt I Dwelt in Marble Halls," the nostalgic aria from the nineteenth-century opera *The Bohemian Girl*, was covered by Irish singer Enya for the 1993 Martin Scorsese adaptation of Edith Wharton's *The Age of Innocence* (1920). Enya was also the voice of soundtrack for the Peter Jackson adaptation of *The Lord of the Rings* movies. However, "Marble Halls" had a number of blackface parodies in the nineteenth century, including "I Dreamt I Dwelt in Hotel Halls," complete with racial slurs and offensive language. See Mahar, *Behind the Burnt Cork Mask*.

26 Brooks, *Bodies in Dissent*; Whitted, "'And the Negro Thinks in Hieroglyphics.'"

27 Kendi, *Stamped from the Beginning*; Hall, "The Spectacle of the Other."

28 Hall, *Representation*, 263; emphasis in the original.

29 Ricoeur, *Memory, History, Forgetting*.

30 McClintock, *Imperial Leather*; Young, *Colonial Desire*.

31 Alexander, *The New Jim Crow*; Carby, *Race Men*; Roberts, *Killing the Black Body*.

32 Morrison, *Playing in the Dark*, 6.

33 Morrison, *Playing in the Dark*, 38.

34 Said, *Culture and Imperialism* (New York: Knopf, 1993), 69.

35 Morrison, *Playing in the Dark*, 9.

36 Xie, "Rethinking the Identity of Cultural Otherness," 13.

37 Morrison, *Playing in the Dark*, 9–10; my emphasis.

38 Pollock, *Colormute*.

39 It should be noted that there are decolonial counter-traditions within science fiction. See, for example, Cashbaugh, "A Paradoxical, Discrepant, and Mutant Marxism." However, by far the most popular narratives are those that center

on invasion and conquest and that position space as a "frontier" that humanity should explore and settle as if by divine decree.

40 Rieder, *Colonialism and the Emergence of Science Fiction*.

41 Bould and Vint, "Political Readings," 103.

42 Bould and Vint, "Political Readings," 106.

43 Jenkins, *Textual Poachers*, xxix; emphasis mine.

44 Xie, "Rethinking the Identity of Cultural Otherness," 13.

45 Digital activist CaShawn Thompson (@thepbg on Twitter) founded the hashtag #BlackGirlMagic in 2013, a shortened version of the saying "Black girls are magic." Thompson's idea for the tag resonates with my own experiences: "As a kid, I was really introverted and I loved fairytales. I had a big imagination and all these magical ideas that weren't rooted in reality, and when I saw the women in my family running businesses, raising families, making a way out of no way, to me as a little girl it just seemed like magic. As a child, I literally thought that black women were magic, so when I put it out there, it wasn't a new concept for me but I'm glad it resonated with other black women and girls" (Ebony F., "As Black Girl Magic Turns Four Years Old").

46 Sealey-Ruiz, "Editorial: Why Black Girls' Literacies Matter."

47 Muhammad and Haddix, "Centering Black Girls' Literacies," 301. Other important scholars working in the burgeoning field of Black girlhood studies are Ruth Nicole Brown, Aimee Meredith Cox, Bettina Love, and Monique W. Morris.

CHAPTER 2. LAMENTATIONS OF A MOCKINGJAY

1 Fisher, "Precarious Dystopias."

2 For more about racial unrest in twentieth-century Detroit, I highly recommend Sugrue, *The Origins of the Urban Crisis*.

3 Since 1967, there have been frequent references in popular culture to Detroit as post-American and/or postapocalyptic—for instance, in *RoboCop*. An essay that looks at the life and death of Detroit over its three centuries of existence as an odd liminal space within the United States is Herron's "Detroit Borderama."

4 Gay, "What We Hunger For."

5 Patterson, *Slavery and Social Death*; Hunter, "The Persistent Problem of Colorism."

6 Clawson and Trice, "Poverty as We Know It."

7 Although I read *The Hunger Games* several times before seeing the first movie in March 2012, it is likely that I transferred Collins's description of the first Avox that Katniss meets to Cinna, who is definitely described as having brown hair.

8 "Named for the Zulu and Xhosa word for 'power,' Amandla [Stenberg] was born in Los Angeles, California, to Karen Brailsford, a writer, and Tom Stenberg, a businessman. Her mother is African American and her father is Danish (and of part Inuit-Greenlandic ancestry)" (Brailsford, "Amandla Stenberg").

9 The casting of Oladayo A. "Dayo" Okeniyi as Thresh, as well as rock star Lenny Kravitz as Cinna, was also noted as problematic by fans. However, Amandla

Stenberg's character, Rue, received by far the most screen time in the first *Hunger Games* movie, and received the brunt of the hate.

10 Thomas, "The Pleasures of Dreaming."

11 Rieder, *Colonialism and the Emergence of Science Fiction.*

12 A magical Negro is a character written solely to assist White protagonists resolve conflict and reach their goals in a story. See Hughey, "Cinethetic Racism"; Glenn and Cunningham, "The Power of Black Magic."

13 Collins, *The Hunger Games*, 8.

14 Dubrofsky and Ryalls, "*The Hunger Games*."

15 Collins, *The Hunger Games*, 8.

16 Collins, *The Hunger Games*, 12.

17 Collins, *The Hunger Games*, 22–23.

18 Collins, *The Hunger Games*, 25.

19 Collins, *The Hunger Games*, 25.

20 Bernstein, *Racial Innocence*, 7.

21 Collins, *The Hunger Games*, 41.

22 Collins, *The Hunger Games*, 74.

23 Dubrofsky and Ryalls, "*The Hunger Games*," 396.

24 Dubrofsky and Ryalls, "*The Hunger Games*," 403.

25 Although fan responses in the real world are examined later in this chapter, here I would like to note the role of authenticity in the intersections between televised state violence and the neoliberal imperative of using visual technologies to market the body (in this case, through becoming a contestant on reality TV), both phenomena that *The Hunger Games* were explicitly designed to provide commentary upon.

26 Collins, *The Hunger Games*, 44–45.

27 Dubrofsky and Ryalls, "*The Hunger Games*," 396.

28 Morrison, *Playing in the Dark*, 5.

29 Lea, "To Kill a Mockingjay?"

30 I would like to acknowledge contemporaneous work done by my colleagues Antero Garcia and Marcelle Haddix in identifying Rue as the true heroine of the series in their "The Revolution Starts with Rue" "Reading YA with 'Dark Brown Skin.'"

31 Lee, *To Kill a Mockingbird.*

32 Collins, *The Hunger Games*, 42–43.

33 It is notable that Collins's mockingjay is also part jabberjay, which brings to mind blue jays, which are native to North America. In myths of the Chinook people, the blue jay is a trickster figure. According to the Cornell Lab of Ornithology: "Thousands of Blue Jays migrate in flocks along the Great Lakes and Atlantic coasts, but much about their migration remains a mystery. . . . No one has worked out why they migrate when they do" ("Blue Jay: Life History," *All About Birds*, www. allaboutbirds.org). Therefore, it is perhaps unsurprising that a jabberjay would

subvert its original purpose of "jabbering" surveillance of the Capitol and begin "jabbering" songs of freedom.

34 Collins, *The Hunger Games*, 38.

35 Collins, *The Hunger Games*, 42.

36 Collins, *The Hunger Games*, 42.

37 Although call and response is found in music and storytelling in cultures from around the world, in the United States it is a central feature of African American music, religious worship, and discourse. Call and response is thus associated with both the catharsis of music and the endurance of the oppressed.

38 Collins, *The Hunger Games*, 45–46.

39 Collins, *The Hunger Games*, 69.

40 Collins, *The Hunger Games*, 74.

41 Collins, *The Hunger Games*, 98.

42 Collins, *The Hunger Games*, 98–99.

43 Collins, *The Hunger Games*, 98–99.

44 Rue is referred to in Luke 11:42: "But woe unto you, Pharisees! For ye tithe mint and rue and all manner of herbs." The herb has been used in the traditional cuisine of Ethiopia for thousands of years.

45 The original chorus of "The Yellow Rose of Texas" (found at http://www.sonsofdewittcolony.org/), which has been changed for modern sensibilities, reveals West's association with flowers and beauty despite her status as "mulatto" and "colored":
    She's the sweetest rose of color this darky ever knew,
    Her eyes are bright as diamonds, they sparkle like the dew,
    You may talk about your Dearest May and sing of Rosa Lee,
    But the yellow rose of Texas beats the belles of Tennessee.

46 Collins, *The Hunger Games*, 99.

47 Collins, *The Hunger Games*, 99.

48 Collins, *The Hunger Games*, 108.

49 Collins, *The Hunger Game*, 126.

50 Throughout the first book, Thresh provides the perfect, if stereotypical, foil for Rue: he is described as "strong, sullen and silent." He appears far less than Rue does, which (as I mention in chapter 2) is a pattern I have found throughout mainstream young adult fantasy and science fiction. It is notable that while Rue's place in the narrative supports Katniss's story, Thresh is clearly positioned to add depth to Rue, as all of his appearances outside of those with all the tributes are related to her. Katniss, for her part, thinks that if she were Thresh's size, she could "get away with sullen and hostile and it would be just fine!," which, in light of the historic and contemporary treatment of Black men in the United States, is problematic—especially since Katniss lives and Thresh does not. See also Dubrofsky and Ryalls, "The Hunger Games," 402.

51 Collins, *The Hunger Games*, 145.

52 Collins, *The Hunger Games*, 157, 159.

53 Collins, *The Hunger Games*, 183–184.

54 It can be argued that Katniss's altruism toward Rue is actually *sparked* by Rue's choice to save her life:

> I call Rue's name in a hushed whisper and the eyes appear, wide and alert, at once. She points up to the nest again. I hold up my knife and make a sawing motion. She nods and disappears. There's a rustling in a nearby tree. Then the same noise again a bit father off. I realize she's leaping from tree to tree. It's all I can do not to laugh out loud . . . I imagine her flying around the training equipment never touching the floor. (Collins, *The Hunger Games*, 185)

55 Hamilton, *The People Could Fly*.

56 Collins, *The Hunger Games*, 185.

57 Collins, *The Hunger Games*, 199–202.

58 Collins, *The Hunger Games*, 200.

59 Collins, *The Hunger Games*, 202–203.

60 Collins, *The Hunger Games*, 204–205.

61 Collins, *The Hunger Games*, 200–201. Left untreated, the tracker jacker stings would have eventually killed Katniss, as they did another tribute.

62 Collins, *The Hunger Games*, 200–201.

63 Collins, *The Hunger Games*, 211–212.

64 Isaiah 40:6 (King James Version).

65 Collins, *The Hunger Games*, 236.

66 Another conflation between girl characters and birds can be found in the 1911 version of J. M. Barrie's classic *Peter Pan* (http://etc.usf.edu/):

> "You are too late," he cried proudly, "I have shot the Wendy. Peter will be so pleased with me."
>
> "This is no bird," he said in a scared voice. "I think this must be a lady." "A lady?" said Tootles, and fell a-trembling.
>
> "And we have killed her," Nibs said hoarsely . . . "A lady to take care of us at last," said one of the twins, "and you have killed her!"
>
> "She is dead," he said uncomfortably. "Perhaps she is frightened at being dead."

67 Collins, *The Hunger Games*, 231–232.

68 Collins, *The Hunger Games*, 233.

69 Collins, *The Hunger Games*, 233.

70 Torkelson, "Somewhere between Hair Ribbons and Rainbows."

71 Ringlestein, "Real or Not Real," 382.

72 Dubrofsky and Ryalls, "*The Hunger Games*," 402; my emphasis.

73 Sharpe, *In the Wake*, 80.

74 A recent digital humanities study of the genre disparities in African American children's literature can be found in Nel, *Was the Cat in the Hat Black?*, 167–201.

75 Bernstein, *Racial Innocence*, 4.

76 Bernstein, *Racial Innocence*, 16.

77 Nel, "Was the Cat in the Hat Black?"

78 DiAngelo and Sensoy, "Getting Slammed."
79 Leonardo and Porter, "Pedagogy of Fear"; Dumas, "'Losing an Arm'"; Anagnosto-poulos, Everett, and Carey, "'Of Course We're Supposed to Move On.'"
80 In the first edition of *The Hunger Games*, Katniss thinks to herself that she needs to kill Rue's murderer on page 243. She finds Peeta on page 244, and from that point on, mentions of Rue become utilitarian rather than personal:

   p. 254 "I've got two water bottles and Rue's water skin"

   p. 258 "the camp Rue and I made"

   p. 263 "I came upon a bush of Rue's berries"

   p. 267 "I mince groosling until it's practically mush and mash some of Rue's roots."

   p. 267 In reference to Thresh, the other District 11 tribute not needing the food stores at the Cornucopia: "I've got a feeling he must share some of Rue's knowledge on how to feed yourself from the earth."

   Thus, Rue has moved from being associated with *innocence* in Katniss's story to being associated with the protagonist's *survival*. Rue's removal from the Games has emotional resonance only if the tale is focalized through Katniss's point of view. From a critical counterstorytelling perspective, Rue dies so that Katniss can live.
81 Collins, *The Hunger Games*, 285–286.
82 Collins, *The Hunger Games*, 293.
83 Collins, *The Hunger Games*, 304.
84 Here is a link to all the mentions of Rue in *Catching Fire* (retrieved July 1, 2015): https://books.google.com/books?id=FN5wMOZKTYMC&printsec=frontcover&dq=catching+fire&hl=en&sa=X&ei=kXQ5Vf6OK_P9sATE8IGoBA&ved=0CB4Q6AEwAA#v=onepage&q=Rue&f=false.
85 Here is a link to all the mentions of Katniss in *Mockingjay* (retrieved July 1, 2015): https://books.google.com/books?id=Iw_gHtk4ghYC&printsec=frontcover&dq=mockingjay&hl=en&sa=X&ei=HHU5VfO9DouosASeh4HIDg&ved=0CB4Q6AEwAA#v=onepage&q=Rue&f=false.
86 Losen et al., *Are We Closing the School Discipline Gap?*. See also Alexander, *The New Jim Crow*.
87 Brown's "For Tamir, Who Was Stolen" is an evocative, lyrical elegy for twelve-year-old Tamir Rice, slain by police in 2014 for playing with a toy gun in a public park.
88 Myers, "The Apartheid of Children's Literature"; Aronson, "Guest Post"; xojane, "Are Black People Really Not Relatable?"
89 Brewster, "She Has No Idea," does a fine job of demonstrating the way that Collins uses conventions of the young adult genre to create reader sympathy and engagement with Katniss (as well as the ethical dilemmas elided in the process).
90 Bishop, "Mirrors, Windows, and Sliding Glass Doors."
91 Bernstein, *Racial Innocence*.
92 Morrison, *Playing in the Dark*, 9–10.
93 Morrison, *Playing in the Dark*, 38.

94 Stewart, "Racist *Hunger Games* Fans Are Very Disappointed." Stewart quotes from the actual tweets, as did an article in *Business Insider* that I quoted in "Asieybarbie's 'I Am Beautiful' Campaign and Sleepy Hollow's Orlando Jones." As a veteran of fandom myself, I prefer to keep the discourse anonymous, since it does not paint these fans in a positive light, and they may have changed their positions since they first reacted to the sight of Amandla Stenberg as Rue.

95 Stewart, "Racist *Hunger Games* Fans Are Very Disappointed."

96 Stewart, "Racist *Hunger Games* Fans Are Very Disappointed."

97 See xojane, "Are Black People Really Not Relatable?"

98 Garcia and Haddix, "The Revolution Starts with Rue."

99 prismatic-bell, "Can We Just Stop and Talk about This for a Minute?"; emphasis in the original.

100 Hamilton, *The People Could Fly.*

101 The final line of Dunbar, "Sympathy," is, "I know why the caged bird sings!"

102 Maya Angelou, *I Know Why the Caged Bird Sings* (New York: Random House, 1969).

103 Billy Taylor, "I Wish I Knew How It Would Feel to Be Free," as famously sung by Nina Simone on her 1967 album *Silk & Soul.*

104 An explanation of the Sankofa bird and concept can be found at "Sankofa: Sankofa Is the Official Black Student Union of UIS," University of Illinois, Springfield, http://www.uis.edu/africanamericanstudies (retrieved October 29, 2018).

105 Leonardo and Porter, "Pedagogy of Fear."

CHAPTER 3. A QUEEN OUT OF PLACE

1 Mendlesohn, *Rhetorics of Fantasy.*

2 Bunny DeBarge's "A Dream" has been sampled fifteen times and covered once. See http://www.whosampled.com/DeBarge/A-Dream/sampled (retrieved October 29, 2018). Beyond her cover of "Time Will Reveal" from DeBarge's *In a Special Way*, the music and imagination of Janelle Monae is also worthy of further study by those interested in theorizing Black characters in fantasy and fairy tales. The persona Janelle has developed across all her studio albums, Cindi Mayweather, is a Black queer feminist posthuman reading of the Cinderella story (English and Kim, "Now We Want Our Funk Cut").

3 Christgau, "Consumer Guide."

4 Funes, "Merlin Conjures Up Camelot."

5 Christopoulos, Karakantza, and Levaniouk, *Light and Darkness in Ancient Greek Myth and Religion. Greek Studies*; Guerlac, "Can There Be Colors in the Dark?"

6 Painter, *The History of White People.*

7 Tolkien, "On Fairy-Stories."

8 Card, *How to Write Science Fiction & Fantasy.*

9 Todorov, *The Fantastic*, 25.

10 Benton, *Secondary Worlds*, 23.

11 Bhabha, *The Location of Culture*, 2.
12 Gutiérrez, "Developing a Sociocritical Literacy in the Third Space."
13 Totlis, "The Dream as Space, Time and Emotion."
14 Elliott, "Decolonizing the Imagination."
15 Brand, *A Map to the Door of No Return.*
16 Commander, *Afro-Atlantic Flight*, 5. Cynthia B. Dillard also considers the challenges and the promise of African Diasporic return and remembering, asking, "How do racial/cultural memories make demands on [our] present projects?" ("Re-Membering Culture").
17 Tolkien, *The Silmarillion.*
18 Young, *Race and Popular Fantasy Literature.*
19 Tolkien, "Letter to Milton Waldman [1951]."
20 Wright, *Physics of Blackness.*
21 Kris Swank, "Black and Liminal in Camelot."
22 Bradford, *The Middle Ages in Children's Literature*, 7.
23 Britton, "From the *Knight's Tale* to *The Two Noble Kinsmen*," 65.
24 Loomba, *Shakespeare, Race, and Colonialism.* See also refer to Burton and Loomba, *Race in Early Modern England.*
25 Britton, "From the *Knight's Tale* to *The Two Noble Kinsmen*," 68.
26 Heng, *Empire of Magic*, 68.
27 Cohen and Steel, "Race, Travel, Time, Heritage," 103.
28 Jones, "The Dragon's Call," aired September 20, 2008 (BBC).
29 Fulton, "A Woman's Place."
30 The first two of the four books in the Chrysalis Queen quartet have been published to date: Nancy McKenzie, *Guineveres' Gift* (New York: Knopf Books for Young Readers, 2008), and Nancy McKenzie, *Guineveres' Gamble* (New York: Knopf Books for Young Readers, 2009). The animated series *Princess Gwenevere and the Jewel Riders* (created by Robert Mandell for Bohbot Entertainment) ran September 9, 1995–December 12, 1996 (syndication).
31 Bradford, "Uncovering Hidden Black History."
32 Snead and MacCabe, *White Screens, Black Images.*
33 Jones, "The Mark of Nimueh," aired October 4, 2008 (BBC).
34 Jones, "The Mark of Nimueh."
35 Michie, "To Kill the King," aired December 6, 2008 (BBC).
36 Jones, "Le Morte d'Arthur," aired December 13, 2008 (BBC).
37 Overman, "The Once and Future Queen," aired September 26, 2009 (BBC).
38 Overman, "The Once and Future Queen."
39 Overman, "The Once and Future Queen."
40 Overman, "Lancelot and Guinevere," aired October 10, 2009 (BBC).
41 Watkins, "Lancelot du Lac," aired November 26, 2011 (BBC).
42 Michie (part 1) and Jones (part 2), "The Sword in the Stone," December 17 and 24, 2011 (BBC).

43 Actress Angel Coulby, in an interview with the *Los Angeles Times*, stated that the famous love triangle between Lancelot, Guinevere, and Arthur would not have been appropriate for a family show:

> The audience is a family audience, and obviously there are a lot of other storylines within the original legend that probably wouldn't have been appropriate for our show. There's all sorts of stuff, incest and all sorts of things which wouldn't have gone down well with a family audience. So I think they did pretty well to factor in all the important points. Like the Arthur, Gwen and Lancelot love triangle—that could have been the death of the relationship between Arthur and Gwen, but instead they put a twist on it that made it possible for us to sort of carry on the series and for us get to the end point that they'd always planned. . . . Although I kind of like the stories, so I think right now is maybe the time to start reading the books. ("'Merlin'")

44 Jones, "The Dark Tower," aired November 10, 2012 (BBC).

45 The "Dark Tower" is a well-known location throughout fantastic literature. In the *Lord of the Rings* trilogy, Tolkien used the title *The Two Towers* "since the events recounted in it are dominated by Orthanc, the citadel of Saruman, and the fortress of Minas Morgul that guards the secret entrance to Mordor; it tells of the deeds and perils of all the members of the now sundered fellowship, until the coming of the Great Darkness." Robert Browning's poem "Childe Roland to the Dark Tower Came" inspired Stephen King's famous "Dark Tower" series. In the character of *Merlin*'s Gwen, a dark queen imprisoned within a dark tower, there are some perhaps coincidental echoes of Countee Cullen's famous Harlem Renaissance poem, "From the Dark Tower":

> We were not made to eternally weep.
> The night whose sable breast relieves the stark,
> White stars is no less lovely being dark,
> And there are buds that cannot bloom at all
> In light, but crumple, piteous, and fall;
> So in the dark we hide the heart that bleeds,
> And wait, and tend our agonizing seeds.

46 Easter eggs in television culture are inside jokes, hints, and callbacks to previous episodes or the larger canon, such as a book or comic that the show is based on. TV Tropes gives the history of the Easter egg in fan cultures, which comes from game developers, in "Easter Egg," TV Tropes.

47 Julian Jones, "The Dark Tower," *Merlin*, season 5, episode 6, directed by Ashley Way, aired November 10, 2012 (BBC).

48 Jones, "The Dark Tower."

49 Jones, "The Dark Tower."

50 Jones, "The Hollow Queen," aired November 24, 2012 (BBC).

51 McBrien, "With All My Heart," aired November 24, 2012 (BBC).

52 A case in point is that in the very next episode, McBride, "The Kindness of Strangers" (aired December 8, 2012 [BBC]) Gwen has only the following six lines:

1. "It is, my lord."
2. "Yes, that looks perfect."
3. "Over here?"
4. "Yes, he has changed, hasn't he?"
5. "Arthur."
6. "That is so sweet."

53 Sherman, "Source, Authority, and Audience in the BBC's *Merlin*," 91.

54 Hero Complex, "'Merlin' Co-creator Julian Murphy on Series' Emotional Conclusion." *Los Angeles Times*, February 6, 2013. http://herocomplex.latimes.com/.

55 Tassja, "The Unbearable Whiteness of Being Part IV."

56 Einylondon, comment on Tassja, "The Unbearable Whiteness of Being Part IV."

57 Edwards, "Casting, Plotting, and Enchanting: Arthurian Women in Starz's *Camelot* and the BBC's *Merlin*."

58 Zahrawithaz, "What It Means to Me to Have a Black Guinevere."

59 Hero Complex, "'Merlin' Co-Creator Julian Murphy on Series' Emotional Conclusion." *Los Angeles Times*, February 6, 2013. http://herocomplex.latimes.com/.

60 Wilken, "'Merlin' Showrunner Shares His Thoughts on the Season Finale."

61 Organization for Transformative Works, "Works in Merlin (TV)."

62 According to Fanlore.org, slash fanfiction is "a type of fanwork in which two (or more) characters of the same sex or gender are placed in a sexual or romantic situation with each other. *Slash* can also be a verb; *to slash* is to create a slash fanwork or to interpret the chemistry between the characters in the source text as homoerotic" (retrieved October 17, 2017, from https://fanlore.org/wiki/Slash).

63 zerosorez, "How Merlin BBC Saved My Life." Reddit, LGBT subreddit, n.d., retrieved October 17, 2017, from https://www.reddit.com/r/lgbt/comments/3bxiql/how_merlinbbc_saved_my_life/.

64 Wilken, "'Merlin' Showrunner Shares His Thoughts on the Season Finale."

65 Brandon, "I Am Getting More and More Sick of Homophobia."

66 BBC Merlin Confessions, "The Way that Femslashers Are Treated in This Fandom Is disgusting . . . ," retrieved October 17, 2017, http://gnimaerd.tumblr.com/post/31398782563/lovepb13-bbcmerlinconfessions-the-way-that.

67 BBC Merlin Confessions, "The Way that Femslashers Are Treated in This Fandom."

68 According to Fanlore.org, "'femslash' is derived from 'female slash', and refers to a genre of fan fiction featuring female characters involved in a romantic or sexual relationship. In English, it is the most common media fandom term for homosexual relationships between female characters" (https://fanlore.org/wiki/Femslash).

69 Eurasian Sensation, "How Come There's a Black Click in *Merlin*?"

70 Eurasian Sensation, "How Come There's a Black Click in *Merlin*?"

71 Elliott, *Remaking the Middle Ages*, 214.

72 Swank, "Black and Liminal in Camelot."

73 Personal communication, June 8, 2014. Also cited in Thomas and Stornaiuolo, "Restorying the Self."

74 Sherman, "Source, Authority, and Audience in the BBC's *Merlin*," 82.

75 Wymer, "A Quest for the Black Knight."

76 BBC Arts, "Colour-Blind Casting."

77 Clarke, "BBC Conjures Up More 'Merlin.'"

78 Appadurai, *Modernity at Large*; Nakamura, *Cybertypes*.

79 Tollerton, "Multiculturalism, Diversity, and Religious Tolerance in Modern Britain and the BBC's *Merlin*," 115.

80 Tollerton, "Multiculturalism, Diversity, and Religious Tolerance in Modern Britain and the BBC's *Merlin*," 117.

81 Hurley, "Seeing White," 221.

82 Duncan, "Critical Race Ethnography in Education," 93–94.

CHAPTER 4. THE CURIOUS CASE OF BONNIE BENNETT

1 "Stan" is fandom slang for an obsessive fan. It comes from an Eminem song, "Stan." In 2010s digital discourse on sites like Tumblr, "stanning" is an alternate word for one's current favorite fandom.

2 Smith, *The Vampire Diaries: The Awakening,, The Vampire Diaries: The Struggle, The Vampire Diaries: The Fury*, and *The Vampire Diaries: Dark Reunion*.

3 Romano, "How the Creator of 'Vampire Diaries' Used Kindle Worlds to Get Back at Her Publisher."

4 Graham, "Kat Graham."

5 Nel, *Was the Cat in the Hat Black?*, 169.

6 Cohen, "Monster Theory," 17.

7 Cohen, "Monster Theory," 19.

8 "Sleeping with a Vampire."

9 Brooks, "Finding the Humanity in Horror," 7.

10 "Horror Blackademics."

11 Although I do not treat it here, there is an extensive literature about the connection between fears of vampires and anti-Semitism. One relevant example is Stratton's "Buffy the Vampire Slayer."

12 White, *Speaking with Vampires*. It is also notable that similar rumors of White/European vampirism and consumption of Black bodies exist throughout the African Diaspora, whether metaphorical or representative of true beliefs.

13 Levine and Parks, *Undead TV*.

14 Rosenberg, "The Way We Were."

15 Pinchevsky, "Fan Fiction Is Finally Legitimized with Kindle Worlds."

16 Thomas, "Asieybarbie's 'I Am Beautiful' Campaign and Sleepy Hollow's Orlando Jones."

17 Bridgeman, "Brigman Award Winner."

18 Kligman and Stanton, "162 Candles."

19 Lisa was a character on ABC's *Saved by the Bell*, which ran from 1989 to 1993, and was played by Lark Voorhies for the entire run of the series. Originally conceived as a Jewish character, Lisa is described by Klosterman as a "wildly unlikable rich

Black girl; vain clotheshorse; unrequited love interest of Screech," the nerdy guy who served as the plot's comic relief (*Being Zach Morris*, 139). In contrast, in real life, Voorhies was featured in Black teen magazines. My friends and I noticed her hair and clothes, and many still note her as one of the most beautiful Black actresses of our generation. Since the show's popularity predated the digital age, it was not known to Gen-X audiences that Voorhies dated a number of young actors, including Mark-Paul Gosselaar, who played Zack Morris, the handsome young White male lead on the show. Yet it was beyond the imagination of the writers of the teen television of my youth to represent what Voorhies's life as a young Black woman was like, and the relationship between Voorhies and Gosselaar was largely kept out of the press. Although there were Black girls on Gen-X teen television who led full lives, they seemed to be primarily located on Black sitcoms, with a few exceptions notable for their rarity (Robin Givens's character on *21 Jump Street* comes to mind, as well as the Black BFF on *Felicity*).

20 Kligman and Stanton, "162 Candles."
21 Ross, "Reunions! Death! Team Bonnie and Damon!"
22 Narducci, "The Last Dance."
23 Young, "Crying Wolf."
24 See, for instance, Dries, "The Sacrifice," and Meyer, Septien, and Narducci, "As I Lay Dying."
25 Young and Reynolds, "Dead Man on Campus."
26 Meyer, Septien, and Narducci, "As I Lay Dying."
27 Sonneshine, "Ghost World."
28 Young and Reynolds, "Dead Man on Campus."
29 Roberts, *Killing the Black Body*; Carby, *Race Men*; Alexander, *The New Jim Crow*.
30 McClintock, *Imperial Leather*; Hartman, *Scenes of Subjection*.
31 Young and Charbonneau, "Because the Night."
32 Young and Charbonneau, "Because the Night."
33 Young and Dries, "The Walking Dead."
34 Matthews and Finch, "For Whom the Bell Tolls."
35 Dries and Young, "Home."
36 Swift, "*Vampire Diaries* Finale Recap."
37 Carter, "How *The Vampire Diaries* Wronged Bonnie Bennett."
38 Carter, "How *The Vampire Diaries* Wronged Bonnie Bennett."
39 Lenhart, "Teens, Social Media, and Technology Overview."
40 Meredith Clark is a groundbreaking scholar of the digital social phenomenon of Black Twitter. Her "To Tweet Our Own Cause" is an essential starting place for understanding the critical dimensions of this work. Vine was a social media platform (2012–2017) where users could share and circulate six-second looping video clips. It was notable for the ways that young people of color used the service to showcase their creativity and engage in social commentary. See, for instance, Chow, "A Moment of Silence for the Black and Brown Talent that Grew on the Vine." In "We Need to Talk about Digital Blackface in Reaction GIFs," Jackson

connects the proliferation of Black people in the visual humor of memes, also known as "reaction GIFs," to past instantiations of Blackface and racist caricature.

Images of black people, more than anyone else, are primed to go viral and circulate widely online—in trauma, in death, and in memes. Reaction GIFs are an uneasy reminder of the way our presence is extra-visible in life, every day, in ways that get us profiled, harassed, mocked, beaten, and killed. Long before the Internet or television, merry racist characters like pickaninnies and coons circulated in the same social space as lynching postcards. Being on display has always been a precarious experience for Black folks. Scholars such as Tina Campt and artists like Martine Syms consider what it means for Black images to be reproduced as stock visuals in history and culture.

41 RaceFail '09 was one of the first wide-ranging racial controversies in science fiction and fantasy fandom during the digital age. Although observers differ about when the debate was first sparked, RaceFail was ignited after in January 2009, when author Elizabeth Bear published a blog post about "Writing the Other" that raised many questions and led to both objections to her point of view and as support across multiple websites, platforms, and communities. It was reignited after the May 2009 publication of Patricia Wrede's novel *The Thirteenth Child*, featuring an alternate New World where Native Americans did not exist. Fanlore provides many relevant links on its RaceFail page: https://fanlore.org/wiki/Race-Fail_%2709.

42 Evans and Darling, "The Power of Black Women in Fandom."

43 Ransby, "The Class Politics of Black Lives Matter." .

44 Bonilla and Rosa, "#Ferguson."

45 Nuñez, "Loving *Vampire Diaries*."

46 Sparky, "*The Vampire Diaries*."

47 Anders, "Why Can't *The Vampire Diaries* Just Let Bonnie Bennett Be Awesome?"

48 Blackwelder, "What Would *The Vampire Diaries* Have Been Like without Bonnie Bennett?"

49 Gibson, "7 Reasons Bonnie Bennett Deserves to be the Leading Lady on *The Vampire Diaries*."

50 Kerney, "21 Problems that Only Bonnie Bennett from *The Vampire Diaries* Understands."

51 Carter, "How *The Vampire Diaries* Wronged Bonnie Bennett."

52 Carter, "How *The Vampire Diaries* Wronged Bonnie Bennett."

53 As documented in Thomas and Stornaiuolo, "Restorying the Self," researching fandom can be difficult for many reasons: the desire for privacy among fans, the challenges of verifying real-world identities in virtual communities, threats of legal action from copyright holders, and the possibility of social ridicule for online activities. Furthermore, past practices of critics and researchers have (rightly, in my view) led some from nondominant, minoritized backgrounds to distrust our motives and intentions. Therefore, I asked fans of Bonnie to chat with me via Tumblr or Twitter about the way they felt her character had been treated only if

they felt comfortable, to share as much or as little as they wished, and to let me
know whether they wanted me to use their real name or a pseudonym.

54 Selah Mitchell, personal communication, February 13, 2015.

55 Selah Mitchell, personal communication, February 15, 2015.

56 Natandy Thomas, personal communication, February 20, 2016.

57 Natandy Thomas, personal communication, February 20, 2016.

58 Much like the previous chapter's discussion of DeBarge's "A Dream," R&B song-
stress Anita Baker's 1990 album *Compositions* featured the single "Fairy Tales,"
which also deconstructed the promises of the fantastic for Black women and girls.
In the most powerful part of the song, Baker sings:

> You never came to save me
> You let me stand alone
> Out in the wilderness
> Alone in the cold
> I found no magic potion
> No horse with wings to fly
> I found the poison apple
> My destiny to die
> No royal kiss could save me
> No magic spell to spin
> My fantasy is over
> My life must now begin.

Once again, the counternarrative teaches Black girls and women that they
must save themselves within the waking dream of the fantastic. The song was
released as a single in December 1990 and was a Top 10 Billboard R&B hit.

59 James and St. John. "Why *The Vampire Diaries*' Treatment of Bonnie Bennett—
and Her Fans—Continues to Bite."

60 Stokes, "*The Vampire Diaries* Recap."

61 For relevant examples, see the "Book Bonnie" tag on Tumblr.com.

62 Henderson, "The Culture behind Closed Doors."

63 In 2017 and 2018, there was considerable consternation over the casting of
Amandla Stenberg (discussed in chapter 2 as the actress playing Rue) as Starr
Carter in the movie adaptation of Angie Thomas's blockbuster young adult
novel *The Hate U Give*. Readers of the novels complained that the dark-
skinned girl on the novel's cover led them to believe that Starr was also dark.
Although conversations about colorism in casting are not new, Stenberg's
casting as Starr led to broader conversations about how Black children and
teens are represented in mass media and entertainment. See Onyejiaka, "Hollywood's Colorism Problem" and Rao, "*The Hate U Give* Illustrator Disappointed."

64 Federal Communications Commission, "Children's Educational Television."

65 Click, Aubrey, and Behm-Morawitz, *Bitten by Twilight*; Jenkins, *Convergence
Culture*; Levine and Parks, *Undead TV*.

66 Sexton, "The Social Life of Social Death: On Afro-Pessimism and Black Optimism." Here, Sexton is citing philosopher Lewis Gordon's 1997 book *Her Majesty's Other Children: Sketches of Racism from a Neocolonial Age*: "Now, recall my point about the two dominant principles of racist ideology: (1) be white, but above all, (2) don't be black. We can call the first *the principle of white supremacy*; and we can call the second *the principle of black inferiority*" (63, emphasis added).

67 Hartman, *Lose Your Mother*; Sexton, "People-of-Color-Blindness."

68 Du Bois, *The Souls of Black Folk*.

69 During the 2010s, television and film saw the rise of characters who were neither heroes nor villains, but somewhere in between. These characters are sometimes referred to as being "morally gray"—somewhere between black and white. See McMahon, "The Rise of Morally Gray Characters."

70 Natandy Thomas, personal communication, February 20, 2016. The quotation from Kat Graham also be found in Peterson, "The Vampire Diaries' Kat Graham on the Surprising Differences between Bonnie Bennett and Kat Graham."

71 Ebony Elizabeth (@Ebonyteach), Twitter posts, March 10, 2017, 10:10 pm–10:16 pm, https://twitter.com/Ebonyteach/status/840399589274456064 through https://twitter.com/Ebonyteach/status/840401030412156928.

CHAPTER 5. HERMIONE IS BLACK

1 As of October 2017, I was listed on Fanlore.org, the Wiki for fandom history (https://fanlore.org/wiki/Ebony_Elizabeth_Thomas). Whenever I muse to my classes that I have a Fanlore page, but not one on Wikipedia, a student inevitably replies with something like, "Yes, but a Fanlore page is much cooler."

2 For more about my fanfiction *Trouble in Paradise* and the 2006 controversy, see its Fanlore page: https://fanlore.org/wiki/Trouble_in_Paradise.

3 #MagicInNorthAmerica was a hashtag protest against J. K. Rowling's erasure of Native American culture, history, and contemporary peoples after the Pottermore feature of the same name was released in the spring of 2016. On her blog, *Native Appropriations*, Cherokee scholar Adrienne Keene writes:

> The problem . . . is that we as Indigenous peoples are constantly situated as fantasy creatures. Think about *Peter Pan*, where Neverland has mermaids, pirates . . . and Indians. Or on Halloween, children dress up as monsters, zombies, princesses, Disney characters . . . and Indians. Beyond the positioning as "not real," there is also a pervasive and problematic narrative wherein Native peoples are always "mystical" and "magical" and "spiritual"—able to talk to animals, conjure spirits, perform magic, heal with "medicine" and destroy with "curses." Think about Grandmother Willow in *Pocahontas*, or Tonto talking to his bird and horse in *The Long Ranger*, or the wolfpack in *Twilight* . . . or any other number of examples. (Keene, "Magic in North America")

> Nambe Pueblo scholar and activist Debbie Reese of *American Indians in Children's Literature* created a useful resource guide to the controversy on her

website, "Native People Respond to Rowling," March 10, 2016, https://americanindiansinchildrensliterature.blogspot.com/2016/.

In solidarity with Native and Indigenous scholars and activists, I storified my Tweets about the matter at https://storify.com/Ebonyteach/the-trouble-with-magicinnorthamerica.

4   Excerpt is from Thomas, *Trouble in Paradise*, chapter 6, "Curiouser and Curiouser," and Hamilton, *The People Could Fly*.

5   Between the publication of *Harry Potter and the Goblet of Fire* in 2000 and *Harry Potter and the Half-Blood Prince* in 2005 (which effectively settled the shipping question), advocates of the Harry and Hermione and Ron and Hermione pairings engaged in extensive textual and semiotic warfare over whose reading of the *Harry Potter* novels was most correct. As an advocate of the Harry and Hermione pairing, I participated with enthusiasm in these debates, controversies, and flame wars, engendering quite a bit of justified animosity.

6   Post, AngieJ LiveJournal, http://angiej.livejournal.com/2006/08/16/.

7   Sharpe, *In the Wake*.

8   @RelicUA, tweet, "I think poor non-white people are in a state of quantum super-position, such that they only exist when the narrative requires #TWiBNation." Twitter, December 6, 2016, https://twitter.com/relicUA/status/806323165798469633.

9   According to physicist and feminist theorist Karen Barad, "Superpositions represent ontologically indeterminate states—states with no determinate fact of the matter concerning the property in question." She goes on to note that "superpositions embody quantum indeterminacy" (*Meeting the Universe Halfway*, 265).

10 Margaret Rouse, a writer and director at WhatIs.com, provides a layperson's definition of the famous physics experiment known as the Schrödinger's cat paradox:

In 1935, Erwin Schrödinger proposed an analogy to show how superposition would operate in the everyday world: the somewhat cruel analogy of Schrödinger's cat. . . . We place a living cat into a steel chamber, along with a device containing a vial of hydrocyanic acid. There is, in the chamber, a very small amount of a radioactive substance. If even a single atom of the substance decays during the test period, a relay mechanism will trip a hammer, which will, in turn, break the vial and kill the cat. The observer cannot know whether or not an atom of the substance has decayed, and consequently, cannot know whether the vial has been broken, the hydrocyanic acid released, and the cat killed. Since we cannot know, the cat is both dead and alive according to quantum law, in a superposition of states. It is only when we break open the box and learn the condition of the cat that the superposition is lost, and the cat becomes one or the other (dead or alive). This situation is sometimes called *quantum indeterminacy* or *the observer's paradox*: the observation or measurement itself affects an outcome, so that the outcome as such does not exist unless the measurement is made. (That is, there is no single outcome unless it is observed.) (http://whatis.techtarget.com/)

11 Jefferson, *Notes on the State of Virginia.*

12 Wanzo, "African American Acafandom and Other Strangers"; Carrington, *Speculative Blackness.*

13 Excerpt is from *Paradise Lost*, chapter 1, "The Talented Dr. Granger."

14 Bennett, "What a Racebent Hermione Really Represents."

15 Breianna Harvey, personal communication, November 12, 2015. Originally cited in Thomas and Stornaiuolo, "Restorying the Self."

16 Lorde, *Zami*, 5.

17 Adichie, "The Danger of a Single Story."

18 Thomas and Stornaiuolo, "Restorying the Self."

19 J. K. Rowling, "Canon: brown eyes, frizzy hair and very clever. White skin was never specified. Rowling loves black Hermione." Twitter status, December 21, 2015, https://twitter.com/jk_rowling/status/678888094339366914.

20 Tosenberger, "'Oh My God, the Fanfiction!'"

21 Gonzalez, "J. K. Rowling says that Hermione Should Have Married Harry, not Ron."

22 Incidentally, Rowling's revelation that she'd chosen the romances that ended her series for personal reasons is something that I predicted more than thirteen years earlier in a post on the Harry Potter for Grownups Yahoo! Group. See ebonyink@hotmail.com, "Freudian/Lacanian Support for H/H (long)," December 19, 2000. http://groups.yahoo.com/neo/groups/HPforGrownups/conversations/messages/7284.

23 John Green, "Books belong to their readers." Twitter status, February 1, 2014, https://twitter.com/realjohngreen/status/429797089569439744.

24 Smagorinsky, "If Meaning Is Constructed, What Is It Made From?"

25 Kukkonen, "Navigating Infinite Earths," 39–40.

26 Kukkonen, "Navigating Infinite Earths," 40.

27 Along with comics, theater can illuminate paths toward diversifying the fantastic. There is a long tradition of Black versions of classical stories on stage, mostly hailing African Diasporic spaces outside the United States. For instance, Marcel Camus's *Black Orpheus* and Orson Welles's *Voodoo Macbeth* are retellings of Greek and Shakespearean tragedy, respectively. Trinidadian American poet and children's writer Rosa Guy initially wrote *My Love, My Love: The Peasant Girl* as a retelling of the "Little Mermaid" fairy tale, but it has found Tony Award–winning success in its Broadway musical incarnation as *Once on This Island.*

28 Kukkonen, "Navigating Infinite Earths," 42.

29 "Superman Image Gallery," SupermanHomepage.com, http://www.superman-homepage.com/.

30 Kukkonen, "Navigating Infinite Earths," 42.

31 The name of the doctor's famous spacetime ship is the TARDIS, an acronym for "Time and Relative Dimension in Space." For an explanation of what has become known as "TARDIS transcendentalism," see Ireland, "This Planet Has Four Walls."

32 Kukkonen, "Navigating Infinite Earths," 43.

33 Thomas and Stornaiuolo, "Restorying the Self."

34 Vasquez, "Critical Ethnography and Pedagogy."

35 Gee, *Situated Language and Learning.*

36 Jenkins, Greene, and Ford, *Spreadable Media.*

37 Bond and Michelson, "Writing Harry's World."

38 Wright, *Physics of Blackness.*

39 Sousanis, *Unflattening.*

40 Sklar, "Narrative as Experience."

41 Garcia and Haddix, "The Revolution Starts with Rue."

42 Xie, "Rethinking the Identity of Cultural Otherness," 1.

43 Philip and Garcia, "The Importance of Still Teaching the iGeneration."

44 Thompson, "Brave New World of Digital Intimacy."

45 Gee and Hayes, *Language and Learning in the Digital Age*; boyd, "Why Youth ⬚ Social Network Sites," 7.

46 Ong, *Orality and Literacy*; Pettitt, "Before the Gutenberg Parenthesis" Sauerberg, "The Encyclopedia and the Gutenberg Parenthesis."

47 Smagorinsky, "If Meaning Is Constructed, What Is It Made From?"

48 The idea of "reading and/or writing the self into existence" was inspired by Vasquez, "Critical ethnography and pedagogy." See also Rooks, "Writing Themselves into Existence."

49 Larrick, "The All-White World of Children's Books."

50 Gay, *Culturally Responsive Teaching*; Ladson-Billings and Tate, "Toward a Critical Race Theory of Education"; Paris, "Culturally Sustaining Pedagogy."

51 Miranda and DiGiacomo, "'Hamilton's' Lin-Manuel Miranda on Finding Originality, Racial Politics."

52 Bacon. "An African Voice."

53 Holmes, "Having Hermione Look Like Me Is Amazing."

54 Bennett, "What a Racebent Hermione Really Represents."

55 Barrie, *The Annotated Peter Pan.*

56 Rankine and Loffreda, "On Whiteness and the Racial Imaginary."

57 Rankine, Loffreda, and Cap, *The Racial Imaginary.*

58 Bishop, "Reflections on the Development of African American Children's Literature."

59 Kane, "The 2016 #BlackSpecFic Report."

60 Carroll, "Back At You."

BIBLIOGRAPHY

Adichie, Chimamanda Ngozi. "The Danger of a Single Story." TED video. July 2009. www.ted.com.

Alexander, Michelle. *The New Jim Crow: Mass Incarceration in the Age of Colorblindness*. New York: The New Press, 2012.

Anagnostopoulos, Dorothea, Sakeena Everett, and Carleen Carey. "'Of Course We're Supposed to Move On, but Then You Still Got People Who Are Not over Those Historical Wounds': Cultural Memory and US Youth's Race Talk." *Discourse & Society* 24, no. 2 (2013): 163–185.

Anders, Charlie Jane. "Why Can't *The Vampire Diaries* Just Let Bonnie Bennett Be Awesome?" *iO9*, October 31, 2014. http://io9.gizmodo.com.

Angelou, Maya. *I Know Why the Caged Bird Sings*. New York: Random House, 1969.

Appadurai, Arjun. *Modernity at Large: Cultural Dimensions of Globalization*. Minneapolis: University of Minnesota Press, 1996.

Aronson, Sarah. "Guest Post: Sarah Aronson on 'It's Okay if You Don't Like My Unlikeable Protagonist." Cynthia Leitich Smith's Cynsations blog, October, 22, 2013. http://cynthialeitichsmith.blogspot.com.

Attebery, Brian. *Stories about Stories: Fantasy and the Remaking of Myth*. Oxford, UK: Oxford University Press, 2014.

Bacon, Katie. "An African Voice." *Atlantic*, August 2, 2000. www.theatlantic.com.

Barad, Karen. *Meeting the Universe Halfway: Quantum Physics and the Entanglement of Matter and Meaning*. Durham, NC: Duke University Press, 2007.

Barrie, James M. *The Annotated Peter Pan: Centennial Edition*, edited by Maria Tatar. New York: W. W. Norton, 2014.

BBC Arts. "Colour-Blind Casting: The Untold Story of Black and Asian Shakespeare." April 27, 2015. www.bbc.co.uk.

Bennett, Alanna. "What a 'Racebent' Hermione Really Represents." *Buzzfeed*, February 1, 2015. www.buzzfeed.com.

Benton, Michael. *Secondary Worlds: Literature Teaching and the Visual Arts*. Philadelphia: Open University, 1992.

Bernstein, Robin. *Racial Innocence: Performing American Childhood from Slavery to Civil Rights*. New York: New York University Press, 2011.

Bhabha, Homi. *The Location of Culture*. London: Psychology Press, 1994.

Bishop, Rudine Sims. "Reflections on the Development of African American Children's Literature." *Journal of Children's Literature* 38, no. 2 (2012): 5–13.

———. "Mirrors, Windows, and Sliding Glass Doors." *Perspectives* 6, no. 3 (1990): ix–xi.

Blackford, Holly Virginia. *Out of This World: Why Literature Matters to Girls*. New York: Teachers College Press, 2004.

Blackwelder, Carson. "What Would *The Vampire Diaries* Have Been Like without Bonnie Bennett?" *Wetpaint*, February 6, 2015. www.wetpaint.com.

Bond, Ernest L., and Nancy L. Michelson. "Writing Harry's World: Children Co-Authoring Hogwarts." In *Critical Perspectives on Harry Potter*, edited by Elizabeth E. Heilman, 309–327. New York: Routledge, 2008.

Bonilla, Yarimar, and Jonathan Rosa. "#Ferguson: Digital Protest, Hashtag Ethnography, and the Racial Politics of Social Media in the United States." *American Ethnologist* 42, no. 1 (2015): 4–17.

Bould, Mark, and Sherryl Vint. "Political Readings." In *Cambridge Companion to Fantasy Literature*, edited by Edward James and Farah Mendlesohn, 103. Cambridge, UK: Cambridge University Press, 2012.

boyd, danah. "Why Youth ⬚ Social Network Sites: The Role of Networked Publics in Teenage Social Life." In *Youth, Identity, and Digital Media Volume*, edited by David Buckingham, 119–142. Cambridge, MA: MIT Press, 2007.

Bradford, Clare. *The Middle Ages in Children's Literature*. London: Palgrave Macmillan, 2015.

———. *Reading Race: Aboriginality in Australian Children's Literature*. Melbourne: Melbourne University Press, 2001.

Bradford, K. Tempest. "Uncovering Hidden Black History, on Screen and on the Page." *Code Switch*, National Public Radio, 2015.

Brailsford, Karen. "Amandla Stenberg." IMDb Mini Biography. Retrieved October 29, 2018, from www.imdb.com.

Brand, Dionne. *A Map to the Door of No Return: Notes to Belonging*. Toronto: Vintage Canada, 2012.

Brandon. "I Am Getting More and More Sick of Homophobia." *Farmer of the Dicks: Wonder, Ramblings, and Wankery* (blog), June 11, 2011. tinyhipsterboy.tumblr.com.

Brewster, Hilary. "She Has No Idea. The Effect She Can Have." In *The Politics of Panem*, edited by Sean P. Connors, 169–188. Rotterdam: Sense Publishers, 2014.

Bridgeman, Mary. "Brigman Award Winner—Forged in Love and Death: Problematic Subjects in *The Vampire Diaries*." *Journal of Popular Culture* 46, no. 1 (2013): 3–19.

Britton, Dennis Austin. "From the *Knight's Tale* to *The Two Noble Kinsmen*: Rethinking Race, Class and Whiteness in Romance." *postmedieval: a journal of medieval cultural studies* 6, no. 1 (2015): 64–78. doi:10.1057/pmed.2015.3.

Brooks, Daphne. *Bodies in Dissent: Spectacular Performances of Race and Freedom, 1850–1910*. Durham, NC: Duke University Press, 2006.

Brooks, Kinitra. "Finding the Humanity in Horror: Black Women's Sexual Identity in Fighting the Supernatural." *Poroi* 7, no. 2 (2011): Article 7. doi:10.13008/2151-2957.1098.

Brooks, Kinitra D. *Searching for Sycorax: Black Women's Hauntings of Contemporary Horror*. New Brunswick, NJ: Rutgers University Press, 2017.

Brown, Jeffrey A. *Black Superheroes, Milestone Comics, and Their Fans.* Jackson: University Press of Mississippi, 2000.

Brown, Stacia L. "For Tamir, Who Was Stolen." Stacialbrown.com, 2014.

Browning, Robert. "Childe Roland to the Dark Tower Came." 1855. https://www.bartleby.com.

Burton, Jonathan, and Ania Loomba. *Race in Early Modern England: A Documentary Companion.* Springer, 2016.

Carby, Hazel V. *Race Men.* Cambridge, MA: Harvard University Press, 2009.

Card, Orson Scott. *How to Write Science Fiction & Fantasy.* Writer's Digest Books, 2001.

Carrington, André M. *Speculative Blackness: The Future of Race in Science Fiction.* Minneapolis: University of Minnesota Press, 2016.

Carroll, Rebecca. "Back at You: Ntozake Shange, Poet, Playwright, and Fiery Author of 'For Colored Girls Who Have Considered Suicide/When the Rainbow Is Enuf' Minces No Words." *Mother Jones,* January/February 1995: 69.

Carter, Kristen. "How *The Vampire Diaries* Wronged Bonnie Bennett." *Black Girl Nerds,* April 21, 2017. https://blackgirlnerds.com/.

Cashbaugh, Sean. "A Paradoxical, Discrepant, and Mutant Marxism: The Emergence of a Radical Science Fiction in the American Popular Front." *Journal for the Study of Radicalism* 10, no. 1 (2016): 63–106.

Chow, Kat. "A Moment of Silence for the Black and Brown Talent that Grew on the Vine." *Code Switch,* National Public Radio, October 28, 2016. www.npr.org.

Christgau, Robert. "Consumer Guide." *Village Voice,* February 21, 1984. www.robert-christgau.com.

Christopoulos, Menelaos, Efimia D. Karakantza, and Olga Levaniouk, eds. *Light and Darkness in Ancient Greek Myth and Religion. Greek Studies: Interdisciplinary Approaches.* Lanham, MD: Lexington Books, 2010.

Clark, Meredith. "To Tweet Our Own Cause: A Mixed-Methods Study of the Online Phenomenon of Black Twitter." PhD diss., University of North Carolina, Chapel Hill, 2014.

Clarke, Steve. "BBC Conjures Up More 'Merlin.'" *Variety,* October 25, 2010.

Clawson, Rosalee A., and Rakuya Trice. "Poverty as We Know It: Media Portrayals of the Poor." *Public Opinion Quarterly* 64, no. 1 (2000): 53–64.

Click, Melissa A., Jennifer Stevens Aubrey, and Elizabeth Behm-Morawitz, eds. *Bitten by Twilight: Youth Culture, Media, & the Vampire Franchise.* New York: Peter Lang, 2010.

Cohen, Jeffrey Jerome. "Monster Culture: Seven Theses." In *Monster Theory: Reading Culture,* edited by Jeffrey J. Cohen, 1–23. Minneapolis: University of Minnesota Press, 1996.

Cohen Jeffrey Jerome, and Karl Steel. "Race, Travel, Time, Heritage." *postmedieval: a journal of medieval cultural studies* 6, no. 1 (2015): 98–110. doi:10.1057/pmed.2014.39.

Collins, Suzanne. *The Hunger Games.* New York: Scholastic, 2008.

Commander, Michelle D. *Afro-Atlantic Flight: Speculative Returns and the Black Fantastic.* Durham, NC: Duke University Press, 2017.

Cook, Daniella Ann, and Adrienne D. Dixson. "Writing Critical Race Theory and Method: A Composite Counterstory on the Experiences of Black Teachers in New Orleans Post-Katrina." *International Journal of Qualitative Studies in Education* 26, no. 10 (2013): 1238–1258.

Cooperative Children's Book Center, University of Wisconsin, Madison. "A Few Observations on Publishing in 2013."

Cullen, Countee. "From the Dark Tower." Reprinted in Eugenia W. Collier, "I Do Not Marvel, Countee Cullen." *College Language Association Journal* 11 no. 1 (1967). www.english.illinois.edu.

DiAngelo, Robin, and Özlem Sensoy. "Getting Slammed: White Depictions of Race Discussions as Arenas of Violence." *Race Ethnicity and Education* 17, no. 1 (2014): 103–128.

Dillard, Cynthia B. "Re-Membering Culture: Bearing Witness to the Spirit of Identity in Research." *Race Ethnicity and Education* 11, no. 1 (2008): 87–93.

Dries, Caroline. "The Sacrifice." *The Vampire Diaries*, season 2, episode 10. Directed by Ralph Hemecker. Burbank, CA: The CW, 2010.

Dries, Caroline, and Brian Young. "Home." *The Vampire Diaries*, season 5, episode 22. Directed by Chris Grismer. Burbank, CA: The CW, 2014.

Du Bois, William Edward Burghardt. *The Souls of Black Folk*, edited by Brent Hayes Edwards. New York: Oxford University Press, 2008 [1903].

Dubrofsky, Rachel E., and Emily D. Ryalls. "*The Hunger Games*: Performing Not-Performing to Authenticate Femininity and Whiteness." *Critical Studies in Media Communication* 31, no. 5 (2014): 395–409.

Dumas, Michael J. "'Losing an Arm': Schooling as a Site of Black Suffering." *Race Ethnicity and Education* 17, no. 1 (2014): 1–29.

Dunbar, Paul Laurence. "Sympathy." Retrieved October 25, 2018, from www.poetryfoundation.org.

Duncan, Garrett Albert. "Critical Race Ethnography in Education: Narrative, Inequality and the Problem of Epistemology." *Race Ethnicity and Education* 8, no. 1 (2005): 93–114. doi: 10.1080/1361332052000341015.

"Easter Egg." *TV Tropes*. Retrieved October 17, 2017, from http://tvtropes.org/.

Ebony F. "As Black Girl Magic Turns Four Years Old, CaShawn Thompson Has a Fresh Word for All the Magical Black Girls." Blavity, February 12, 2017. https://blavity.com/as-blackgirlmagic-turns-four-years-old-cashawn-thompson-has-a-fresh-word-for-all-the-magical-black-girls.

Eddo-Lodge, Reni. "Call Out Culture: What We Can Learn from 'To JK Rowling, from Cho Chang.'" *The F Word: Contemporary UK Feminism*, April 2013.

Edwards, Jennifer C. "Casting, Plotting, and Enchanting: Arthurian Women in Starz's *Camelot* and the BBC's *Merlin*." *Arthuriana* 25, no. 1 (2015): 57–81.

Einylondon. Comment on Tassja, "The Unbearable Whiteness of Being Part IV: Guinevere, Racism, and the Tyranny of Beauty." *Irresistable Revolution* (blog), January 13, 2012. http://irresistable-revolution.blogspot.com.

Elliott, Andrew B. R. *Remaking the Middle Ages: The Methods of Cinema and History in Portraying the Medieval World*. Jefferson, NC: McFarland, 2010.

Elliott, Zetta. "Decolonizing the Imagination." *The Horn Book*, March/April 2010.

English, Daylanne K., and Alvin Kim. "Now We Want Our Funk Cut: Janelle Monáe's Neo-Afrofuturism." *American Studies* 52, no. 4 (2013): 217–230.

Eurasian Sensation. "How Come There's a Black Click in *Merlin*?" *Eurasian Sensation* (blog), July 25, 2009. http://eurasian-sensation.blogspot.com.

Evans, Kerri, and Britta Darling. "The Power of Black Women in Fandom." *Black Enterprise*, September 22, 2015. www.blackenterprise.com.

Federal Communications Commission. Children's Educational Television. Last updated November 6, 2017. https://www.fcc.gov.

Fisher, Mark. "Precarious Dystopias: *The Hunger Games, In Time*, and *Never Let Me Go*." *Film Quarterly* 65, no. 4 (2012): 27–33.

Forest, Danielle E., K. L. Garrison, and Sue C. Kimmel. "'The University for the Poor': Portrayals of Class in Translated Children's Literature." *Teachers College Record* 117, no. 2 (2015): 1–40.

Fulton, Helen. "A Woman's Place: Guinevere in the Welsh and French Romances." *Quondam et Futurus* 3, no. 2 (1993): 1–25.

Funes, Juliette. "Merlin Conjures Up Camelot, 'Smallville' Style." *Los Angeles Times*, August 20, 2009. http://herocomplex.latimes.com.

Garcia, Antero, and Marcelle Haddix. "Reading YA with 'Dark Brown Skin': Race, Community, and Rue's Uprising." *ALAN Review* 42, no. 2 (2015): 37–44.

———. "The Revolution Starts with Rue." In *The Politics of Panem: Challenging Genres*, edited by Sean P. Connors, 203–217. Rotterdam: Sense Publishers, 2014.

Gates, Henry Louis. *The Signifying Monkey: A Theory of Afro-American Criticism*. New York: Oxford University Press, 1988.

Gay, Geneva. *Culturally Responsive Teaching: Theory, Research, and Practice*. New York: Teachers College Press, 2010.

Gay, Roxane. "What We Hunger For." *The Rumpus*, April 12, 2012. https://therumpus.net/2012/04/what-we-hunger-for/.

Gee, James Paul. *Situated Language and Learning: A Critique of Traditional Schooling*. Psychology Press, 2004.

Gee, James Paul, and Elisabeth Hayes. *Language and Learning in the Digital Age*. Abingdon, UK: Routledge, 2011.

Gibson, Kelsie. "7 Reasons Bonnie Bennett Deserves to be the Leading Lady on *The Vampire Diaries*." *Bustle*, June 1, 2015. https://www.bustle.com.

Glenn, Cerise L., and Landra J. Cunningham. "The Power of Black Magic: The Magical Negro and White Salvation in Film." *Journal of Black Studies* 40, no. 2 (2009): 135–152.

Gonzalez, Robbie. "J. K. Rowling says that Hermione Should Have Married Harry, not Ron." *Io9*, February 2, 2014. https://io9.gizmodo.com.

Graham, Kat. "Kat Graham." IMDb Mini Biography. Retrieved October 25, 2018, from https://www.imdb.com.

Guerlac, Henry. "Can There Be Colors in the Dark? Physical Color Theory before Newton." *Journal of the History of Ideas* 47, no. 1 (1986): 3–20.

Gutiérrez, Kris D. "Developing a Sociocritical Literacy in the Third Space." *Reading Research Quarterly* 43, no. 2 (2008): 148–164.

Hall, Stuart. *Representation: Cultural Representations and Signifying Practices*. London: Sage, 1997.

———. "The Spectacle of the Other." In *Discourse Theory and Practice: A Reader*, edited by Margaret Wetherell, Stephanie Taylor, and Simon J. Yates, 324–344. London: Sage, 2001.

Hamilton, Virginia. *The People Could Fly: American Black Folktales*, vol. 1. New York: Knopf Books for Young Readers, 1985.

Hartman, Saidiya V. *Scenes of Subjection: Terror, Slavery, and Self-Making in Nineteenth-Century America*. Oxford, UK: Oxford University Press, 1997.

———. *Lose Your Mother: A Journey Along the Atlantic Slave Route*. New York: Macmillan, 2008.

Hellekson, Karen, and Kristina Busse, eds. *Fan Fiction and Fan Communities in the Age of the Internet: New Essays*. Jefferson, NC: McFarland, 2006.

Henderson, Felicia D. "The Culture behind Closed Doors: Issues of Gender and Race in the Writers' Room." *Cinema Journal* 50, no. 2 (Winter 2011): 145–152.

Heng, Geraldine. *Empire of Magic: Medieval Romance and the Politics of Cultural Fantasy*. New York: Columbia University Press, 2003.

Herron, Jerry. "Detroit Borderama: Parts 1–3." *Places Journal* (2010): n.p. doi:10.22269/100706.

Holmes, Anna. "White until Proven Black: Imagining Race in *Hunger Games*." *New Yorker*, March 30, 2012.

Holmes, Sarah. "Having Hermione Look like Me Is Amazing." *BBC News*, December 23, 2015. www.bbc.com.

Horning, Kathleen T., Merri V. Lindgren, and Megan Schliesman. "A Few Observations on Publishing in 2013." *CCBC Choices 2014*. http://ccbc.education.wisc.edu.

"Horror Blackademics: Black Women in Vampire Fiction." *Graveyard Shift Sisters*, September 9, 2014.

Howard, Sheena C., and Ronald L. Jackson II, eds. *Black Comics: Politics of Race and Representation*. London: A&C Black, 2013.

Hughey, Matthew W. "Cinethetic Racism: White Redemption and Black Stereotypes in 'Magical Negro' Films." *Social Problems* 56, no. 3 (2009): 543–577.

Hunter, Margaret. "The Persistent Problem of Colorism: Skin Tone, Status, and Inequality." *Sociology Compass* 1, no. 1 (2007): 237–254.

Hurley, Dorothy L. "Seeing White: Children of Color and the Disney Fairy Tale Princess." *Journal of Negro Education* 74, no. 2 (2005): 221–232.

Ireland, Andrew. "This Planet Has Four Walls: How Early *Doctor Who* Narrative Was Influenced by Techniques and Technology to Overcome the Confines of Studio Recording." The Media School, Bournemouth University, UK. Retrieved October 25, 2018, from http://eprints.bournemouth.ac.uk.

Irvine, Jacqueline Jordan. *Educating Teachers for Diversity: Seeing with a Cultural Eye*. New York: Teachers College Press, 2003.

Jackson, Lauren Michele. "We Need to Talk about Digital Blackface in Reaction GIFs." *Teen Vogue*, August 2, 2017.

Jackson, Sandra, and Julie E. Moody-Freeman, eds. *The Black Imagination: Science Fiction, Futurism and the Speculative*. New York: Peter Lang, 2011.

James, Kendra, and Jordan St. John. "Why *The Vampire Diaries'* Treatment of Bonnie Bennett—and Her Fans—Bites." *Racialicious*, April 10, 2012.

Jefferson, Thomas. *Notes on the State of Virginia*, 1781. https://www.pbs.org.

Jenkins, Henry. *Convergence Culture: Where Old and New Media Collide*. New York: New York University Press, 2006.

———. *Textual Poachers: Television Fans & Participatory Culture*. New York: Routledge, 1992.

Jenkins, Henry, Joshua E. Greene, and Sam Ford. *Spreadable Media: Creating Value and Meaning in a Networked Culture*. New York: New York University Press, 2013.

Jones, Julian. "The Hollow Queen." *Merlin*, season 5, episode 8. Directed by Alice Troughton. White City, West London, UK: BBC, 2012.

———. "The Dark Tower." *Merlin*, season 5, episode 6. Directed by Ashley Way. White City, West London, UK: BBC, 2012.

———. "The Mark of Nimueh." *Merlin*, season 1, episode 3. Directed by James Hawes. White City, West London, UK: BBC, 2008.

———. "Le Morte d'Arthur." *Merlin*, season 1, episode 13. Directed by David Moore. White City, West London, UK: BBC, 2008.

———. "The Dragon's Call." *Merlin*, season 1, episode 1. Directed by James Hawes. White City, West London, UK: BBC, 2008.

Kane, Cecily. "The 2016 #BlackSpecFic Report." *Fireside Fiction* (blog), July 24, 2017. https://firesidefiction.com.

Keene, Adrienne. "Magic in North America: The Harry Potter Franchise Veers Too Close to Home." *Native Appropriations*, 2016. https://nativeappropriations.com.

Kendi, Ibram. *Stamped from the Beginning: The Definitive History of Racist Ideas in America*. New York: Random House, 2017.

Kerney, Viktor T. "21 Problems that Only Bonnie Bennett from *The Vampire Diaries* Understands." *Buzzfeed*, April 20, 2015. https://www.buzzfeed.com.

King, Stephen. *The Dark Tower VII: The Dark Tower*. Hampton Falls, NH: Grant, 2004.

Kligman, Barbie, and Gabrielle G. Stanton. "162 Candles." *The Vampire Diaries*, season 1, episode 8. Directed by Rick Bota. Burbank, CA: The CW, 2009.

Klosterman, Chuck. *Being Zach Morris: An Essay from Sex, Drugs, and Cocoa Puffs*. New York: Scribner, 2010, Kindle ed.

Kukkonen, Karin. "Navigating Infinite Earths: Readers, Mental Models, and the Multiverse of Superhero Comics." *StoryWorlds: A Journal of Narrative Studies* 2, no. 1 (2010): 39–58. doi:10.1353/stw.0.0009.

Ladson-Billings, Gloria. "From the Achievement Gap to the Education Debt: Understanding Achievement in US Schools." *Educational Researcher* 35, no. 7 (2006): 3–12.

Ladson-Billings, Gloria, and William Tate IV. "Toward a Critical Race Theory of Education." *Teachers College Record* 97, no. 1 (1995): 47–68.

Larrick, Nancy. "The All-White World of Children's Books." *Saturday Review* 48, no. 37 (1965): 63–65.

Lea, Steven. "To Kill a Mockingjay? Was Suzanne Collins 'Inspired' by Gregory Peck/ Harper Lee Classic?" *Philadelphia Inquirer*, April 10, 2012.

Lee, Carol D. *Signifying as a Scaffold for Literary Interpretation: The Pedagogical Implications of an African American Discourse Genre*. Urbana, IL: National Council of Teachers of English, 1993.

Lee, Harper. *To Kill a Mockingbird*. New York: Warner, 1982 [1960].

Lee and Low Books. "Why Hasn't the Number of Multicultural Books Increased in Eighteen Years?" New York, June 17, 2013.

Lenhart, Amanda. "Teens, Social Media, and Technology Overview." Pew Research Center: Internet and Technology, April 9, 2015. www.pewinternet.org.

Leonardo, Zeus, and Ronald K. Porter. "Pedagogy of Fear: Toward a Fanonian Theory of 'Safety' in Race Dialogue." *Race Ethnicity and Education* 13, no. 2 (2010): 139–157.

Levine, Elana, and Lisa Ann Parks. *Undead TV: Essays on Buffy the Vampire Slayer*. Durham, NC: Duke University Press, 2007.

Loomba, Ania. *Shakespeare, Race, and Colonialism*. New York: Oxford University Press, 2002.

Lorde, Audre. *Zami: A New Spelling of My Name*. Berkeley, CA: Crossing Press, 1982.

Losen, Daniel, Cheri Hodson, Michael A. Keith II, Katrina Morrison, and Shakti Belway. *Are We Closing the School Discipline Gap?* Los Angeles, CA: The Center for Civil Rights Remedies, February 2015. http://civilrightsproject.ucla.edu.

Łuksza, Agata. "Sleeping with a Vampire." *Feminist Media Studies* 15, no. 3 (2015): 429–443.

MacCann, Donnarae. *White Supremacy in Children's Literature: Characterizations of African Americans, 1830–1900*. New York: Routledge, 2013.

Macunaima. "Why Myth-Making Is Dangerous for Subordinate Peoples." Message board post, Brazzil.net Forum, 2003.

Mahar, William John. *Behind the Burnt Cork Mask: Early Blackface Minstrelsy and Antebellum American Popular Culture*. Champaign: University of Illinois Press, 1999.

Mafe, Diana Adesola. *Where No Black Woman Has Gone Before: Subversive Portrayals in Speculative Film and TV*. Austin: University of Texas Press, 2018.

Matthews, Brett, and Elisabeth Finch. "For Whom the Bell Tolls." *The Vampire Diaries*, season 5, episode 4. Directed by Michael Allowitz. Burbank, CA: The CW, 2013.

McBrien, Richard. "The Kindness of Strangers," *Merlin*, season 5, episode 10. Directed by Declan O'Dwyer. White City, West London, UK: BBC, 2012.

———. "With All My Heart." *Merlin*, season 5, episode 9. Directed by Alice Troughton. White City, West London, UK: BBC, 2012.

McClintock, Anne. *Imperial Leather: Race, Gender, and Sexuality in the Colonial Contest*. London: Routledge, 2013.

McGillis, Roderick, ed. *Voices of the Other: Children's Literature and the Postcolonial Context*, 2nd ed. New York: Routledge, 2013.

McMahon, Andrew. "The Rise of Morally Gray Characters and Stories in Entertainment." *Nerd Stash*, 2017. https://thenerdstash.com.

Mendlesohn, Farah. *Rhetorics of Fantasy*. Middletown, CT: Wesleyan University Press, 2008.

"'Merlin': Angel Coulby Talks Gwen's Journey from Servant to Queen." *Los Angeles Times*, April 29, 2013. http://herocomplex.latimes.com.

Meyer, Turi, Al Septien, and Michael Narducci. "As I Lay Dying." *The Vampire Diaries*, season 2, episode 22. Directed by John Behring. Burbank, CA: The CW, 2011.

Milner, H. Richard. "Rethinking Achievement Gap Talk in Urban Education." *Urban Education* 48, no. 1 (2013): 3–8.

Michie, Jake. "A Lesson in Vengeance." *Merlin*, season 5, episode 7. Directed by Alice Troughton. White City, West London, UK: BBC, 2012.

———. "To Kill the King." *Merlin*, season 1, episode 12. Directed by Stuart Orme. White City, West London, UK: BBC, 2008.

Michie, Jake (part 1), and Julian Jones (part 2). "The Sword in the Stone." *Merlin*, season 4, episodes 12 and 13. Directed by Alice Troughton. White City, West London, UK: BBC, 2011.

Miranda, Lin-Manuel, and Frank DiGiacomo. "'Hamilton's' Lin-Manuel Miranda on Finding Originality, Racial Politics (and Why Trump Should See His Show)." *Hollywood Reporter*, August 12, 2015. www.hollywoodreporter.com.

Morrison, Toni. *Playing in the Dark: Whiteness and the Literary Imagination*. Cambridge, MA.: Harvard University Press, 1992.

Muhammad, Gholnecsar E., and Marcelle Haddix. "Centering Black Girls' Literacies: A Review of Literature on the Multiple Ways of Knowing of Black Girls." *English Education* 48, no. 4 (2016): 299–336.

Myers, Christopher. "The Apartheid of Children's Literature." *New York Times*, March 15, 2014.

Myers, Walter Dean. "Where Are the People of Color in Children's Books?" *New York Times*, March 16, 2014.

Nakamura, Lisa. *Cybertypes: Race, Ethnicity, and Identity on the Internet*. New York: Routledge, 2013.

Narducci, Michael. "The Last Dance." *The Vampire Diaries*, season 2, episode 18. Directed by John Behring. Burbank, CA: The CW, 2011.

Nel, Philip. *Was the Cat in the Hat Black? The Hidden Racism of Children's Literature, and the Need for Diverse Books*. New York: Oxford University Press, 2017.

———. "Was the Cat in the Hat Black?: Exploring Dr. Seuss's Racial Imagination." *Children's Literature* 42, no. 1 (2014): 71–98.

Nevins, Jess. "The Black Fantastic: Highlights of Pre–World War II African and African-American Speculative Fiction." *io9*, September 27, 2012. http://io9.gizmodo.com.

Older, Daniel José. "Diversity Is Not Enough: Race, Power, Publishing." *Buzzfeed*, April 17, 2014. www.buzzfeed.com.

Ong, W. J. *Orality and Literacy*. London: Routledge, 2013.

Onyejiaka, Tiffany. "Hollywood's Colorism Problem Can't Be Ignored Any Longer." *Teen Vogue*, August 22, 2017. https://www.teenvogue.com/story/hollywoods-colorism-problem-cant-be-ignored.

Organization for Transformative Works. "Works in Merlin (TV)." *Archive of Our Own*. Retrieved October 17, 2017, from http://archiveofourown.org.

Overman, Howard. "Lancelot and Guinevere." *Merlin*, season 2, episode 4. Directed by David Moore. White City, West London, UK: BBC, 2009.

———. "The Once and Future Queen." *Merlin*, season 2, episode 2. Directed by David Moore. White City, West London, UK: BBC, 2009.

Nikolajeva, Maria. "Fantasy." In *The Greenwood Encyclopedia of Folktales and Fairy Tales*, edited by Donald Haase. Westport, CT: Greenwood Publishing Group, 2007.

Nuñez, Kismet. "Loving *Vampire Diaries*: Why History, Slavery, and Race in Fandom Matters." *AntiJemimaLife*, December 2, 2011. https://nunezdaughter.wordpress.com.

Painter, Nell Irvin. *The History of White People*. New York: W. W. Norton, 2010.

Paris, Django. "Culturally Sustaining Pedagogy: A Needed Change in Stance, Terminology, and Practice." *Educational Researcher* 41, no. 3 (2012): 93–97.

Patterson, Orlando. *Slavery and Social Death*. Cambridge, MA: Harvard University Press, 1982.

Peterson, Price. "*The Vampire Diaries*' Kat Graham on the Surprising Differences between Bonnie Bennett and Kat Graham." TV.com, May 10, 2012. www.tv.com.

Pettitt, Thomas. "Before the Gutenberg Parenthesis: Elizabethan-American Compatibilities." Paper presented at "Media in Transition 5: Creativity, Ownership. and Collaboration in the Digital Age," Massachusetts Institute of Technology, 2007.

Philip, Thomas, and Antero Garcia. "The Importance of Still Teaching the iGeneration: New Technologies and the Centrality of Pedagogy." *Harvard Educational Review* 83, no. 2 (2013): 300–319.

Pinchevsky, Carol. "Fan Fiction Is Finally Legitimized with Kindle Worlds." *Forbes*, May 22, 2013.

Pollock, Mica. *Colormute: Race Talk Dilemmas in an American School*. Princeton, NJ: Princeton University Press, 2004.

prismatic-bell. "Can We Just Stop and Talk about This for a Minute?" Tumblr blog post, 2013. http://leseanthomas.tumblr.com.

Rankine, Claudia and Beth Loffreda. "On Writers and the Racial Imaginary: Where Writers Go Wrong in Imagining the Lives of Others." *Lithub*, 2015. https://lithub.com.

Rankine, Claudia, Beth Loffreda, and Max King Cap, eds. *The Racial Imaginary: Writers on Race in the Life of the Mind*. Albany, NY: Fence Books, 2015.

Ransby, Barbara. "The Class Politics of Black Lives Matter." *Dissent* 62, no. 4 (2015): 31–34.

Rao, Sameer. "*The Hate U Give* Illustrator Disappointed With Movie For Casting Light-Skinned Actress." *Colorlines*, August 2, 2018.

Reese, Debbie. "Patricia Wrede's Thinking as She Wrote *The Thirteenth Child*." *American Indians in Children's Literature* (blog), June 2009. https://americanindiansin-childrensliterature.blogspot.com.

Ricoeur, Paul. *Memory, History, Forgetting*. Chicago: University of Chicago Press, 2004.

Rieder, John. *Colonialism and the Emergence of Science Fiction*. Middletown, CT: Wesleyan University Press, 2008.

Riggs, Marlon T. *Ethnic Notions*. San Francisco: California Newsreel, 1987. Film.

Ringlestein, Yonah. "Real or Not Real: *The Hunger Games* as Transmediated Religion." *Journal of Religion and Popular Culture* 25, no. 3 (2013): 372–387. doi: 10.3138/jrpc.25.3.372.

Roberts, Dorothy. *Killing the Black Body: Race, Reproduction, and the Meaning of Liberty*. New York: Vintage, 1999.

Romano, Aja. "How the Creator of 'Vampire Diaries' Used Kindle Worlds to Get Back at Her Publisher." *Daily Dot*, February 10, 2014.

Rooks, Noliwe. "Writing Themselves into Existence: The Intersection of History and Literature in Writings on Black Women." *Iowa Journal of Literary Studies* 10, no. 1 (1989): 51–63.

Rosenberg, Leah A. "The Way We Were: Ritual, Memory, and Television." In *Television and the Self: Knowledge, Identity, and Media Representation*, edited by Kathleen M. Ryan and Deborah A. Macey, 11–25. Lanham, MD: Lexington Books, 2013.

Ross, Robyn. "Reunions! Death! Team Bonnie and Damon! What to Expect from *The Vampire Diaries* Season Finale." *TV Guide*, May 14, 2014.

Said, Edward W. *Culture and Imperialism*. New York: Knopf, 1993.

Sauerberg, L. O. "The Encyclopedia and the Gutenberg Parenthesis." Paper presented at "Media in Transition 6: Stone and Papyrus, Storage and Transmission." Cambridge, MA: Massachusetts Institute of Techology, April 2009.

Schalk, Sami. *Bodyminds Reimagined: (Dis)ability, Race, and Gender in Black Women's Speculative Fiction*. Durham, NC: Duke University Press, 2018.

Schoenberg, Nara. "Slavery in Children's Books: What Works?" *Chicago Tribune*, February 15, 2016.

Sealey-Ruiz, Yolanda. "Editorial: Why Black Girls' Literacies Matter: New Literacies for a New Era." *English Education* 48, no. 4 (2016): 291–292.

Sexton, Jared. "People-of-Color-Blindness: Notes on the Afterlife of Slavery." *Social Text* 28, no. 2 (2010): 31–56.

———. "The Social Life of Social Death: On Afro-Pessimism and Black Optimism." *In-Tensions* 5, no. 1 (2011): 1–47.

Shapiro, Lila. "Can You Revise a Novel to Make It More Woke?" *Vulture*, February 2018.

Sharpe, Christina. *In the Wake: On Blackness and Being*. Durham, NC: Duke University Press, 2016.

Sherman, Jon. "Source, Authority, and Audience in the BBC's *Merlin*." *Arthuriana* 25, no. 1 (2015): 82–100.

Sklar, Howard. "Narrative as Experience: The Pedagogical Implications of Sympathizing with Fictional Characters." *Partial Answers: Journal of Literature and the History of Ideas* 6, no. 2 (2008): 481–501.

Smagorinsky, Peter. "If Meaning Is Constructed, What Is It Made From? Toward a Cultural Theory of Reading." *Review of Educational Research* 71, no. 1 (2001): 133–169.

Smith, L. J. *The Vampire Diaries: Dark Reunion*, vol. 4. New York: HarperCollins & 17th Street Productions, 1992.

———. *The Vampire Diaries: The Fury*, vol. 3. New York: HarperCollins & 17ᵗʰ Street Productions, 1992.

———. *The Vampire Diaries: The Struggle*, vol. 2. New York: HarperCollins & 17ᵗʰ Street Productions, 1991.

———. *The Vampire Diaries: The Awakening*, vol. 1. New York: HarperCollins & 17ᵗʰ Street Productions, 1991.

Snead, James A., and Colin MacCabe. *White Screens, Black Images: Hollywood from the Dark Side*. London: Psychology Press, 1994.

Solórzano, Daniel G., and Tara J. Yosso. "Critical Race Methodology: Counter-Storytelling as an Analytical Framework for Education Research." *Qualitative Inquiry* 8, no. 1 (2002): 23-44.

Sonneshine, Rebecca. "Ghost World." *The Vampire Diaries*, season 3, episode 7. Directed by David Jackson. Burbank, CA: The CW, 2011.

Sousanis, Nick. *Unflattening*. Cambridge, MA: Harvard University Press, 2015.

Sparky. "*The Vampire Diaries*: What People of Colour Do When They're Not Snack Food." *Fangs for the Fantasy*, September 30, 2011. www.fangsforthefantasy.com.

Stephens, John. "Between Imagined Signs and Social Realities: Representing Others in Children's Fantasy and Folktale." *International Research in Children's Literature* 4, no. 2 (2011): v–viii.

Stewart, Dodai. "Racist *Hunger Games* Fans Are Very Disappointed." *Jezebel*, March 26, 2012. https://jezebel.com/5896408/racist-hunger-games-fans-dont-care-how-much-money-the-movie-made.

Stokes, Rebecca. "*The Vampire Diaries* Recap: Bonnie Bennett Should Just Stay Dead." *Cafe Mom: The Stir*, October 31, 2013. http://thestir.cafemom.com.

Stratton, Jon. "Buffy the Vampire Slayer: What Being Jewish Has to Do with It." *Television & New Media* 6, no. 2 (2005): 176–199.

Sugrue, Thomas J. *The Origins of the Urban Crisis: Race and Inequality in Postwar Detroit*. Princeton, NJ: Princeton University Press, 2014.

Suler, John. "The Online Disinhibition Effect." *Cyberpsychology & Behavior* 7, no. 3 (2004): 321–326.

Swank, Kris. "Black and Liminal in Camelot." Paper delivered at "Tales after Tolkien: Medievalism and Twenty-First Century Fantasy Literature," 48th International Congress on Medieval Studies, Kalamazoo, MI, May 12, 2013. https://www.academia.edu.

Swift, Andy. "*Vampire Diaries* Finale Recap: Break on Through." *TV Line*, May 15, 2014. https://tvline.com.

Tassja, "The Unbearable Whiteness of Being Part IV: Guinevere, Racism, and the Tyranny of Beauty." *Irresistable Revolution* (blog), January 13, 2012. http://irresistable-revolution.blogspot.com.

Thomas, Ebony Elizabeth. "Asieybarbie's 'I Am Beautiful' Campaign and Sleepy Hollow's Orlando Jones: Visual Representation Matters." *The Dark Fantastic: Race and the Imagination in Children's and YA Books, Media and Fandom Culture* (blog), July 6, 2014. http://thedarkfantastic.blogspot.com.

———. "Curiouser and Curiouser." *Trouble in Paradise. A Harry Potter Fanfic by AngieJ* (also known as Ebony Elizabeth). Retrieved October 25, 2018, from http://teland. com.

———. "The Imagination Gap in #Kidlit and #YAlit: An Introduction to the Dark Fantastic." *The Dark Fantastic: Race and the Imagination in Children's and Young Adult Literature, Media, and Fan Cultures* (blog), June 10, 2014. http://thedarkfantastic. blogspot.com.

———. "The Pleasures of Dreaming: How L. M. Montgomery Shaped My Lifeworlds." In *A Narrative Compass: Stories That Guide Women's Lives*, edited by Betsy Gould Hearne and Roberta Seelinger Trites, 80–95. Urbana-Champaign: University of Illinois Press, 2009.

———. "The Talented Dr. Granger." *Paradise Lost. A Harry Potter Fanfic by AngieJ* (also known as Ebony Elizabeth). Retrieved October 25, 2018, from http://dreaming-in-color.net.

Thomas, Ebony Elizabeth, and Amy Stornaiuolo. "Restorying the Self: Bending toward Textual Justice." *Harvard Educational Review* 86, no. 3 (2016): 313–338.

Thompson, Clive. "Brave New World of Digital Intimacy." *New York Times*, September 7, 2008.

———. "I'm So Totally, Digitally Close to You." *New York Times*, September 5, 2008.

Todorov, Tzvetan. *The Fantastic: A Structural Approach to a Literary Genre*. Cleveland, OH: Case Western Reserve University Press, 1973.

Tolkien, J. R. R. "Letter to Milton Waldman [1951]." In *JRR Tolkien, The Letters of JRR Tolkien*, edited by Humphrey Carpenter. Boston: Mariner Books, 2000.

———. "On Fairy-Stories." In J. R. R. Tolkien and Christopher Tolkien, *The Monsters and the Critics and Other Essays*. London: Allen & Unwin, 1983.

———. *The Silmarillion*. Boston: Houghton Mifflin, 1977.

———. *The Lord of the Rings Vol. I: The Fellowship of the Ring*. London: Allen & Unwin (1954): 423.

———. *The Lord of the Rings Vol. II: The Two Towers*. London: Allen & Unwin, 1954.

Tollerton, David C. "Multiculturalism, Diversity, and Religious Tolerance in Modern Britain and the BBC's *Merlin*." *Arthuriana* 25, no. 1 (2015): 113–127.

Torkelson, Anne. "Somewhere between Hair Ribbons and Rainbows: How Even the Shortest Song Can Change the World." In *The Hunger Games and Philosophy: A Critique of Pure Treason*, edited by George A. Dunn and Nicolas Michaud, 26–40. New York: John Wiley & Sons, 2012.

Tosenberger, Catherine. "'Oh My God, the Fanfiction!': Dumbledore's Outing and the Online Harry Potter Fandom." *Children's Literature Association Quarterly* 33, no. 2 (2008): 200–206.

Totlis, Athanasios. "The Dream as Space, Time and Emotion." *North American Journal of Medical Sciences* 3, no. 6 (2011): 302–315.

Vasquez, Vivian. "Critical Ethnography and Pedagogy: Bridging the Audit Trail with Technology." Keynote address presented at the 35th Annual Ethnography in Education Forum, University of Pennsylvania, March 2014.

Wanzo, Rebecca. "African American Acafandom and Other Strangers: New Genealogies of Fan Studies." *Transformative Works and Cultures* 20 (2015): n.p. https://journal.transformativeworks.org.

Watkins, Lucy. "Lancelot du Lac," *Merlin*, season 4, episode 9. Directed by Justin Molotnikov. White City, West London, UK: BBC, 2011.

We Need Diverse Books. "About WNDB." Retrieved October 25, 2018, from https://diversebooks.org.

White, Luise. *Speaking with Vampires: Rumor and History in Colonial Africa.* Berkeley: University of California Press, 2000.

Whitted, Qiana. "'And the Negro Thinks in Hieroglyphics': Comics, Visual Metonymy, and the Spectacle of Blackness." *Journal of Graphic Novels and Comics* 5, no. 1 (2014): 79–100.

Wilken, Selina. "'Merlin' Showrunner Shares His Thoughts on the Season Finale." *Hypable*, January 21, 2013. www.hypable.com.

Womack, Ytasha. *Afrofuturism: The World of Black Sci-fi and Fantasy Culture.* Chicago: Chicago Review Press, 2013.

Wright, Michelle M. *Physics of Blackness: Beyond the Middle Passage Epistemology.* Minneapolis: University of Minneapolis Press, 2015.

Wymer, Kathryn. "A Quest for the Black Knight: Casting People of Color in Arthurian Film and Television." Medievalists.net, 2014. www.medievalists.net.

Xie, Shaobo. "Rethinking the Identity of Cultural Otherness: The Discourse of Difference as Unfinished Project." In *Voices of the Other: Children's Literature in the Postcolonial Context*, edited by Roderick McGillis, 1–16. London: Routledge, 1999.

xojane. "Are Black People Really Not Relatable?." Xojane.com, July 5, 2012.

Young, Brian. "Crying Wolf." *The Vampire Diaries*, season 2, episode 14. Directed by David von Acken. Burbank, CA: The CW, 2011.

Young, Brian, and Charlie Charbonneau. "Because the Night." *The Vampire Diaries*, season 4, episode 17. Directed by Garreth Stover. Burbank, CA: The CW, 2013.

Young, Brian, and Caroline Dries. "The Walking Dead." *The Vampire Diaries*, season 4, episode 22. Directed by Rob Hardy. Burbank, CA: The CW, 2013.

Young, Brian, and N. Reynolds. "Dead Man on Campus." *The Vampire Diaries*, season 5, episode 8. Directed by R. Hardy. Burbank, CA: The CW, 2013.

Young, Elizabeth. *Black Frankenstein: The Making of an American Metaphor.* New York: New York University Press, 2008.

Young, Helen. *Race and Popular Fantasy Literature: Habits of Whiteness.* London: Routledge, 2015.

Young, Kevin. *The Grey Album: On the Blackness of Blackness.* Minneapolis, MN: Graywolf Press, 2012.

Young, Robert J. C. *Colonial Desire: Hybridity in Theory, Culture and Race.* London: Routledge, 2005.

Zahrawithaz. "What It Means to Me to Have a Black Guinevere." *Zahrawithaz LiveJournal*, October 13, 2009. http://zahrawithaz.livejournal.com.

INDEX

achievement gap, 178n18

actors, 168; Kravitz, Lenny, 38, 181n9; Okeniyi, Oladayo A. "Dayo," 181n9; Somerhalder, Ian, 119

actresses: Coulby, Angel, 12, 69, 79, 93, 94, 95, 96, 102, 104, 188n43; Dobrev, Nina, 108, 118, 130; Gavankar, Janina, 111; Graham, Kat, 111, 133, 134, 190n4; Guy, Jasmine, 111; Lawrence, Jennifer, 40; Lawson, Bianca, 11; McGrath, Katie, 97, 98; Stenberg, Amandla, 39, 58, 61–62, 181n8, 186n94, 193n63; White, Persia, 111; Williams, Natashia, 111

African Americans: actors, 104, 190n19; call and response, 183n37; casting, 136–138; and classic stories, 196n27; escapism in literature, 49; folktales, 50, 63; *The Hunger Games* (Collins), 50; identity, 73–74, 177n1, 179n10; mockingbird symbolism, 45; poetry, 186n101; social disparities in literature, 50, 184n74; teen internet usage, 128; theme of return, 75, 187n16; traditional literary characters, 50

Africana studies, 21, 101

African Diaspora, 196n27

Africanist presence, 118

afrofuturism, 8, 9, 178n27. *See also* dark fantastic, the

agency: and Bennett, Bonnie (*The Vampire Diaries*), 117, 122, 135; and Gwen (*Merlin*), 78, 93; and the imagination gap, 6; readers' interpretations of, 153, 154

allochronism, 106

alternate history, 159

alternate universe, 159–160

alternate worlds, 157

animalization, 49, 52, 62

anti-Semitism, 190n11

Anna (*The Vampire Diaries*), 122

antagonists, 126, 131; the Dark Other, 28

anti-Blackness, 138, 140–141

Appalachia, 53

Arthur, King (*Merlin*): characterization, 69, 78; dark fantastic cycle, 80–93; and Gwen, 79–80, 85, 88–89, 96–100, 188n43; and haunting, 90–92; and hesitation, 80–84; and Merlin, 96–100; transmedia storytelling, 69

Arthuriana: and authenticity of Gwen, 94–102; Gwen, 187n30; and inclusivity, 103, 105; transmedia storytelling, 69, 90

audience engagement, 59

audiences. *See* readers; viewers

authenticity, 42–43, 93–102, 182n25

autoethnographic experiences: childhood, 1–2, 36–37, 66–69; and fanfiction, 144–150, 152–153; as a fangirl, 108–109, 137–138; as a writer, 15–18

Bennett, Bonnie (*The Vampire Diaries*): Black fangirls, 128–129, 130–135, 137–141, 153; casting of, 111; character development, 130–131; characterization, 110–111; dark fantastic cycle, 116–127, 134–137; fandoms, 130; and innocence, 112; as a monster, 115, 134–135; responses, 130–134; v. McCullough, Bonnie, 126, 134, 135

ABOUT THE AUTHOR

Ebony Elizabeth Thomas is Associate Professor in the Literacy, Culture, and International Educational Division at the University of Pennsylvania's Graduate School of Education. A former Detroit Public Schools teacher and National Academy of Education/Spencer Foundation Postdoctoral Fellow, she is an expert on diversity in children's literature, youth media, and fan studies.

POSTMILLENNIAL POP

General Editors: Karen Tongson and Henry Jenkins

Puro Arte: Filipinos on the Stages of Empire
Lucy Mae San Pablo Burns

Spreadable Media: Creating Value and Meaning in a Networked Culture
Henry Jenkins, Sam Ford, and Joshua Green

Media Franchising: Creative License and Collaboration in the Culture Industries
Derek Johnson

Your Ad Here: The Cool Sell of Guerrilla Marketing
Michael Serazio

Looking for Leroy: Illegible Black Masculinities
Mark Anthony Neal

From Bombay to Bollywood: The Making of a Global Media Industry
Aswin Punathambekar

A Race So Different: Performance and Law in Asian America
Joshua Takano Chambers-Letson

Surveillance Cinema
Catherine Zimmer

Modernity's Ear: Listening to Race and Gender in World Music
Roshanak Kheshti

The New Mutants: Superheroes and the Radical Imagination of American Comics
Ramzi Fawaz

Restricted Access: Media, Disability, and the Politics of Participation
Elizabeth Ellcessor

The Sonic Color-Line: Race and the Cultural Politics of Listening
Jennifer Lynn Stoever

Diversión: Play and Popular Culture in Cuban America
Albert Sergio Laguna

Antisocial Media: Anxious Labor in the Digital Economy
Greg Goldberg

Open TV: Innovation beyond Hollywood and the Rise of Web Television
Aymar Jean Christian

Missing More Than Meets the Eye: Special Effects and the Fantastic Transmedia Franchise
Bob Rehak